COMMERCIALIZING
CHILDHOOD

Ellen,

Thanks for your interest!

Paul Ringel

A volume in the series
Studies in Print Culture and the History of the Book

Edited by
Greg Barnhisel
Robert A. Gross
Joan Shelley Rubin
Michael Winship

COMMERCIALIZING CHILDHOOD

*Children's Magazines, Urban Gentility, and
the Ideal of the American Child, 1823–1918*

PAUL B. RINGEL

University of Massachusetts Press
Amherst and Boston

ISBN 978-1-62534-191-4 (paper); 190-7 (hardcover)

Designed by Dennis Anderson
Set in Adobe Caslon Pro by House of Equations, Inc.
Printed and bound by Sheridan Books, Inc.

Library of Congress Cataloging-in-Publication Data
Ringel, Paul B., 1968–
Commercializing childhood : children's magazines, urban gentility, and the ideal
of the American child, 1823–1918 / Paul B. Ringel.
pages cm. — (Studies in print culture and the history of the book)
Includes bibliographical references and index.
ISBN 978-1-62534-191-4 (pbk. : alk. paper) —
ISBN 978-1-62534-190-7 (hardcover : alk. paper)
1. Children's periodicals, American—History—19th century.
2. Children's periodicals, American—History—20th century.
3. Children—Books and reading—United States—History—19th century.
4. Children—Books and reading—United States—History—20th century.
5. Child consumers—United States—History—19th century.
6. Child consumers—United States—History—20th century. I. Title.
PN4878.R68 2015
051.083—dc23
2015024890

British Library Cataloguing in Publication Data
A catalogue record for this book is available from the British Library.

For Eri,
and for Mom and Dad

CONTENTS

ACKNOWLEDGMENTS

I DO NOT have a simple explanation for my interest in nineteenth-century children's magazines and their training of child consumers. I didn't have children when I began this process, although I have two now. I think being the son of a pediatrician and a teacher laid the foundation for this interest, as did being a person who, even as an adult, gets paralyzed by consumer choices. Most often, though, I describe the experience in terms befitting the subject; I simply fell down the rabbit hole, and got curiouser and curiouser with each surprising, and at times shocking, new piece of evidence that I found. What I do know is the exact moment when that fall began. I was in the John Hay Library at Brown University when the librarian, who was assisting me in researching an only slightly related subject, pulled down a book and said something along the lines of "It's not what you're looking for, but this is pretty interesting." The book was *Under Dewey at Manila; or, the War Fortunes of a Castaway*, Edward Stratemeyer's boys' novel about the Spanish-American War. At the time, I did not know that the author was the future publisher of the Bobbsey Twins, Hardy Boys, and Nancy Drew; I was simply fascinated by the idea of explaining complex foreign policy decisions in a manner that children could understand. Stratemeyer's prolific and remarkably successful career was just one of the unexpected twists that emerged as I explored back to the religious revivals of the 1820s and forward through World War I in my efforts to understand how adult Americans explained the dizzying changes of the nineteenth century to the nation's children.

I wish I knew that librarian's name so that I could thank her individually, but I did not know at the time that this moment would launch me on a more than decade-long endeavor. Instead, I have to settle for making her a representative of the dozens of helpful librarians whose generosity of time and knowledge were vital to my research. There are too many people to list here, but a few staffs and individuals deserve special mention. The de Grummond Children's Literature Collection at the University of Southern Mississippi awarded me an Ezra Jack Keats Fellowship that allowed me to spend two weeks exploring its wonderfully rich archives. Brandeis University librarians were instrumental to getting my dissertation (which ultimately became this book) off the ground. Carolyn E. Shankle, a specialist in the University of North Carolina–Greensboro's Martha Blakeney Hodges Special Collections and University Archives, preserved my sanity near the frantic end of this process by helping me to procure images for the book, including the cover illustration. Finally, the librarians at High Point University have handled my relentless research and professorial requests with skill, equanimity, and kindness. I particularly want to thank David Bryden, who somehow got me access to every database I needed, and especially Bob Fitzgerald, who obtained hundreds of documents for me from around the globe without ever flinching or failing.

A long line of wonderful teachers and mentors has left an indelible mark on my scholarship and my career. (The usual caveats apply: they get credit for the accomplishments; the flaws herein are all mine.) Steve Ward and Mo Randall started me down this road at Roxbury Latin, whether they know it or not; and Elaine Abelson, Jeff Nunokawa, Sean Wilentz, and the other marvelous history and English professors I encountered at Princeton University intrigued me, pushed me, and whetted my appetite for graduate school. Once I got there, thanks to an Irving and Rose Crown Fellowship from Brandeis University, I had the great luck to learn from and work with Jackie Jones, Mickey Keller, Michael Willrich, and David Hackett Fischer. The research for this book began under the tutelage of Jim Kloppenberg, who never abandoned the project even after he moved across the river to Harvard University, and ended its dissertation stage under the guidance of Jane Kamensky. Their combined wisdom, wit, patience, and savvy remain my model for how to treat my own students. Scott Casper addded valuable insights as my outside dissertation reader. During the revision process, John Cooper generously read every word of the manuscript and offered invaluable intellectual and practical advice. I can't thank him, Jane, Jim, and the rest of my teachers enough for their time and attention.

The graduate program at Brandeis was wonderful because of not only its faculty but also the cohort of friends and colleagues who continue to be my core academic support group. Emily Straus, Molly McCarthy, Eben Miller, Ben Irvin, Greg Renoff, Will Walker, Hilary Moss, and Jeff Wiltse all helped this project along, whether through feedback on drafts, conversations, or long-distance pep talks.

The vibrant academic community of the North Carolina Piedmont Triad has given me a new set of supportive colleagues and friends. My colleagues in the history department at High Point University have all helped in unique ways. I particularly want to thank Philip Mulder and Lauren Brown for their thoughtful commentary on drafts, and Rick Schneid and Larry Simpson for their overall support of my teaching and scholarship. Outside the department, Dinene Crater showed me the ropes and helped me find my way innumerable times. Paige Meltzer offered incredibly helpful comments on late drafts. Heather Setzler, Phil and Allison Slaby, Heidi Verhaal Levine, and Thaddeus Ostrowski helped me to keep me going by plying me with food and alcohol, distracting me with sports, or just letting me vent. Mark Setzler and Dave Levine were my rocks throughout this process: they listened to all of my nonsense, gave much of it back, and dragged me through.

Brian Halley, my editor at University of Massachusetts Press, has offered unflagging support for this book. The anonymous readers gave me positive feedback and incredibly insightful perspectives on how to improve the manuscript. Managing editor Carol Betsch and copyeditor Dawn Potter made incalculable improvements to the final product. Parts of chapter 4 previously appeared in a different form and are republished with permission: "Thrills for Children: The *Youth's Companion,* the Civil War, and the Commercialization of American Youth," in *Children and Youth during the Civil War Era,* ed. James Alan Marten (New York: New York University Press, 2012).

Most of all, I want to thank my family. Deb, Scott, Dana, Pat, Susan, Larry, Peggy, Liz, and Marshall, you have lived with this project for way too long and have had to deal with my cutting out of way too many family events. You are always supportive, and I don't tell you enough how much I appreciate it. Julia and Sam, you have never known a time when I wasn't working on this book. I tried not to miss anything major, even if it meant taking longer to finish, but I hope now we'll start a new story of our own.

Three people need extra thanks. Mom and Dad, you gave me the freedom and courage to change course. You let me move back in when I was a broke graduate student. And you always encouraged me, even when you didn't understand. Eri, I don't think you had any idea what you were getting into when you started dating a late-stage graduate student. I scared you with my nighttime writing rituals. I dragged you away from your job and family to this strange new place where you built us a home and a community and yourself a new career. I left you with the kids too many weekends and asked you to edit too many drafts. You hold everything together, and I couldn't have done it without you.

COMMERCIALIZING
CHILDHOOD

Introduction

A SUNDAY school teacher stands at the edge of a freshly dug grave, surrounded by a group of boys. He points to a small coffin lying next to the grave. As the boys look toward the coffin, the teacher offers them a warning: "Young persons are apt to think that their time of life is not the best time to become serious,—still there are many warnings given, to show them that *they* are mortal and may die while young. Some of the little boys who attend our Sabbath school can remember George Cook. For a short time he attended the school with them—but he is dead!" George was stricken "at play, [when] a shoe was thrown carelessly against his head," and "while he was sick . . . something which he said, makes us hope that he went to heaven. He was heard to say . . . 'I love you, my parents, but I love my Saviour better.'" "Warn[ing] the boys against throwing stones or sticks at each other . . . [and] against playing on the Sabbath day," the teacher ended by telling them "what George said before he died, and how he prayed, [how] he exhorted them to obey their parents and their teacher, to repent of their sins, and to pray to the Saviour to pardon them and fit them for heaven."[1]

"George Cook" opened the November 1823 debut issue of the *Teacher's Offering, or Sabbath Scholar's Magazine.* This publication, which the American Sunday School Union renamed the *Youth's Friend* in 1825, was the first children's magazine to flourish in the United States, reaching a circulation of 10,000 subscribers by 1827.[2] "George Cook" introduces the magazine's premise, drawn from orthodox Protestant theology, that children are by nature sinful creatures. This belief prompted the *Youth's Friend* editors to discourage children from play, which orthodoxy presented as a corrupting distraction from their obligation to save their souls from eternal damnation. The editors also avoided overtly commercial practices such as advertising,

Sunday school students and their teacher gather around the coffin of George Cook. From *Youth's Friend*, 1823. Courtesy of the Lois Lenski Collection of Early American Children's Literature, Martha Blakeney Hodges Special Collections and University Archives, University Libraries, University of North Carolina at Greensboro.

which they viewed as potentially debasing for unredeemed young minds. The magazine encouraged young readers to acknowledge their innate depravity and abandon faith in their own decision-making capacity, deferring instead to moral authorities such as Sunday school teachers and parents and above all recognizing and embracing God's omnipotent power to determine their eternal fate.

Nearly a century later, in May 1911, the children's magazine *St. Nicholas* began the serial story "Dorothy the Motor-Girl." The heroine, recently disabled by a fall from a horse, won an automobile through a newspaper puzzle contest. The joy of winning the car, along with time spent outdoors on motoring excursions, helped to restore her health. However, when her father faced financial ruin due to the machinations of a large corporation, Dorothy sold her prized possession to pay for her older brother's final year at Yale. Ultimately, her father's business venture succeeded, enabling him to repurchase her automobile and return it to Dorothy at a party celebrating her generosity and selflessness.[3]

Like the *Youth's Friend*, *St. Nicholas* thrived, garnering critical acclaim and achieving consistent monthly sales of about 70,000 copies for more than half a century after its 1873 founding.[4] Yet "Dorothy" diverged starkly from "George Cook" in the message it conveyed to young readers. Its author displays a more optimistic, liberal Protestant perspective on children's nature, celebrating her heroine's intellectual capabilities (Dorothy's victory in the puzzle contest) and inherent benevolence (her sacrifice of her car for her brother) through her commercial and leisure activities. Rather than encouraging children to defer to adults and divine will, the author promotes their self-improvement and intervention into traditionally adult worlds of business and finance. Support for these actions comes from not just Dorothy's parents or teachers but also a distant, market-based culture of consumption. The rest of *St. Nicholas*—a glossy corporate magazine filled with advertisements for children's sporting goods, summer camps, and breakfast cereals—reinforced these messages.

Dorothy the Motor-Girl celebrates the arrival of her car. From *St. Nicholas*, 1911. Courtesy of the Early Juvenile Literature Collection, Martha Blakeney Hodges Special Collections and University Archives, University Libraries, University of North Carolina at Greensboro.

The perspectives on childhood presented in these stories were somewhat extreme for their eras: by the 1820s many Americans had abandoned
belief in infant depravity, and few would have embraced the therapeutic
value of consumer culture for children as ardently as "Dorothy" did in the
1910s. Nonetheless, they were not anomalous. Nor were they indicative of
a broad ideological shift within American society, for the divide between
these magazines' liberal and orthodox Protestant approaches to childrearing
was a constant feature in the industry throughout the nineteenth century.[5]
The *Juvenile Miscellany,* a liberal publication proclaiming that children "can
act from good principle" and exposing them to the diverse wonders of
distant cultures, was a commercial and critical sensation when it appeared
in 1826, yet evangelical Sunday school publications that urged children to
focus inward on their inherently sinful natures continued to prosper into
the 1850s.[6] The latter genre had lost much of its appeal by the onset of the
Civil War, but its influence persisted in the *Youth's Companion,* the nation's
best-selling children's magazine (and one of the highest circulating periodicals of any genre) during the last quarter of the nineteenth century. The
Companion, which reached an audience of more than half a million weekly
customers by the early 1890s, continued to present an orthodox view of
children as peculiarly vulnerable to the physical and moral temptations
of modern society, even as *St. Nicholas* succeeded by promoting children's
capacity for flourishing under the same conditions.[7]

As the contrast between "George" and "Dorothy" exemplifies, American
children's magazines of both ideological perspectives integrated their beliefs
with the growing consumer demands of both adults and children to create
new methods for instructing young readers. The *Companion,* for example,
changed from a magazine that refused to cater to children's interests into
one that immersed its young readers in consumer culture. By the 1890s,
it was providing entertainment and advice from celebrity authors such as
Theodore Roosevelt and Mark Twain (both of whom also contributed to
St. Nicholas) and giving away grand pianos, vacations, and substantial cash
prizes to children who sold the most subscriptions. This approach, like
that of *St. Nicholas* during the same period, indicates that children's active
participation in commercial cultures of consumption and leisure was largely
accepted in the United States by the eve of World War I (though this was,
and continues to be, controversial).

From its emergence in the 1820s until the onset of its declining cultural
influence in the 1910s, the American children's magazine industry worked
to facilitate this shift by defining and legitimizing young readers' expand-

ing roles as consumers. Because the industry constantly needed to monitor and adapt its appeals to earn repeat customers, and because it succeeded in gaining weekly or monthly access to millions of American homes over the course of the century, its practices offer unique insights into this process of legitimization. They reveal that the process was gradual and intermittent, due to the tensions between the magazines' primary goals of shaping children's values and earning profits as well as their audiences' diverse and inconsistent demands. These practices also reveal that the key to success in the industry was construction of an editorial formula that combined stable beliefs about children's nature with flexible responses to families' constantly changing relationships with the expanding market economy.

In this book, I examine how producers of children's magazines created and maintained these formulas, focusing particularly on the cultural conditions that spawned and sustained the magazines that shaped the industry's editorial paradigms.[8] These examples should lead us to reconsider our understanding of how and why children's market relationships intensified over the course of the nineteenth century. Many scholars have viewed children's integration into consumer cultures as a process instigated by corporate and intellectual elites during the late nineteenth and early twentieth centuries, but children's magazines reveal the limitations of this interpretation.[9] Children's access to these cultures did grow significantly after the Civil War as publishers increasingly marketed products directly to young readers, and they grew again in the early twentieth century when retailers and advertisers began to adopt the same approach. Yet marketing to children in the United States began as early as the 1820s, when American production of children's magazines, books, and toys first became economically sustainable.[10]

Producers and consumers of these products quickly recognized the influence that such goods could exert on young readers. As an 1824 review of the *Youth's Friend* claimed, "the mode of periodical instruction from the press, is attended with many advantages; especially when directed to the young."

> Every parent whose children are able, and are permitted to read a newspaper, know with what joy they hail its arrival. If this paper be expressly designed for the young, it will be received with still higher pleasure; and if it comes in the child's *own name*, he will place upon it an inestimable value. Let the Youth's Magazine be called *his own paper*, and how will the juvenile reader clasp it to his bosom in ecstacy [*sic*] as he takes it from the Post-Office. And if instruction from any source will deeply affect his heart, it will when communicated through the medium of this little pamphlet.[11]

This assessment was not just a harbinger of future commercial practices; it was an early step in an ongoing effort to employ consumer products as instruments for shaping children's behaviors.

A focus on the similarities between "George" and "Dorothy" highlights the tenets of this longer tradition. Both stories begin with a presumption, newly predominant in the United States after the American Revolution, that adults could shape children's moral, intellectual, and social development through instruction and other environmental influences.[12] Both adopt a sentimental approach to this shaping process, seeking to inspire young readers' appropriate behavior by way of emotional appeals rather than rational discourse. In so doing, both also strengthened the link between children's education and domestic, increasingly feminized environments.[13] The appearance of these stories in commercial publications suggests a shared belief that the market economy was not necessarily a corrupting influence on those environments, and the fact that these publications were children's magazines indicates a common (if variable) understanding that marketing directly to children could facilitate or even enhance their spiritual, intellectual, and physical development.

The growth patterns of the children's magazine industry further indicate that elites did not primarily drive this practice. Editors were the chief architects of the magazines' formulas. They managed all aspects of production, from selection of written and visual content (at least some of which they often created themselves) to layout, marketing, and, by the mid-1800s, advertising. These editorial positions offered, for much of the century, a tenuous livelihood; and the men and women who held them were marginalized by some combination of financial status, lack of formal education, religious denomination (though all were Protestant), and gender. Yet the most successful children's magazines had editors with long tenures. Nathaniel Willis oversaw the *Companion* for thirty years, Daniel Sharp Ford for forty-two years; Mary Mapes Dodge managed *St. Nicholas* for thirty-two years. Such longevity allowed these editors to employ the market economy to both guide the nation's children and improve their own economic and social standing.[14]

To achieve these goals, editors had to gain the favor of the expanding audience of American families interested in purchasing children's magazines. For much of the century these customers drove the market, establishing expectations to which editors were forced to respond. Extant evidence about this audience is sparse, but the magazines' formulas suggest that the editors believed their customers were predominantly white, Protestant, northern, urban, disproportionately educated, and relatively prosperous. (Children's magazines were not a luxury that most poor families could afford.) From the industry's beginnings in the 1820s, however, subscribers came from not only the elite but also the middle and working classes. Moreover, what the families shared with children's magazine editors was neither economic nor social status but an ambition for advancement and a belief that carefully managed engagement with the market economy could help them and their children to fulfill these aspirations.

This belief was grounded in an expanding system of social evaluation practices that producers and consumers of children's magazines, like many other socially and financially ambitious nineteenth-century Americans, described as gentility.[15] Borrowed from the rituals of eighteenth-century colonial elites who sought to link themselves to the fashionable world of the English aristocracy, nineteenth-century American gentility was constructed upon the belief that individuals, even if they lacked substantial income or prestigious lineage, could improve their status by constructing a public persona that balanced polite manners, Protestant morality, and tasteful display of consumer goods.[16] Children's magazines reveal that ambitious white Americans from a variety of class and denominational backgrounds embraced this opportunity for upward mobility, leading to the emergence of distinct societies that coexisted (sometimes uneasily) within the fluid boundaries of gentility. These publications also illustrate that many Americans feared that the economic and cultural changes that had facilitated their advancement—greater access to consumer products, a more mobile population, the decline in deference to traditional forms of elite authority—might lead to increased moral corruption and excessive democratization. The gentility presented in American children's magazines simultaneously provided a means for furthering the interests of their audiences and checking these frightening tendencies. Although they appeared meritocratic, these performance-based parameters for respectability could be learned only through institutions (such as churches, social clubs, and publications) deemed reputable by those in power. Access to these institutions generally required some degree of wealth as well as exposure to white Protestant cultures, prerequisites that sustained existing social hierarchies by excluding most Americans of other races and religions.

The nineteenth-century American children's magazine industry was a product of this carefully balanced genteel sensibility. As the century progressed, successful publications increasingly offered entertainment for young readers but persisted in emphasizing their didactic role as a "Companion" or "Friend" who would guide American children into reputable conduct amid the moral and cultural complexities of a rapidly urbanizing and industrializing society. Indeed, children's magazines staked their claim as uniquely valuable commercial products on their ability to instill such conduct *through* entertainment, an idea that appealed to genteel parents who were already using market goods to shape and reflect their own behaviors. This alignment explains the industry's trajectory: its emergence during the 1820s and 1830s, its peak influence in the late nineteenth century, and its incipient decline in the 1910s mirrored the course of gentility's reign as a prevailing source of cultural authority in the United States.

Children's magazines' status as successful yet genteel commercial products helps to explain why children became integrated into the nation's consumer cultures over the course of the nineteenth century. Although corporate influences accelerated this process and intellectual elites struggled to shape it, the predominant impetus for this shift, especially before the Civil War, came from the middle and even the margins of respectable white Protestant society. These individuals and families perceived genteel methods of market integration as a way to maximize their children's—and their own—opportunities for economic and social advancement. Children's magazines sought to establish and spread norms for this process, and the industry's accomplishments indicate that millions of families believed these publications' commercial practices to be an effective means of instilling market behaviors that could help young white Americans to thrive in modern society.

CHILDREN'S MAGAZINES were predominantly products of northeastern urban cultures. Although they appeared across the United States over the course of the nineteenth century, the most commercially successful publications emerged from Boston, New York, and Philadelphia. These cities made editors' jobs easier because they not only provided proximity to large audiences and commercial writers but also were among the earliest places in which American ideals about childhood began to change.[17] As genteel families (and those who aspired to gentility) moved into and near these cities, they gradually shifted from viewing childhood as a time of labor to identifying it as a period of development and preparation through education. This move toward accepting young people as "economically useless" correlated with what one scholar has described as the "sacralization" of children as uniquely innocent and vulnerable individuals who needed protection from corrupting commercial influences, increasingly in "domesticated, nonproductive," and feminized environments.[18]

This shift is well documented, but less considered is the fact that it occurred concurrently with efforts to cultivate children as consumers. As prosperous Americans withdrew children from public commercial environments, they also started to recognize the importance of privately employing market products to shape young people's conduct and prepare them for life in an industrializing society. The nation's economic expansion, which increased children's access to commercial goods, intensified these impulses in conjunction and contradiction with one another, leading adults to employ consumer products as instruments to both protect children from market-driven cultures and teach them to navigate the complexities of those cultures.

Children's magazines became vital cultural institutions because they were among the earliest American products to attempt to cater to both of these adult demands. Ironically, because these publications were the creation of one group of adults (editors, writers, and publishers) who were primarily subject to the approval of another group of adults (parents, educators, and other community leaders), they tell us very little about the actual experiences or desires of nineteenth-century children.[19] Instead, they reveal how much the industry's success hinged on meeting these complicated expectations created by the spread of urban gentility. Indeed, children's magazines produced before the growth of these expectations had failed to engage commercial audiences. The *Children's Magazine,* which appeared in Hartford, Connecticut, in 1789, is the first known example of the genre published in the United States. Yet despite having experienced and well-funded editors, it lasted for only four months. For nearly two generations, subsequent magazines had similarly disappointing results.[20] The obstacles of these early innovators were partly technological. Manually operated printing presses ran slowly and often broke down. Paper and ink were scarce and expensive. Primitive distribution networks and a lack of population density in even the largest U.S. cities made reaching audiences a monumental task.[21] In addition to these material challenges, the cultural inducements that eventually convinced American families to subscribe to children's magazines had not fully formed before the 1820s.

Part I of this book, "Establishing Children's Magazines, 1823–1856," covers the period from the founding of the *Teacher's Offering* until the end of *Companion* founder Nathaniel Willis's editorial tenure. In these chapters I examine the shifting social conditions that allowed the first generation of successful American children's magazines to prosper during the second quarter of the nineteenth century. Although the *Teacher's Offering* emerged first from New Haven and then Philadelphia, these conditions developed most maturely in Boston, where the Unitarian Controversy (a conflict between orthodox and liberal Protestant leaders for authority over the city's religious and cultural institutions) instigated the creation of the *Miscellany* and the *Companion*. These two publications, the nation's earliest financially self-sustaining children's magazines, were founded in 1826 and 1827, just eight months and a few city blocks apart.

The editors of these magazines, Lydia Maria Child and Nathaniel Willis, were both products of Boston's artisan class, and their decisions to create these periodicals—as well as the contrasting visions of children that emerged from them—reflected the expanding and diversifying avenues toward gentility that also instigated consumer demand for their publications in this rapidly urbanizing region. Yet their subsequent editorial experiences also reveal the power that commercial audiences already held to limit the boundaries for acceptable idealizations of American childhood. Willis was a printer, editor, and publisher whose "primitive orthodox" faith intertwined with his long-standing opposition to concentrated wealth and elite political authority.[22] By the time he launched the *Companion* in 1827 as part of a city-wide orthodox revival, he had achieved economic stability and community status as a deacon at Park Street Church, and his magazine represented his attempt to assume the traditional role of a gentleman by offering his views on issues of public import. Yet Willis struggled to reconcile his orthodox beliefs and patriarchal pedagogical methods with audience expectations of a more sentimental approach to young readers. Chapter 1 explores how he constructed a compromised editorial formula that both fulfilled his social and evangelical agendas and kept the *Companion* solvent.

Child, a financially straitened young woman who procured her position at the *Miscellany* through the patronage of the city's Unitarian elites, also faced the challenge of squaring her views with those of her audience. In contrast to Willis, she decided not to compromise herself ideologically, thus affirming the growing power of commerce in shaping genteel ideals for American children. Whereas Willis's initially severe portrayal of children's need to acknowledge their innate depravity alienated New England families, Child's enthusiastic and sentimental confidence in young readers and eagerness delighted parents, children, and critics. Yet her ambition to extend the logic of liberal Protestant theology toward the creation of a less hierarchical American society that created new opportunities for women, nonwhites, and the poor—and her desire to employ children as conduits for this process—eventually eradicated her success. Chapter 2 examines how Child gained the favor of genteel New Englanders by balancing her commercial and ideological interests and how her loss of the *Miscellany*'s editorship following her advocacy of abolition in the magazine solidified the industry's socially conservative perspective for the rest of the antebellum period.

The divide between the *Companion*'s orthodox and the *Miscellany*'s liberal Protestantism originated from the local Unitarian controversy in Boston. But as part II, "Commercializing Children's Magazines, 1857–1873," reveals, these magazines established templates that persisted as the industry nationalized during the mid-nineteenth century. Beginning with Daniel Sharp Ford's assumption of the *Companion*'s editorship and continuing through the founding of *St. Nicholas,* these chapters examine how the two distinct ideological types of children's magazines began marketing more directly to young readers while seeking to maintain the approval of the adults who were their primary customers. The impetus for this shift was economic expansion, which dramatically increased the industry's geographic reach and thus commercial potential but also expanded the entertainment options available to young readers, making them less willing to accept the relentlessly didactic fare of antebellum magazines.

Daniel Sharp Ford was among the earliest children's magazine editors to address young Americans as customers whom he needed to please. Like his *Companion* predecessor Willis, he was orthodox in his Protestant faith. Yet whereas Willis perceived his role solely as that of a patriarchal instructor, Ford believed he could enhance both children's moral character and his own profits by also treating them as commercial partners. Chapter 3 considers how he reconciled the two facets of this relationship with his young readers, with a particular focus on his reframing of the sensational tropes of disreputable working-class entertainments into a story genre that I have labeled "genteel sensationalism."

Like Willis and Child before him, Ford struggled to gain audience acceptance for his vision of childhood. His initial efforts to transform the *Companion* from a religious magazine into a more commercially popular publication achieved only limited success, and the onset of the Civil War led him to revert toward Willis's more conservative editorial approach. Ultimately, though, the war accelerated genteel Americans' willingness to accept an expanded consumer role for children. By the end of the conflict, Ford had reintroduced his antebellum blend of commerce and theology to a now enthusiastic audience that propelled the *Companion* to unprecedented commercial success for a children's magazine. Chapter 4 evaluates the wartime conditions that caused this ideological shift and considers why the *Companion*'s individualized approach to self-improvement—drawn from the doctrines of orthodox theology—resonated so effectively with postwar American families.

The acceptance of more active commercial roles for children also broadened commercial interest in the children's magazine industry. Nearly every major publishing house in the United States produced a new children's periodical between 1865 and 1880.[23] This second generation of publications generally was better funded and more connected to the nation's literary elite than the industry's founders were, yet its editors experienced similar difficulties in constructing formulas that met the demands of a commercial audience. One challenge was the ongoing cultural reassessment of childhood. As the nation continued to urbanize and industrialize during the second half of the nineteenth century, people were moving away from older definitions of youth. Once, youth had encompassed a single life stage between infancy and adulthood, extending roughly from the time children could play without adult supervision until they gained economic independence from their parents through work or marriage.[24] During the half century between the Civil War and World War I, however, genteel Americans were increasingly replacing this construction with the concept of an extended childhood. The *Youth's Friend* and the *Miscellany,* for example, were marketed to an audience between the ages of five and fourteen, but *St. Nicholas* strived to maintain readers through the age of eighteen. Appealing to older children required models of young people on the cusp of adulthood, which explains why the characters in "Dorothy" look so much older than those in "George Cook" and why they could independently undertake seemingly adult activities such as motoring excursions. At the same time, editors began to segment their audience within the magazine, delivering content and establishing behavioral expectations that specifically targeted smaller categories of children based on age, gender, and eventually class.

The children's magazine industry reveals that part of the reason for this shift was commercial.[25] Ford's genteel sensational stories, which he filled with a more aggressive ideal of masculinity than the *Companion* had previously displayed, were among the publishing industry's early efforts to attract boy readers during the 1850s. This strategy was based on the assumption (which appears to have been false but nonetheless gained currency during this period) that boys, who often had more physical freedom than girls did and thus greater access to commercial goods, would not read publications that they perceived as feminized. War fiction and dime novels accelerated this trend during the 1860s, and postwar magazines had to address it to remain viable. Ford's editorial formula left him well situated to do so, but his liberal Protestant competition struggled with this issue. Chapter 5 examines how the editors of *Our Young Folks* and the *Riverside Magazine for Young People,* both produced by New England's cultural elite, strived but failed to sufficiently adapt to changing genteel standards for child readers.

Our Young Folks and the *Riverside* also pursued a gendered approach, employing their own versions of previously marginalized fiction—fairy tales and "bad boy" stories—to attract young audiences. Rather than relying on sensationalism, which they perceived as a crass brand of emotional manipulation, the editors sought to elevate young readers' emotions through more realistic, high-quality literature and artwork produced by prominent and rising contributors such as Charles Dickens, Harriet Beecher Stowe, Hans Christian Andersen, and Winslow Homer. They also adopted a communal perspective (derived largely from ideals that shaped the Union war effort) toward building their audience and nurturing young Americans' social and moral development, an approach that contrasted starkly with Ford's message of individualism. Perhaps as problematic as the paternalism of their agenda, however, was their mistrust of commercial relationships with young readers as a means of maximizing their intellectual and moral development.[26]

Like most other children's magazines of the immediate postwar years, *Our Young Folks* and the *Riverside* did not survive the decade. Their failures cannot be entirely attributed to their editorial formulas, for the economic downturn of the early 1870s and individual circumstances also contributed to their decline. Yet *St. Nicholas,* which debuted in 1873 after literally absorbing these magazines, succeeded at the nadir of the U.S. economic downturn by introducing adjustments to the liberal Protestant formula that made it more consumer-friendly. *St. Nicholas* editor Mary Mapes Dodge was a native New Yorker who shared the intellectual ambitions of the New England elite but not their anxieties about market influences. Like Ford, she believed that commercial products could facilitate children's development, but her perspective derived not from orthodox faith but a combination of liberal Protestantism, her New York upbringing, and her gender. Dodge followed *Miscellany* editor Lydia Maria Child's precedent: she displayed faith in children's critical capacities and used the market economy to support herself in a male-dominated publishing business. Unlike Child, though, she did not prioritize social reform. She called her magazine a "pleasure ground" for children, but its pleasures came at a financial and cultural cost. *St. Nicholas* was twice as expensive as any previous American children's magazine, meaning that its readers were predominantly limited to the nation's wealthiest families. Chapter 6 explores how Dodge's embrace of commercial roles for children in *St. Nicholas* continued the industry's process of reinforcing existing social hierarchies.

Part III, "Sustaining Children's Magazines, 1873–1918," covers the *Companion*'s and *St. Nicholas*'s co-reign as the industry's behemoths. During

these decades, external forces persistently tested the magazines' genteel editorial formulas. For much of this time, these formulas proved sufficiently
adaptable to allay the concerns of middle-class and wealthy American
families, who wanted to maintain control over late nineteenth-century
industrialization and urbanization. By the 1910s, however, Ford's and
Dodge's successors were struggling to keep their genteel approach relevant
for young readers, an indication of the onset of their magazines'—and the
industry's—gradually declining cultural influence.

The first major challenge that Ford and Dodge confronted during the
1870s and 1880s was a national debate about children's reading materials. It
was instigated by orthodox white Protestant reformers, who perceived the
urbanization and industrialization that fueled the success of the *Companion*
and *St. Nicholas* as a moral and social threat. These reformers categorized
sensational children's literature as a danger on the level of pornography and
gambling, and public response forced Ford and Dodge to address this issue in their magazines. In chapter 7 I consider those responses, particularly
in the context of postwar urbanization, and argue that the editors needed
to make only minor adjustments to their existing formulas to accommodate those concerns. This flexibility indicated the continuing strength of
gentility as a means for white Protestants to respond to Gilded Age social
pressures.

Greater difficulties for the magazines began to emerge in the 1880s as
young Americans' life experiences increasingly moved away from the model
for which gentility had been created. As children spent more time in school
and in extracurricular activities, and as new sources of cultural authority
ranging from retail industries to medical and social science experts began
to focus on American children's coming-of-age experiences, the *Companion*
and *St. Nicholas* struggled to maintain their identities and their audiences.
Chapter 8 examines these struggles, concluding that the magazines' divergence from their traditional formulas serves as evidence that they and
their industry were ceding the vanguard of marketing to children to less
genteel retailers such as department stores and producers of series books.
This shift, along with the departure of prominent writers and artists from
the industry, was a harbinger of the gradual decline that led to the end of
the *Companion*'s run in 1929 and *St. Nicholas*'s in 1940.

In many ways, the nineteenth-century children's magazine industry was
a victim of its own success in legitimizing children's integration into the
nation's cultures of consumption and leisure. By the early twentieth century,
public responsibility for monitoring and guiding that consumer consciousness had been transferred to either wholly noncommercial institutions

(such as religious institutions and schools) or the retail, advertising, and banking industries that sought to cultivate new generations of unabashed customers.[27] Children's magazines' vital role as a bridge between domestic and commercial cultures became, like the divide that genteel Americans sought to maintain between those cultures, increasingly anachronistic within the broader society. This change helps to explain why the cultural influence of twentieth-century successors such as *Highlights* and *Cricket* remains more narrowly contained in what one scholar has described as the specialized "enclave" of children's literature.[28]

Yet during the nineteenth century, when family's relationships with nonlocal market cultures were new, children's magazines served the vital role of mediating those relationships in a way that facilitated genteel consumer roles for American children. By examining how this process developed, we can learn how ambitious white Protestant families integrated market products into their lives in a way that maintained their cultural advantages over Americans of other races and religions. In doing so, they established respectable forms of commercial behavior for children but also injected an ambivalence about those behaviors that persists in many educated, prosperous American families of the twenty-first century.

PART I

Establishing Children's Magazines
1823–1856

IN THE *YOUTH'S COMPANION,* GIRLS RECEIVED "REFUSE" FOR dinner because they behaved like pigs. Boys drowned while swimming in a river with friends.[1] Indeed, children died in the magazine on nearly a weekly basis, for its founder and editor, Nathaniel Willis, presented childhood as an inherently sinful and thus physically and spiritually dangerous stage of life.

At the same time, just a few blocks from the *Companion*'s office in Boston's Congress Square, *Juvenile Miscellany* editor Lydia Maria Child offered a different perspective. She opened each 1826–27 issue with a stanza from the English poet William Wordsworth:

> We'll talk of sunshine and of song;
> And summer days, when we were young;
> Sweet, childish days, that were as long
> As twenty days are now

In 1828 she replaced that epigram with a couplet, also by Wordsworth:

> The Child is the father of the man;
> And I could wish my days to be
> Bound to each other by natural piety

These selections exemplified her magazine's ideals, which celebrated the inherent benevolence and spirituality of childhood as a paradigm toward which adults should strive to return.[2]

Willis's and Child's similar backgrounds make this contrast between their characterizations of childhood particularly striking. Both grew up in Boston-area artisan families that struggled to achieve financial stability and social respectability amid the cultural changes of the new nation. During their childhood, both moved to the edges of American settlement—Willis to Ohio, Child to Maine—but returned to Boston as young adults seeking economic opportunities. Both believed the United States had sacrificed its ideals in the decades since the American Revolution, and they sought to reinvigorate the values they perceived to be inherent in those ideals. And both adopted the children's magazine, a relatively new commercial product that was just becoming financially sustainable in the 1820s, as the vehicle to communicate their ambitious social visions to New England children and their families.

The disjunction between these editors' similar backgrounds and contrasting ideologies highlights the cultural instability in early nineteenth-century New England societies. This instability—and the leadership vacuum it created—instigated the spread of gentility and consequently the establishment of the children's magazine industry. The *Companion* and the *Miscellany* both emerged from a long-running theological conflict between liberal and orthodox Protestants known as the Unitarian Controversy, which reflected the transforming nature of authority throughout the region during the first third of the century. The controversy officially began in 1805, when a group of self-proclaimed liberal clergymen seized control of the traditionally orthodox faculty of Harvard College, challenging both orthodox religious doctrines (including belief in infant depravity) and the community leadership of the ministers and laymen who held those doctrines.

Both magazines debuted during an 1826–27 surge in this conflict, instigated by an orthodox revival intended to stem liberals' expanding influence over Boston and its environs. Child, whose ambitions had been thwarted by the orthodox patriarchy, accepted the patronage of the Unitarian publishers who gave her the editorship of the *Miscellany*, a magazine founded to promote liberal Protestant beliefs shortly after the revival's outbreak. Willis, like many other workingmen of the era, was angered by what he saw as the corrupting practices of an emerging "cultural oligarchy" and embraced the orthodox revival as a means of restoring Revolutionary virtue to the region. He introduced the *Companion* eight months after the *Miscellany*'s debut, with the specific goal of countering the influence of Child's successful publication.[3]

The fact that the Unitarian Controversy had spilled over from New England's pulpits and town meetings into children's magazines indicates that it was more than a theological debate; it was part of a broader conflict over which people, ideas, and institutions would shape the behaviors of a society that was urbanizing and industrializing at an extraordinary rate. By the 1820s, Boston's population had grown nearly tenfold from its nadir of 6,000 during the British wartime occupation of the 1770s.[4] The city had transformed from an isolated colonial settlement into an international mercantile and nascent manufacturing center with a growing, mobile, and less deferential population. Under these unsettled conditions, local elites' traditional practice of dictating standards of public behavior based on divine sanction of their authority was no longer a realistic method of social governance, and the Controversy was a struggle to determine what form of leadership would replace this fading model.[5]

The introduction of the *Companion* and the *Miscellany* into this conflict was not unprecedented, for the press had already become an instrument through which both sides sought to exert influence. Orthodox evangelicals, following their defeat at Harvard, particularly relied on such publications. By the 1810s, organizations such as the American Tract Society and the American Sunday School Union were producing hundreds of thousands of Bibles, tracts, and periodicals to disseminate their messages to nearly every corner of the nation.[6] The first successful American children's magazine, the American Sunday School Union's *Youth's Friend and Scholar's Magazine,* emerged from this wave of evangelical print, and by 1826 its estimated circulation was between 10,000 and 13,000 subscribers.[7]

The success of the *Youth's Friend* likely inspired the decisions to create the *Companion* and the *Miscellany;* the shops that produced both magazines were located in the same neighborhood as the Boston office of the American Sunday School Union. Willis's and Child's motivations and circumstances, however, differed from those of the committee that edited the *Youth's Friend.* That magazine, subsidized by the organization and provided with a ready-made audience from its national network of Sunday schools, was a quasi-market publication focused predominantly on evangelical concerns. Willis and Child shared these editors' ideological passions (though not, in Child's case, their beliefs) but also used their magazines to strengthen their individual social and economic standings. Willis, who had become a relatively prosperous and respected printer and editor, employed the *Companion* to claim the traditional role of a virtuous gentleman framing debates for the public good. Child, a generation younger and financially insecure, hoped her *Miscellany* editorship would facilitate her economic independence. Because both magazines were independently financed and lacked preexisting readerships, advancing these goals—and their broader ideological agendas—required the development and maintenance of commercial audiences that found value in the publications' childrearing guidance.

Although no data remain to identify those audiences, we can make reasonable inferences from existing evidence. Children's magazines were beyond the financial means of most poor New Englanders. The limited number of poor children who appeared in their pages and the fact that most who did appear came from families that had fallen from prosperity further suggest that Willis and Child identified financially successful families as their primary readers. The content also indicates that the editors believed their subscribers were primarily adult female Protestants who, regardless of their denominational affiliation, held socially conservative views and were deeply sentimental about children. Finally, the fact that these purchasers were willing to accept a commercial product's guidance on the intimate subject of childrearing indicates their comfort with impersonal, market-based relationships, a position that excluded many rural New Englanders of the era.

These inferences suggest that the primary audience for these magazines was an expanding group of relatively prosperous and ambitious coastal New Englanders who embraced the ideals of gentility. The elites of this group, later known as Brahmins, were establishing cultural authority over the region through a genteel model that balanced public presentation of wealth—displayed through a sophisticated consumption of material goods—with advocacy of an optimistic liberal Protestant morality that emphasized individuals' capacity for self-improvement. Other striving members of these communities emulated this success, constructing public identities based upon similar, if less lavish, practices that reflected and (they hoped) facilitated their own social, economic, and spiritual advancement.

Both Willis and Child absorbed this genteel faith in self-improvement, and presented their magazines as instruments that could help families to achieve such goals for their children. Yet both also found elements of this elite version of genteel authority troubling. Willis challenged what he perceived as elites' secularized optimism, while Child employed liberal Protestant values to promote a more democratic genteel vision that also extended opportunities for advancement to women and nonwhites. These efforts to alter emerging standards of gentility achieved limited success. Both magazines found an audience, an indication that genteel society contained diverse perspectives on Protestant theology and consequently on approaches to childrearing. Yet Willis struggled to reconcile his patriarchal Calvinist pedagogical methods with his audience's sentimental and increasingly feminized view of children. Child achieved immediate commercial success and critical acclaim for the *Miscellany*'s optimistic approach to American children, but her attempts to engage young readers as participants in debates on controversial public issues, particularly abolition, eventually led to her dismissal from the magazine.

Willis's and Child's experiences reveal the extent to which their genteel audiences' standards of respectability exerted influence over children's magazines during the second quarter of the nineteenth century. This influence fueled the growth of the *Companion* and the *Miscellany* but also dictated the shape of that growth. Neither Willis nor Child fully met those standards themselves: his faith was too orthodox; she was too poor and too democratic. Thus, they had to mitigate their ideals to meet the expectations of customers who were more interested in reinforcing the existing social order than in changing it. Those expectations coalesced around two primary requirements for children's magazines: a sentimental treatment of childhood, and a corresponding desire to cloister children from the potentially corrupting influences of market cultures and public controversies.

Yet even as audiences pushed Willis and Child to accept these requirements, their patronage of the *Companion* and the *Miscellany* laid a foundation for children's eventual participation in the market cultures their guardians feared. During this period, children's consumer roles remained limited. With the exception of the *Miscellany*, most antebellum publications sought, in the words of Willis, "to do good *to*" rather than *for* young readers.[8] Nevertheless, the popularity of Child's efforts to foster an active role for children as critics of the *Miscellany* as well as the industry's emerging recognition of the didactic value of instigating young readers' consumer desires revealed a nascent public impulse to nurture that desire as a tool for shaping respectable identities. The extended run of Willis's *Companion* and the mercurial one of Child's *Miscellany* reveal the difficulties that editors faced in maintaining such a balance but also illustrate how this genteel impulse spurred the development of children's magazines into a sustainable commercial industry.

CHAPTER 1

Deacon Willis's *Companion*

✳

THE FIRST weekly issue of the *Youth's Companion*, published on June 6, 1827, opened with "The Twins," an anonymous story about James, a young orphan, and Miss S, his neighbor and the Sunday school teacher who oversaw his spiritual education. When James became ill, he told Miss S,

> You know not how much I love you—how much I am obliged to you. Before you taught me, I knew nothing of death—nothing about heaven, or God, or angels. I was a very wicked boy till you met me . . . [but now] I am not afraid to die. You told me, and the Testament tells me, that Christ will suffer little children to come unto him, and though I am a very sinful little boy, yet I think I shall be happy, for I love this Saviour who can save such a wicked boy as I am . . . When I am dead I wish you to tell all the Sabbath scholars how much I love them all—tell them they must all die, and may die young, and tell them to come and measure the grave of little James.—And then prepare to die.

Soon after, Miss S, sitting at James's bedside, "with her own trembling hand, closed his lovely eyes as they shut up in the slumber of death. He fell asleep with a smile—without a struggle."[1]

By the time "The Twins" appeared in the *Youth's Companion*, narratives about pious children's deaths had been staples in New England homes for well over a century. James Janeway's *A Token for Children*, which presented thirteen tales of religious conversions and deaths of "sweet children which feared God," had established the genre in England during the 1670s.[2] His book first appeared in Boston bookshops during the 1680s and was republished in New England in 1700. With the addendum "A Token for the Children of New England," featuring deathbed accounts recounted by eminent Boston clergyman Cotton Mather, it was read and imitated by Americans well into the nineteenth century.[3] Janeway's stories reminded children "about their miserable Condition by Nature," thereby reinforcing New England Calvinists' belief in innate human depravity.[4] Calvinists believed that only God's offering of eternal grace could remove that depravity, but such salvation could not occur until children were old enough to acknowledge their sinfulness and place their eternal fate in God's hands.[5] Unless and until individuals experienced this conversion, they would spend an eternity in hell after their deaths. Because approximately 40 percent of children in seventeenth-century New England died before reaching adulthood, parents pushed their children to begin the process of accepting God's omnipotence as early as possible.[6] Deathbed conversion stories gained favor among these parents, who saw them as a way to remind young readers to take their spiritual obligations seriously.

"The Twins" employed the fundamental elements of the genre, including articulation of children's depravity and focus on preparation for divine judgment. Yet other components of the story softened the traditional message of such narratives. For instance, Janeway's stories included excruciating details of the conversion process: Sarah Howley "brake a vein in her Lungs . . . and oft did spit blood" as she sought redemption; while pleading to God, an unnamed child "would beg and expostulate and weep so that sometimes it could not be kept from the ears of Neighbours."[7] The *Companion* story, however, minimized such agonies, focusing on the accomplishment rather than the process of conversion and directing young readers' attention away from the painful internal struggle required to achieve religious faith. Instead, "The Twins" led children toward a more optimistic message, one drawn from a sentimental culture that was growing increasingly popular among Americans in the early nineteenth century. In contrast to Janeway's tales, this story suggested that sympathy and love, especially when offered by women and children, could facilitate individual journeys toward heavenly rewards.

Nathaniel Willis was the person responsible for introducing this milder version of the conversion story into the *Companion*. Both a printer and a publisher, he edited the magazine from its inception in 1827 through 1856. Yet ironically he was an orthodox Calvinist who displayed little tolerance for such sentiment in his personal theology. A deacon at Boston's Park Street Church (a congregation known as "Brimstone Corner," in part because of its preachers' fiery denunciation of sin), Willis favored a stern, patriarchal approach toward instigating religious awakening in both his church and his home.[8] According to his children, he banned secular entertainments such as dancing; and they recalled that he and the clergy who regularly visited the Willis home would declare that young hearts were "awful hard and dreadful wicked" and that children would go to hell if they did not commit themselves to their faith.[9] In 1819 he even published a pamphlet, "Accounts of the Happy Deaths of Two Young Christians," that adhered to Janeway's model: it emphasized young people's suffering during conversion and did not include a female catalyst who would inspire children to consider their divine fate.[10]

"The Twins," however, tempered such severity and foreshadowed the *Companion*'s increasingly gentler approach as Willis gradually began offering mother-and-child narratives that employed pathos to inspire young readers to reassess the state of their souls. For instance, in 1827, he was still publishing frightening pieces such as the poem "To a Child Who 'Forgot to Pray'":

> Death, on his pale horse, following fast;
> Gains on thy speed, with hell behind;
> Fool, all thy *yesterdays* are past,
> *To-morrow* thou wilt never find;
> *Today* is hastening to eternity;
> *This night thy soul may be required of thee*

Yet by 1856 he was including more compassionate entreaties, such as the poem "The Dying Child":

> But you must first lay me to sleep,
> Where grand-papa is laid;
> Is not the churchyard cold and dark,
> And shan't I feel afraid?
>
> And Should I sleep to wake no more
> Dear mamma, good-bye;
> Poor nurse is kind, but oh! do you
> Be with me when I die.[11]

Willis's mitigation of traditional Calvinist severity, despite his personal connection to a stern and patriarchal faith, was part of a larger pattern of paradox that surrounding his *Companion* editorship. The magazine promoted a deferential faith, yet Willis had worked for decades to weaken the power of social elites whom he perceived as both blasphemous and dangerous to the new nation's democratic potential. He sought to isolate young readers from public life to protect them from the moral and physical dangers of an expanding commercial society, but he conveyed this message through a market product that he encouraged children to identify as their own and pay for with their own money.

Willis's contradictory choices illustrate the difficulties of adapting to the changing nature of cultural authority in early nineteenth-century New England. Like many young men of his generation, Willis struggled to establish economic independence and social respectability under the new nation's tumultuous conditions. In response to these challenges, he was swept into the wave of religious revivals known as the Second Great Awakening. The orthodox community of Boston helped him gain financial stability and social status, and he embraced that increasingly artisanal community's opposition to the growing power of the city's Unitarian elites. These evangelical workingmen viewed the Unitarians' combination of liberal Protestant faith and conservative Federalist politics as betrayals of God and the ideals of the American Revolution, and they sought to circumvent elite power by taking their cause to the public through the press.[12] The *Youth's Friend*, the nation's first sustainable children's magazine, emerged from this wave of religious literature, as did Willis's religious newspaper, *The Boston Recorder*.

By the late 1820s, however, this orthodox community was struggling to remain relevant in Boston and its surrounding towns. Liberal Protestant thought predominated in the majority of Boston's churches and within its power structure. Harriet Beecher Stowe described the atmosphere that was prevailing in 1826, when her father, orthodox minister Lyman Beecher, arrived in Boston:

> Calvinism or orthodoxy . . . was the dethroned royal family wandering like a permitted mendicant in the city where once it had held court . . . All the literary men of Massachusetts were Unitarian. All the trustees and professors of Harvard College were Unitarians. All the elite of wealth and fashion crowded Unitarian churches. The judges on the bench were Unitarian, giving decisions by which the peculiar features of church organization, so carefully ordained by the Pilgrim fathers, had been nullified.[13]

That spring Lyman Beecher instigated an orthodox revival from his pulpit at the newly formed Hanover Street Church, and Willis reaffirmed his commitment to the cause. This time he did so as a community leader, working through his position as a Park Street deacon to facilitate hiring Beecher's son Edward as his church's new minister and founding the *Companion* as an evangelical voice directed at the community's young families. The magazine was not primarily a profit-making venture but an attempt to counter the success of the *Juvenile Miscellany*, the Unitarian-backed children's magazine that debuted in September 1826. Nonetheless, Willis was constantly reminding subscribers to pay their bills on time, an indication that finances were at least a partial concern.

As a successful printer and newspaper publisher, Willis was assuming the traditional gentleman's privilege of offering the public his views on issues of social significance. Yet neither his income nor his environment allowed him to maintain that gentlemanly posture unequivocally. To benefit his evangelical cause and affirm his social standing, he needed to sustain the *Companion* financially, which under contemporary market conditions meant developing the ability to please his subscribers. Thus, his audience's commercial power forced Willis to develop a more genteel editorial approach, one that balanced his religious concerns with commercial needs. The empathetic outlook of "The Twins" exemplified this new approach: rather than emphasizing the orthodox practice of motivating children through fear, it highlighted sentimental methods of nurturing spiritual development, an attitude preferred by many of the respectable women whom he perceived as his primary customers. These women shared Willis's belief in the use of emotion as a tool for spiritual conversion, and a narrative shift toward love and pathos enabled him to establish common ideological ground with these customers without sacrificing his faith's core values.[14]

Willis's adaptations made his *Companion* a pivotal institution in the growth of the children's magazine industry and also revealed the broader shift in conceptions of childhood that were beginning to occur in urbanizing regions of the United States. His competitors during the 1820s and 1830s recognized the value of print media as a persuasive instrument in a more mobile, less deferential society. Moreover, Willis understood that this instrument transformed cultural ideals about childhood from concepts unilaterally handed down by religious and economic elites into products negotiated between buyers and sellers in commercial markets. Although he remained uncomfortable with this relationship, he acknowledged and adjusted to this reality, thus establishing an editorial formula that enabled the *Companion* to promote his religious values for more than three decades, a period that exceeded the run of nearly every other antebellum American children's magazine. Another consequence of his choice would have pleased Willis less: although the fears he shared with his audience about the corrupting influences of market cultures precluded young readers from assuming an active role in this negotiation process during his *Companion* editorship, the changes that he implemented helped to validate children's magazines as a viable commercial product. Consequently, they accelerated the process of legitimizing a genteel role for child consumers in the United States.

NATHANIEL WILLIS's adaptation of the *Companion*'s approach to children derived from three considerations: the crisis of authority that his orthodox community faced, his ambition to help lead the revival of that community's influence, and, most importantly, the changing role of Calvinism in early nineteenth-century New England. To understand this change, we might begin with one word—*peculiar*—which Willis used twice in the editorial that opened his prospectus for the *Companion* on April 16, 1827:

> The capacities of children, and the peculiar situation and duties of youth, require select and appropriate reading. And while adults have various periodical publications, which they consider highly valuable, the younger part of the community seem to require that the same means be prepared for their gratification . . . *This is a day of peculiar care of Youth.* Christians feel that their children must be trained up for Christ. Patriots and philanthropists are making rapid improvements in every branch of education. Literature, science, liberty and religion are extending in the earth. The human mind is becoming emancipated from the bondage of ignorance and superstition. Our children are born to higher destinies than their fathers; they will be actors in a far advanced period of the church and the world. Let their minds be formed, their hearts prepared, and their characters moulded for the scenes and the duties of a brighter day.[15]

The contradictions within Willis's use of *peculiar* illustrate the unique status of children in his orthodox community. As a deacon, he would have been cognizant of the use of the word in Exodus and the First Epistle of Peter, where it describes people who have accepted the omnipotence of divine authority.[16] Willis's choice of the word thus implied that his young readers had a chosen, exalted status, but it also marked them as property, an association affirmed by southerners who just three years later introduced the phrase "peculiar institution" to describe slavery.[17] The idea in both cases was to elevate individuals, materially and spiritually, through their submission. This concept combined the new nation's faith in social progress with the belief of its more orthodox communities that such improvements could occur only through maintenance of a traditional social order.

Willis's ancestry traced back to the earliest separatist settlements in colonial New England, but he did not derive his idea of children as peculiar from those seventeenth-century forebears.[18] Calvinist leaders of that era did not use the term in that context and viewed such notions of human progress as heretical; for these men, recognition of divine omnipotence and abdication to God's will was the ultimate goal, not a step toward salvation or material prosperity.[19] Their writings for and about children focused on innate depravity, not the possibilities of individual or community salvation. For example, John Cotton's 1646 catechism *Milk for Babes,* one of the earliest writings for children in colonial New England and a staple in orthodox homes for more than two hundred years after its publication, taught children that "I was conceived in sinne, and born in iniquity" and "my corrupt nature is empty of grace, bent unto sinne, and onely unto sinne, and that continually." This emphasis on the hopelessness of the human condition without God's saving intervention was common in texts read by seventeenth-century American children.[20]

Willis's *Companion* and other early nineteenth-century evangelical writings for children retained this message but also incorporated an alternative perspective that highlighted young people's spiritual potential. Janeway's *A Token for Children* had instigated that shift during the late 1600s, presenting stories of children whom one historian of children's literature has described as "manifestly more holy than their elders ... *good* children, going to their heavenly reward."[21] Janeway did not deny human depravity; instead, he claimed that properly instructed children had the capacity to develop into pious Christians. He described these children as "rough stone[s] [who] may prove a pillar in the temple of God" and commanded parents to instruct and catechize their offspring, who "are not subjects incapable of the grace of God." Such a belief remained unusual enough to press Janeway into offering a justification of the veracity of his book's accounts: "What is presented is faithfully taken from experienced, solid Christians, some of them in no way related to the children, who, themselves, were eye and ear witnesses of God's works of wonder; or from my own knowledge, or from reverend godly ministers, and from persons that are of unspotted reputation, for holiness, integrity, and wisdom: and several passages are taken verbatim, in writing, from their dying lips. I may add many other excellent examples, if I have any encouragement from this piece."[22]

Despite the popularity of Janeway's text, doubts about children's capacity for piety persisted. Nearly a half-century later, Jonathan Edwards, one of New England's leading ministers, noted that "it has heretofore been looked upon as a strange thing, when any have seemed to be savingly wrought upon, and remarkably changed in their childhood."[23] Edwards's comment suggests that this opinion was changing in colonial America, as does his use of the concept of Christians as a peculiar people—a concept that Willis borrowed nearly a century later.[24] They reflect New Englanders' growing faith in human agency and the need for orthodox clergy to reconcile their faith with this democratizing cultural impulse.

In eighteenth-century writings for children, the predominant solution to this dilemma was the "fire and brimstone" technique of spiritual instruction, which emphasized God's omnipotence while acknowledging individuals' capacity to make decisions that improved their chances for salvation. A popular version of this formula appeared in Isaac Watts's *Divine Songs,* originally published in England in 1715 but circulated widely in the colonies after 1730.[25] These verses for younger children focused less on abstract concerns of divine judgment and more on young people's mundane responsibilities. Nonetheless, the consequences of misbehavior remained terrifying:

> Have you not heard what dreadful plagues
> Are threaten'd by the Lord,
> To him that breaks his father's laws,
> Or mocks his mother's word?
>
> What heavy guilt upon him lies!
> How cursed is his name!
> The ravens shall pick out his eyes,
> And eagles eat the same.[26]

The poem details the horrors of misconduct while implying that children could avoid such a fate, in this case by deferring to God's natural hierarchy through obedience of their parents.

This genre of eighteenth-century evangelical children's literature provided a model for the *Companion;* but as in the deathbed stories, Willis softened the details and the tone of the message. The *Companion*'s 1831 story "The Busy Bee," for example, presented a "lady" preparing a birthday feast for two girls, Jane and Fanny. Jane, the good girl, receives orange slices, a roasted apple, and honey, whereas Fanny gets orange peels, apple rinds, "and the other refuse of the feast." When both girls begin to cry, the woman asks Fanny, "What do you cry for? . . . I know that you heartily love, and have for a long time sought after every thing that is hurtful, filthy, and bad; and, like a pig, you have delighted in wallowing in mire. I therefore am resolved to indulge you. As you love what is filthy, you shall enjoy it, and shall be treated like a pig." When Fanny begs for forgiveness and promises "she [will] never again seek after wickedness, and delight in it," the "lady" responds:

> Fanny, . . . it is very easy for little girls to make fine promises, and to say, "I will be good," and, "I am sorry I have behaved ill." But I am not a person who can be satisfied with words, any more than you can be with orange-peel and skins of apples. I must have deeds, not words. Turn away from your sins, and call upon your God to help you to repent of your past evil life. If you do not

wish to partake of the portion of dogs and swine and unclean creatures in the world to come, you must learn to hate sin in this present world.

"The Busy Bee" may horrify twenty-first-century readers, but it also reduces the stakes of Fanny's "wickedness" in comparison to the punishments delineated in earlier evangelical children's literature. Rather than dying or having her eyes pecked out by ravens, she is served garbage instead of delicacies. Moreover, the *Companion*'s female authority figure reasons with Fanny, offering a veiled warning about eternal consequences rather than explicitly detailing the violent fate awaiting young sinners. The *Companion* indicates that Fanny responds to this approach, forsaking her evil habits and receiving a feast equal to Jane's at her next birthday.[27] This positive ending also contrasts with earlier texts, which used the threat of damnation to motivate young readers to transform their behavior.

Like the gradual eighteenth-century shift toward acceptance of children's capacity for piety, Willis's softening of his predecessors' evangelical practices was a response to the public's growing belief in individual empowerment.[28] The goals of the two shifts were different, however, because the status of Calvinists in the early eighteenth century was much different from their subsequent status in the nineteenth century. Jonathan Edwards and (in England) Isaac Watts were members of the educated elite who approached young readers as part of an effort to maintain the theological and social status quo in their communities. By Willis's time, New England's elites largely had abandoned Calvinism, and orthodox Congregational churches were populated predominantly by artisans such as Willis who were disenchanted with the economic and political direction of their society.[29] For these men, faith became an instrument for reform rather than preservation, yet for Willis religion was also a vehicle for achieving the economic stability and social respectability that had eluded him during his youth. His ascension within Boston's orthodox community linked him, albeit problematically, to the growing segment of Americans who were embracing gentility as a means of self-advancement; and it impelled him to forge the ideological compromise that sustained the *Youth's Companion*.

WILLIS'S RESPECTED status in his church and community at the time of the *Companion*'s founding belied a tumultuous upbringing that exemplified the challenges that many young artisans faced in the new nation's rapidly changing society. Born in Boston in 1780, in the midst of the revolution, he was the son of a printer devoted to the patriot cause. The elder Willis had allegedly participated in the Boston Tea Party and supported independence as editor of the *Independent Chronicle* from 1774 to 1784. After the war and the death of Nathaniel's mother, his father moved west, founding a series of newspapers in Virginia and Ohio during the 1780s and 1790s. Young Nathaniel joined his father and new stepmother in Virginia in 1787 and worked as his father's assistant until he returned to Boston to apprentice at the *Chronicle* in 1796.[30]

The Willis family's constant mobility during Nathaniel's childhood suggests that his father's patriotism did not result in economic success. Financial struggle and migration were common during these decades: the war had ravaged the new states' economies, and its conclusion sparked a wave of travelers in search of new opportunities.[31] Nathaniel followed this pattern of mobility, apprenticing in Boston until 1803 and then moving with his new wife to Portland, Maine, where he accepted an offer to edit a new newspaper, the *Eastern Argus.*

A group of Republican businessmen had established the *Argus* to incite opposition to the Federalist elites who were controlling the city's government. Thus, Willis's position placed him in the midst of the intense political conflicts spreading throughout the nation during this period. He justified his new employers' faith, making "the *Argus* the most widely circulated newspaper published in Maine [and] the most extensive in advertising" within a year of his arrival. However, in 1806 he wrote an article attacking a local Federalist candidate as "swindler, . . . a dissembler, . . . [and] a drunkard," and he was sued and found guilty of libel. Unable to pay the fine, which his financiers also refused to pay, Willis went to prison for one hundred days.[32]

Willis's struggles during this period led him, like many of his contemporaries, to turn to evangelical religion. Although he previously had displayed little interest in spiritual matters, preferring to dance and spend "my Sabbaths roving the fields and reading newspapers," he attended an autumn 1807 service led by Reverend Edward Payson, the young minister of the Second Congregational Church in Portland. Willis "became a constant hearer" of Payson's message and converted during the winter of 1807–8.[33]

His faith further strained his position in Portland. When he published more religious articles in the *Argus,* his backers complained about his "milk-and-water" publication. Willis resigned and, after a failed attempt to start a religious newspaper, opened a grocery store in 1809. However, the combination of a struggling economy and Willis's refusal to sell liquor killed the venture, creating additional financial problems that he spent years working to eliminate.[34]

The Willises returned to Boston in the spring of 1812 and joined the newly established Park Street Church, which was dedicated to restoring "the primitive orthodoxy of New England"in response to what its members viewed as the region's decaying faith.[35] In this community, Willis shifted from battling Maine's political elites to opposing the spread of Unitarianism, the liberal Protestant faith increasingly associated with Boston's wealthiest citizens. He established a print shop on State Street and contributed his printing and publishing services to the orthodox cause.[36] In 1816, he founded the *Boston Recorder,* one of the earliest religious newspapers in the United States, and became a strong public advocate for traditional Protestant beliefs.

Willis's business endeavors brought him the financial success and social respectability he had been seeking for more than a decade, and he cultivated an image that publicized this success. In 1819, he purchased a large home on Atkinson (later Congress) Street that included a guest room the family called the "Prophet's Chamber," where visiting religious dignitaries stayed when they preached to the city's orthodox congregations. Willis's proudest achievement, though, was his appointment as a deacon at the Park Street Church: for the rest of his life he insisted upon that honorific as a symbol of his status.[37]

As he rose within his religious community's economic and social hierarchy, he also privately affirmed his devotion within his family. Biographers of Willis's two famous children, writers Nathaniel Parker Willis and Sara Willis Parton (who published under the pseudonym Fanny Fern), characterize the household as patriarchal. Family life centered around obedience and discipline, particularly on the Sabbath. On that day, Willis forbade all games, toys, and secular books. Parton recalled "the distasteful and barbarous routine of being routed out of bed to attend long recitation and prayers before breakfast" as well as more severe aspects of her father's demeanor:

> "Father is coming!" and little, round faces grow long, and merry voices are hushed, and toys are hustled into the closet; and mamma glances nervously at the door; and baby is bribed with a lump of sugar to keep the peace; and father's business face relaxes not a muscle; and the little group huddle like timid sheep in a corner, and tea is dispatched as silently as if speaking were prohibited by the statute book; and the children creep like culprits to bed, marveling that baby dare crow so loud, now that "Father has come."

Other evidence mitigates Parton's severe assessment of her father, for instance, his willingness to send her to the school of Catharine Beecher, who shared Sara Willis's skepticism about orthodox faith. Nevertheless,

Nathaniel Willis clearly ran a household that strictly adhered to the dictates of his orthodox faith.[38]

Like his Calvinist forefathers, Willis viewed the family as a paternalistic microcosm of society; and just as he sought to dictate his beliefs to his children, he used the *Recorder* to shape his community's faith. Although he claimed he would not "admit the Unitarian controversy into the *Recorder* because the paper was intended as a vehicle of [religious] intelligence," the term *Unitarianism* in fact appeared in the paper seventy times between 1817 and 1824. In nearly every case, the writer was critical of "Unitarian Universalism," arguing, for instance, that the "statement of the views of Unitarians with regard to future punishment . . . must be considered by every friend to evangelical truth as threatening the most serious injury to the interests of piety."[39] The negative consequences of Willis's Portland experiences had not led him to retreat from advocacy in his publications.

Thus, when Lyman Beecher arrived in Boston in the spring of 1826 and insisted on "a united and simultaneous effort to rescue from perversion the doctrines and institutions of our fathers," Willis answered the call.[40] His choice to contribute by way of a children's magazine was a response to the success of the *Juvenile Miscellany*, a liberal Protestant publication that had appeared just three months after the launch of Beecher's revival. Willis later indicated that he had developed his ideas—first, for a children's department in the *Recorder;* then for the *Companion*—from the Bible stories he told to his own children. Yet this explanation is not credible: the *Recorder* ran without a children's department until the month when the *Miscellany* debuted a few blocks from his print shop; and his oldest child, to whom he presumably had proselytized since infancy, turned twenty that year.[41]

The *Companion* gave Willis an opportunity to confirm his status as a virtuous, public-minded citizen in the mold of revolutionary-era New England artisans such as Benjamin Franklin (who had apprenticed at the *Independent Chronicle* two generations earlier). Indications that Willis aspired to this status include his refusal to accept advertising in the *Companion*, a decision that contrasted with his previous practices at the *Argus* and the *Recorder*.[42] Despite his evangelical goals, he also refrained from partisan advocacy in the *Companion*. The motto "No Sectarianism, No Controversy" appeared on the magazine's masthead for all thirty years of his tenure; and in contrast with his editorializing in the *Recorder*, he largely upheld this commitment, avoiding criticism of Unitarians even as he continued to promote orthodox beliefs. Yet as his constant bill collecting shows, Willis was either incapable or unwilling to produce the new magazine as a wholly philanthropic enterprise.[43] To maintain the *Companion* and the religious and personal ambitions it represented, he needed to make his orthodox faith marketable to a commercial audience.

WHEN WILLIS looked for a model that blended such religious and commercial concerns, one publication must have drawn his immediate attention: the *Youth's Friend and Scholar's Magazine.* Although he never acknowledged the *Youth's Friend* as an influence on the *Companion,* he almost certainly was aware of the earlier magazine. Its publisher, the American Sunday School Union, had a satellite office just a few blocks from Willis's print shop on Washington Street. Moreover, as an advocate of Sunday schools, he would have been familiar with the organization's role in spreading those institutions across the nation.[44] Particularly convincing evidence of his awareness is the similarity of the two magazines' pedagogical approaches. Both based their methods on orthodox Protestant doctrines. Although the union stated its commitment to interdenominational cooperation, most of the men on its Committee on Publications came from orthodox backgrounds.[45] For instance, Frederick Adolphus Packard, the organization's corresponding secretary and the committee's leading ideological force, privately dismissed "the beggarly elements of ethics and natural philosophy" in liberal Protestantism and viewed "the doctrines of revealed religion" as the only way to fully engage children's "affections" in religious faith.[46] Yet editors at both the *Youth's Friend* and the *Companion* recognized the value of consumer products as tools for spiritual instruction.

The *Youth's Friend* had begun its life as the *Teacher's Offering,* a local publication of the New Haven Sunday School Union, and on the title page of its 1823–24 bound edition the magazine offered a verse from the Book of Proverbs: "Buy the truth and sell it not."[47] In 1825, when the American Sunday School Union took control of the *Teacher's Offering* and renamed it the *Youth's Friend,* that epigram disappeared, and no further commentaries linked commerce and religious faith. Yet the tension between those two concerns remained central to the publication's message.[48] In fact, the *Teacher's Offering* had initially been created in response to concerns about how to reward children appropriately for good behavior at Sunday schools. In the preface to the first issue, the New Haven teachers who had produced the magazine explained their efforts:

> Being convinced that the usual mode of rewarding children in Sabbath Schools is not attended with the best effects, . . . we are decidedly of the opinion that the formation of a library and the publication of a small Monthly Magazine, (which will be devoted entirely to the interests of the Sabbath

Schools) will be more useful to the children more satisfactory to parents, and less expensive. The Committee would suggest to Teachers of Sabbath Schools, the propriety of presenting the "TEACHER'S OFFERING" as a monthly reward for punctual attendance, correct recitation and good behaviour.[49]

During this era, "the usual mode of rewarding children in Sabbath Schools" meant giving students tickets for proper recitation of Bible verses. Children then turned in those tickets for prizes—usually books—or traded them with peers. Mark Twain later satirized this system in *The Adventures of Tom Sawyer,* and many parents and instructors of the time also criticized the arrangement. They believed that such rewards created environments of envy and competition, which sparked commercially oriented behaviors such as haggling and bargaining among young entrepreneurs, and that the practice failed to instill meaningful understanding of sacred texts.[50]

Although the *Teacher's Offering* offered an alternative to the ticket system, its editors faced the same challenge: how could they make their product enticing to young readers without sacrificing its religious value? Their strategy depended on their ability to convince children that this product that had been created for them had inherent value, and in the *Youth's Friend* the American Sunday School Union continued that approach even as it abstained from acknowledging the calculations behind it. The 1825 name change to the *Youth's Friend* followed a trend toward more companionate titles; in 1824, for example, British evangelical organizations had founded two children's magazines: the *Child's Friend* and the *Child's Companion.*[51] The editors of the *Youth's Friend* explained the intent of the title change in a piece in which a boy proclaims his preference for the new title because "it is more like what is our own, and you know we like what is our own."[52]

Willis followed this naming trend, a choice that supports my hypothesis that he knew about the *Youth's Friend* and its success. He also followed that magazine's practice of explaining to parents the value of emphasizing that the publication was specifically for children. In the announcement for his new magazine, he noted, "We apprehend some will object that another paper is *unnecessary* and *expensive,*" but suggested, "If our youth would consider the COMPANION *their own paper,* they would be willing to pay for it themselves."[53] A few months later, he relayed this message directly to his young audience: "The *Youth's Companion* is intended to be *your own* paper. We wish each of you to have it come in your own name, and to pay for it with your own earnings, or other pocket money. We advise your parents to give you the first reading of it . . . and always to speak of it as *the children's paper.*" Later in the same issue, he affirmed this point in an article that explained how a child might make "Good Use of a Shilling." He suggested "laying by" two cents a month to pay in advance for next year's volume of the *Companion* at a cheaper price.[54]

Like the *Youth's Friend*, the *Companion* did not extend young readers' consumer role to include influence over the content of the magazine. In accordance with predominant educational practices of the era, both publications treated children as recipients rather than active participants in the learning process.[55] The magazines' policies suggested that the existence of a product created specifically for young people should in itself offer sufficient appeal to young readers; they need not also expect entertainment from it. As the *Youth's Friend* asserted in "The Beginning," the magazine's "great object" was "to do good to those who read it . . . Let its readers begin with the desire to get good from it. Let them desire it so much as to pray that they may be profited by all they find in it. Do not be all the time looking for something amusing or extraordinary . . . The main thing with us all, in the use of books ought to be to improve our minds and to obtain good advice as to our conduct in life."[56]

Willis used similar language in a letter to author Lydia Sigourney, describing how he "endeavor[ed] to do good *to* the young."[57] His goal of "doing good to children" framed the relationship between magazine and reader as patriarchal and predominantly unilateral. Both the *Youth's Friend* and the *Companion* sought to engage children as consumers insofar as such a role increased their interest in religious instruction. Once engaged, however, readers became receptacles into which the editors "convey[ed] a vast amount of information" so that "the influence of the Holy Spirit may carry conviction home."[58]

Perhaps the most noticeable link between the two magazines' pedagogies was their predilection for introducing children's deaths into nearly every issue. "George Cook," the story that opened the *Teacher's Offering*'s first issue (as well as the introduction to this book), established a pattern of reminding young readers that death—and divine judgment—lurked around every corner. A similar story, "The Death of Francis A. Brown," features a five-year-old boy, "obedient to his parents and teachers, fond of his book, and of school, and . . . quite forward in learning." Yet he likes "to make himself heard," and one day steps upon a box to "speak [his] piece" but instead falls and breaks his neck.[59] Such stories suggested that children courted destruction by crossing the boundaries of deferential behavior.

In both the *Youth's Friend* and the *Companion*, such frightening tales mingled with less dire ones, an indication that nineteenth-century orthodoxy for children was less severe than its eighteenth-century counterpart had been. The *Youth's Friend* often replaced terrifying rhetoric with more compassionate language. When one of the children in "The Sabbath; or, The Three Cousins" proclaims, "I wish the Sabbath day was dead," the narrator directly addresses the audience: "'What a profane speech,' I think I hear some of you say; 'how could any little boy be so wicked as to utter it?' Ah, my dear children, look into your own hearts, and you will perhaps discover something of the same feeling, though you dare not utter the words. Do you never wake on a Sabbath morning and wish it was Monday? And are you never tired of the day, and glad when it draws to a close?'" Rather than condemning blasphemy and predicting imminent damnation, the story encouraged readers to assess their own faults rigorously, delivering a traditional religious message in a more sympathetic manner.[60]

The *Youth's Friend*'s appeals to young consumers and its softened orthodoxy were similar to, and probably an influence upon, the *Companion*'s. Yet the economic and theological conditions of the magazines were quite distinct. The *Youth's Friend* was subsidized by a national organization with a stated goal of interdenominational cooperation, whereas the *Companion* was financially independent and had been created in the midst of a local denominational conflict. These differences forced Willis to confront directly the inherent contradictions of genteel ambitions for American children, and to construct a commercially sustainable editorial formula under those volatile circumstances.

ONE PRIMARY theological distinction between the *Youth's Friend* and the *Companion* was their treatment of children's redemption. Both magazines embraced Janeway's faith in the possibility of youthful salvation, but the American Sunday School Union also promoted a sentimental belief that such children's spiritual purity might guide others toward the divine path. Willis's magazine generally avoided this subject, focusing instead on the message that the struggle for salvation was an intensely personal and isolating experience.

The majority of *Youth's Friend* stories about pious children focused on the consequences rather than the process of salvation. As in the *Companion*, these narratives eliminated most of the agonizing details prevalent in Janeway's deathbed conversions; but the *Youth's Friend* also often removed the deathbed. Wayward children died regularly in that magazine, but its editors were more interested than Willis was in exploring the ways in which pious youth might benefit society. Indeed, the editors suggested that piety could save children's lives. In "The Orphan Boys," for example, the piety of two brothers who prefer to starve rather than sell their Bible so astounds a merchant that he gives them food to sustain them.[61] Likewise, in "The Knowledge of a Little Boy Astonishing a Priest," the devotion and learning of a pious child thwart the conversion efforts of a "Popish" Irish priest.[62]

Converted children in *Youth's Friend* stories often had a positive spiritual influences on adults, particularly fathers bedeviled by alcohol. The heroine of "Hannah More; or, The Advantages of Sunday Schools" experiences conversion at Sunday school, "but the beneficial influence of her introduction to the Sunday-school [do] not stop here." Her fervent prayers for her father, who spends most of his earnings in a nearby saloon, finally shame him into sobriety and religious conversion. The story extends beyond her father's moment of epiphany to describe his continuing struggles (in contrast to the relative ease of Hannah's conversion), but her instruction and support help him maintain his commitment and restore family order and happiness.[63]

Hannah's place at home and in church—particularly as juxtaposed with her father's place in the saloon—exemplifies the way in which the *Youth's Friend* connected pious children to domestic environments. Yet the magazine's use of this emerging sentimental trope linking piety and the home did not extend to presenting those environments as realms of feminine authority. Stories mentioned fathers more often than mothers, and those mothers who did appear were not active child rearers. Instead, they provided a passive form of moral ballast; stories such as "She Sobbed Herself to Death" taught children that their sinful conduct could literally destroy their mothers.[64] Such minimal, reactive female roles reflected the patriarchal focus of the American Sunday School Union's all-male Committee of Publications.

The *Companion* gradually adopted a similar formula of mixing orthodox theology and sentiment, but in the process Willis increasingly emphasized women's—rather than children's—power to exert positive influence on individual and national moral development. He did not begin with this approach; in early issues, children in the *Companion*'s stories were self-absorbed and more isolated than their counterparts in the *Youth's Friend* or the *Miscellany* were. Few appeared in peer settings, many were orphans, and most of the spiritual mentors who did appear were male. Dying children occasionally implored people "to struggle hard to come after me," but these narratives focused on each individual's assessment of their spiritual fate rather than the sentimental, social value of conversion.[65]

"A Death Bed Scene of a Child Six Years Old," which appeared in the first issue, exemplifies this formula. The dying boy becomes "an anxious inquirer after the way of salvation," asking, "Shall I be happy after death?" His father responds optimistically because the son has been a good, obedient child who attended church and read his Bible, but the boy confesses, "I did not love any of these things. I was afraid of you, or I should never have done them." Finally, when his minister tells him that "faith is the only way to obtain the Saviour, . . . light appear[s] to break in upon his soul—anxiety [is] removed, and he seem[s] to look upon death with joy."[66] This six-year-old's prodigious eloquence (a feature common among Calvinist children, who were trained to explore and express any hint of their developing faith) and lack of social consciousness reflect Willis's primary concern during his community's religious crisis: promoting orthodox beliefs and an individual, faith-based path to salvation.

Willis's aversion to sentimentalizing children extended to the *Companion*'s format. Unlike the *Youth's Friend* and the *Miscellany*, which appeared in the pocket-sized chapbook form traditional for juvenile books, the *Companion* was a broadsheet filled with dense text and few illustrations. Whereas the stories in the magazine portrayed children's moral development as an intensely personal and selfish experience, the child-focused but adult-formatted publication suggested that childrearing was a community responsibility with profound social implications. It was this responsibility, rather than children, that Willis sentimentalized in the *Companion*. His commercial strategy was inherent in the name of the magazine, as he emphasized in his first editorial: "We are all much *influenced* by our associates; and especially in early life—Children imperceptibly imitate other persons, & speak, and feel, and act like them . . . We do feel that we claim a high standing, and assume no mean responsibleness, when we propose to become the frequent *Companions* of children & youth."[67] This sociable relationship made the magazine more vital by linking its growth to children's development. Willis hinted at this connection, telling young readers, "If you like it yourselves, . . . show it to your little cousins and mates; and talk about what you read in it when you see them."[68]

Such a strategy came close to characterizing children as commercial spokespeople for the magazine. The *Companion*'s second editor, Daniel Sharp Ford, adopted this policy three decades later; but Willis shied away from it, positioning the magazine instead as a vehicle to "entertain . . . children and insensibly instruct them, . . . occupy leisure hours, and turn them to good account, . . . sanction and aid parental counsel and pulpit admonition, . . . [and] in an easy and familiar manner, warn against the ways of transgression, error, and ruin, and allure to those of virtue and piety."[69] This amiable perspective had little to do with Willis's actual editorial relationship with young readers during the next thirty years, but its sentiment foreshadowed the magazine's impending turn to women as its pedagogical and commercial partners.

Willis never explained this turn, but perhaps he hinted at his reasons in "A Father's Dying Advice," in which a minister apologizes to his children for his strict pedagogical methods: "Sometimes I have dealt strictly with you in matters which I believed would bring harm to your souls, and grieve the Spirit of God; and I have exerted my paternal authority to prevent mischief; but it was all done out of love to you. However, it may have happened, that I have sometimes been too severe: If this has been the case, I beg you, my dear children, to forgive me; O, forgive your poor dying father!"[70] Given what we know of Willis's daughter's reaction to his teaching practices, we might be tempted to read this passage as a message to his own children, but the lack of additional evidence makes such an interpretation speculative. Nor do we have any indication of complaints about the *Companion*'s early instructional methods. Whatever its motivation, the retreat from orthodox pedagogical practices in "A Father's Dying Advice" mirrored the *Companion*'s shift toward instructional policies that genteel families of the time would have deemed more feminine.

In the *Companion*'s prospectus, Willis stated that "the contents of the proposed work . . . will not take the form of discussion," thus affirming a long-standing orthodox tradition of dictating lessons rather than engaging children as active learners. By the fall of 1827, however, he had reversed that policy, introducing "conversations" between parents and children, a pedagogical form favored predominantly by female writers for children such as Maria Edgeworth and *Miscellany* editor Lydia Maria Child.[71] In January 1828, Willis even reprinted "Mother, What is Death?," a *Miscellany* poem in which a mother gently explains the death of a baby brother to her daughter as evidence of God's omnipotence and saving grace.[72] This turn toward a gentler, more nurturing approach was accompanied by articles praising the "superhuman strength and magnanimity" of women who served tirelessly at the bedside of ailing family members.[73] These pieces, which had little to do with instructing young readers, seem to be an attempt to curry favor with women. The lack of corresponding paeans to men or fatherhood indicates that Willis now saw women as his primary commercial audience.

The *Companion*'s fiction celebrated mothers not only as ballast but also as active conveyers of moral instruction. In "Self-Denial, or, the Two Cousins," for example, Charles decides to participate in a debate on the relative merits of Newton, Bacon, and Locke rather than carouse with "idle young men." He has taken to heart his mother's lesson that "*self-denial* is the basis of all

the virtues" but is mocked by his cousin William, who tells him, "I think you
had better be at your mother's apron strings." Subsequently, William goes
out drinking and commits a murder.[74] Such stories highlighted women's
moral authority within the home, particularly its potential for lasting influence over sons, even after they leave that protective environment and face
the temptations of modern commercial life.

This developing strategy revealed the overlap between Willis's interests
and those of his potential female subscribers. The ability of genteel women
to shape the physical and moral environments of the home was becoming
their primary source of cultural power, and Willis recognized that these
feminized environments could spiritually isolate vulnerable young people
from the commercial hazards of public life. Thus, he encouraged families to construct enticing domestic environments to shield children from
malevolent outside influences:

> As you would not drive your children to seek improper companions abroad,
> seek to make them contented and happy at home. Render their own houses
> pleasant to them, and they will rarely feel a desire to seek happiness in the
> houses of others. Be you their companions and friends, and they will not be
> anxious to seek foreign ones. As far as circumstances will admit, be much
> at home yourselves, and that will keep your children there . . . Do not be
> household tyrants; driving your children from your presence by severity,
> petulance, and ill humour: but conduct yourselves with that affection and
> affability which shall render your return welcome to your family, and draw
> your children in a little crowd of smiling faces round you the moment you
> enter the room.[75]

This statement does not link such an environment explicitly to mothers,
but it sentimentalizes home life in a manner that favors childrearing practices that genteel Americans were coming to perceive as feminine.

A shift toward a more companionate view of the home as a place to nurture and protect children did not mean that Willis eliminated traditionally
male evangelical methods from the magazine. He employed such methods
to frighten young readers away from the temptations of the dangerous outside world, where they could suffer torture at the hands of the Cherokees,
be impressed into a foreign navy, or even surrender to the temptations of
alcohol at the tender age of twelve.[76] He also continued to hector children about their inherent sinfulness and their need to prepare for divine
judgment. Indeed, his attempts to develop an ideological and commercial alliance with genteel women by sentimentalizing their maternal role
was intended to facilitate children's spiritual preparation. By building on
a shared preference for emotion over reason as an instrument for moral

instruction, Willis hoped to keep the *Companion* alive as an instrument for the dissemination of orthodox evangelical doctrines at a time when his religious community and its beliefs were rapidly losing cultural authority. Yet his success in this endeavor also facilitated the growth of a children's magazine industry that extended those sentimental ideals in directions that contravened his beliefs.

CHAPTER 2

Aunt Maria's *Miscellany* and the Limits of Gentility

✳

BENJAMIN AND RACHEL WILSON, the central characters of the story "Adventure in the Woods," are among Boston's earliest settlers. On their journey from England and during their first summer in Massachusetts, the two children encounter exotic animals and plants such as whales, flying fish, corn, and pumpkins. Equally foreign to them are the Indians, whom the children fear. Although the neighboring communities have established peaceful relations, Benjamin and Rachel have "heard frightful stories about . . . [Indians'] wickedness and cruelty—and their dark skin, and long black hair, their strange dresses, and language, [make] them appear very frightful creatures to children who had never seen anything like them before." Yet when a "poor, sick Indian woman, unable to follow her tribe," comes into the village, the children's mother offers her food and invites her to rest in the house. The woman declines the invitation but accepts the food, giving Rachel two bright blue feathers in return.

The next summer, Benjamin and Rachel get lost while hunting for wild fruit outside the settlement. As the sun sets, the "weary and bewildered" children sit on a fallen tree, "weeping bitterly . . . [and] comforting each other with hope of succor." Then Benjamin hears a step and rises to see an old Indian woman. He throws "his arm round his sister, as if to protect her; but of that there [is] no need; for the old woman, kindly stroking Rachel's head, . . . [is] the squaw who had once come to the village for food." The woman makes Rachel understand that she has remembered her kindness and will repay it by leading the children home. "Taking the weary little girl in her arms, as if she had been an infant," she guides them back to the village. Every year thereafter, she comes to visit Benjamin and Rachel, bringing them "some token of remembrance, and returning loaded with

44

presents . . . The children [love] her, and [expect] her yearly visit with pleasure; and they never [see] an Indian, without thinking of their Adventure
in the Wood."[1]

"Adventure in the Woods" was the opening story in the September 1826
debut issue of the *Juvenile Miscellany*. Written by the magazine's editor,
Lydia Maria Francis (who soon married and changed her name to Lydia
Maria Child), it offers a marked contrast to "The Twins," the *Youth's Companion* story that I introduced in chapter 1.[2] "The Twins" concentrates solely
on an unnamed young orphan and his pious female caretaker. The author
provides no historical or geographic context, and events occur in the child's
immediate, familiar environment. The boy's perspective is similarly contained; he predominantly focuses on his imminent divine judgment. Such
a constricted presentation of childhood reflected editor Nathaniel Willis's
goal of keeping children concentrated on their individual spiritual development by isolating them from the dangers and temptations of the world
outside the home.

Child's story is more expansive. She introduces Benjamin and Rachel
as part of a distinctly American community and shows them interacting
with adults from beyond their home, community, and race. She emphasizes
their earthly concerns, particularly the differences that they encounter in
their new society. Child exoticizes these changes but also displays how the
children's upbringing has prepared them to engage with people different
from themselves. Their education has been more ethical than doctrinal:
although their father reads the Bible to them, Child does not distinguish
this experience from the tales he recounts of "Old England." In contrast,
she explicitly identifies their mother's Christian charity to the poor Indian
woman as a direct cause of the children's rescue. By making such narrative
choices, she strives to dissolve rather than erect cultural barriers for children. Her integration of entertainment and instruction—as well as public
and private society—in both this story and her magazine works to teach
young readers how to live an upstanding Christian life in this world rather
than prepares them to achieve salvation in the next.

The contrasting approaches of these tales illustrate their magazines'
divergent responses to the growth of genteel authority in New England
during the second quarter of the nineteenth century. *Companion* editor
Nathaniel Willis manifested his anxiety about this change by reconciling
his orthodox faith with genteel sentimental ideals, focusing particularly on a
shared fear of the moral and physical threats that urbanizing, market-driven
cultures posed for children. Conversely, Child embraced gentility, adopting a liberal Protestant optimism about its potential benefits and bonding

with her audience through their mutual confidence in children's capacity to achieve both individual and national progress in this transforming society.

Child's enthusiastic approach brought the *Miscellany* immediate commercial and critical success. The magazine was, according to one of her biographers, a "sensation." Sarah Josepha Hale's *Ladies' Magazine* urged "every family where there are children" to subscribe, and the *North American Review,* the nation's preeminent literary journal, honored her with an article that described her as "the first woman in the republic."[3] Yet Child's methods also created tensions with her genteel customers that eventually led to the magazine's demise. She extended the logic of liberal Protestantism beyond what much of her audience deemed acceptable, incorporating women, the poor, and nonwhites into a less hierarchical vision of the nation's future. She viewed children, whom many genteel adults wanted to shelter from the outside world, as ideal facilitators of this vision and sought to prepare them to improve society by exposing them to its possibilities rather than shielding them from its dangers. For several years the *Miscellany* thrived despite these tensions because Child carefully balanced her ideological and commercial agendas. But when she expanded her message in 1833 to include abolitionism, her audience quickly abandoned her. Within a year, the publishers removed her as editor; eighteen months later, the magazine folded.

Child's mercurial tenure at the *Miscellany* exposed both the affinities and the conflicts between gentility and liberal Protestantism. The magazine's success reflected genteel New Englanders' growing desire for reading materials that employed nurturing rather than frightening pedagogies to guide children and highlighted women's emerging role as purveyors of those pedagogies. Writers such as Maria Edgeworth and Anna Laetitia Barbauld had produced children's stories in England since the late eighteenth century, but Child's literary success was still rare for American women during the 1820s.[4] She embraced her gender in the *Miscellany,* adopting the authorial persona of the nurturing, rigorous mentor "Aunt Maria," a character who capitalized on changing conceptions of femininity that were leading Americans to view women as particularly qualified to instruct juvenile audiences.[5] Her achievements during the 1820s, along with those of other New Englanders such as Hale, Lydia Sigourney, and Catharine Sedgwick, established commercial possibilities for women in publishing that the expansion and integration of liberal Protestantism and gentility brought to fruition during the next three decades.[6]

Child's *Miscellany* tenure—indeed, her entire career during those years—also revealed the restrictions that genteel society placed on female writers.

Respectable audiences expected women who assumed this public role to limit their subjects to private, domestic lives. Child strained against this restriction, alternately producing ambitious historical novels through which she sought to transcend society's expectations for women (*Hobomok, The Rebels*) and more economically promising books in genres deemed to be acceptable for women writers (*Evenings in New England, The Frugal Housewife*). At the *Miscellany*, she similarly balanced public expectations against her personal aspirations and ideals. "Adventure in the Woods" exemplifies this approach: in it she countered the story's humanitarian message and the integration of children into the public life of a community with the children's inability to help themselves and their rescue by a woman who, despite being of a different race, exhibits the sentimental and nurturing conduct that genteel society celebrated as feminine.

Such compromises were, like Willis's sentimentalizing of his orthodox theology, an effort to balance ideals against public expectations. Yet Child placed more trust in the marketplace than did her competitor. Her underlying assumption during this period was that talent and truth—even if "born in poverty and nurtured in seclusion"—would "set its own high impress" when exposed to commercial audiences, transcending cultural restrictions and enabling her to fulfill ambitions of economic independence and critical reputation.[7] For several years, Boston's genteel elite validated her belief in the democratizing power of the marketplace. The abrupt termination of this support in the aftermath of her abolitionist pronouncements, however, revealed the fragility of her idiosyncratic position as a self-supporting female public figure and the limits of genteel audiences' willingness to accept the potential for social upheaval inherent in liberal Protestant ideals.

Indeed, the fates of the *Companion* and the *Miscellany* highlight the inherent conservatism of nineteenth-century American gentility. Willis's approach—conciliating female readers by adopting a sentimental approach to the increasingly feminine cultural sphere of childrearing—posed little threat to New England society's existing racial and gender hierarchies. In contrast, Child's sentimentality hid neither the radicalism of her ideas nor her growing cultural authority. The fact that readers did not revolt against her ideology until she directed it toward the live controversy of slavery (as opposed to Indians, who were no longer a widespread social concern in New England by the 1820s, or women, who had not yet become one) suggests that they recognized and carefully balanced the social benefits and dangers of her message. They chose to take action when the established social hierarchy seemed to be under threat, thus demonstrating that while gentility created new opportunities for advancement among white

Protestants, it continued to exclude other Americans from the ranks of respectability based on their race, religion, and gender.

Child's tumultuous *Miscellany* experience served as a template and a cautionary tale for other antebellum liberal Protestant writers and editors of children's books and magazines. By following her practice of exposing young readers to the diversity and wonder of the world beyond their local communities, authors such as Jacob Abbott and Samuel Goodrich achieved unprecedented commercial success; but her demise also tempered any impulse to engage young readers in public controversies. A mitigated version of her editorial formula, one that balanced confidence about children and their future against the audience's need to avoid destabilizing extensions of that optimistic faith, became the prototype for liberal Protestant nineteenth-century American children's magazines.

IN RETROSPECT, Lydia Maria Child's decision to advocate abolition in the *Juvenile Miscellany* during the early 1830s seems hubristic. She was a young female editor addressing a topic that her contemporaries considered to be well beyond women's realm, and her male publishing colleagues had expressed opposition to such feminine boldness. An 1829 editorial in the *Yankee and Boston Literary Gazette* commented, "Verily, verily, if our sister-editors get along so merrily, merrily—they will soon be obliged to kill their own mutton. What need have they of . . . the guardianship of he-editors, now they are able not only to mend their own pens, but to mend our manners along with them? not only to sharpen their own instruments, but to bleed *us* with them after they *are* sharpened?"[8] Child may not have seen this particular article, but she knew of the widespread opposition to women writers, who, according to many observers, risked becoming "unsexed" when they ventured beyond their prescribed social roles.[9]

Given such views, she chose to publish both her first book and a later pamphlet attacking the federal government's Indian policies anonymously. But addressing the subject of slavery made her position as a woman writer even more precarious. Although Boston later became a hotbed of abolitionism, support for this stance was meager in the early 1830s. Many of the city's businessmen profited from slavery because their textile mills were prime consumers of southern cotton. Abolitionist minister and editor William Lloyd Garrison found New Englanders' "contempt more bitter, opposition more active, and apathy more frozen" on the subject of abolition "than among slave owners themselves."[10] In 1835, anti-abolitionists attacked Garrison at a public meeting, tied him up, and dragged him through the city's streets. Such violent episodes had not yet occurred when Child introduced the subject in the *Miscellany,* but the young editor knew she was undertaking a formidable challenge.

Yet it is not difficult to reconstruct the logic that might have led her to believe she could overcome these obstacles. Child's commitment to abolition was an extension of her previous efforts to transcend cultural taboos, including provocative attempts to promote the rights of women and Indians. Her writings had enjoyed a decade of critical acclaim and commercial success, an outcome suggesting that her vision, despite its apparent transgressions against genteel mores, aligned with many of her audience's interests and desires. Fundamental to that alignment was a shared belief in children's inherent capabilities. Child affirmed that faith in the *Miscellany*'s introductory editorial:

> I seldom meet a little girl, even in the crowded streets of Boston, without thinking with anxious tenderness, concerning her education, her temper, and her principles. Yes, *principles!* Children can act from good principles, as well as gentleman and ladies. She who never attempts to conceal her own faults; who is ever ready to exclaim, honestly; "No, mama, it was not brother or sister, who did that mischief; it was I, myself,"—has genuine principle. The daughter of a poor, hard working mother, who sits hour after hour, tending her baby brother, and never complains that her arms ache, lest it should add to her mother's trouble; has feeling and conscience too. The boy, who sees a rival come forward, again and again, to receive the prize he has so often wished for himself, and who yet claps louder and louder, with heart-felt joy at his success, is actuated by a principle, as noble, as ever influenced the greatest and the wisest. I have seen many such instances, and they have always warmed my heart, with exceeding love for the dear ones, who could be so generous and pure.[11]

Although the passage retains the moralizing common to American writing for children of this era, it inverts orthodox childrearing practices by celebrating young people's potential for positive behavior rather than emphasizing the dire consequences of juvenile misconduct. Child's insistence that children could "act from good principles" instituted expectations that they would do so, just as her presentation of the normative child as feminine—a choice that she employed throughout her tenure at the *Miscellany*—endowed young women with more cultural legitimacy. Her description of God as "a kind Parent . . . who will help you in every endeavor you make, to be virtuous and religious" further reveals the aspirational model she adopted in contravention of orthodox standards.

Child's repeated insistence on children's capacity for "principles" implied that some of her audience would question this characterization. Orthodox theology remained a powerful, if diminishing, force in Boston during the 1820s. Evangelical ministers such as Lyman Beecher continued to place "fierce pressure" on children "to admit as soon as possible their rebelliousness against God and submit to him lest they risk dying with all their sins upon him."[12] Yet other indicators suggest that a literate New England audience was well prepared for Child's more optimistic message. The region's rapidly urbanizing communities were reassessing beliefs about children as part of the broader questioning of traditional forms of authority that was occurring through the Unitarian Controversy. By 1826, when the *Miscellany* premiered, the majority of churches in these communities had rejected their ancestors' orthodox Calvinist principles—including a belief in infant depravity—in favor of a liberal Protestant conviction that individuals' moral behaviors would allow them to improve both their earthly and divine fates. Earlier in the decade, organizations such as the American Unitarian Association had begun to establish an institutional network for disseminating such ideas, and the turn to outside clergymen (such as Beecher) to lead revivals in Boston suggests that the city's orthodox citizens were on the defensive.[13]

One historian has described Unitarian theology as a "confluence of Protestantism with the Enlightenment." Its followers embraced long-standing European theories about children, such as John Locke's rationalist belief in newborns as "white paper void of all characters, without any ideas" and Jean-Jacques Rousseau's romantic claim in *Émile* that "everything is good as it comes from the hands of the Author of nature; but everything degenerates in the hands of man."[14] Families often engaged with these ideas through the moralistic yet nurturing children's stories of late eighteenth-century British authors such as Anna Laetitia Barbauld and Maria Edgeworth (a scholar of children's literature has called Edgeworth "the patroness of the 1820s" in New England), but local writers also began to adapt these pedagogies for American audiences.[15]

In 1824 Child garnered critical acclaim and commercial success with *Evenings in New England,* a book that explicitly nationalized the methods of Barbauld's *Evenings at Home.* Catharine Sedgwick's popular 1822 novel, *A New-England Tale,* which featured a heroine of almost saintly principles, exemplified the emerging translation of European romantic conceptions of childhood into American sentimental representations of young people as innately spiritual and innocent. Such positive depictions of children appealed not only to the economic and political elites who predominantly joined Unitarian churches but also (as Child's and Sedgwick's work attests) to women constrained by Calvinist patriarchies.

Child's father, Convers Francis, was a prosperous baker who presided over a devoutly orthodox artisanal household similar to Nathaniel Willis's. She later described his "fierce theology" as dominated by an incurable terror of "going to hell," and he insisted that she, too, would "burn hereafter for her apostasy."[16] Child developed an "especial grudge" against this faith, an experience common to American female writers raised during the early nineteenth century. Sedgwick's *A New-England Tale* condemned religious orthodoxy, and the author abandoned the Congregational church despite fears that by adopting the "new faith" she would lose friends, "who would be shocked and deeply wounded by what they consider apostasy."[17] Lyman Beecher's daughter Catharine also struggled with her father's faith, and Nathaniel Willis's daughter Sara later openly castigated her family's religious practices. She argued Sunday should not "be a day for puzzling the half-developed brain of childhood with gloomy creeds" or fettering children with "chains of fear . . . The God *my eyes* see, is not a tyrant, driving his creatures to heaven through fear of hell."[18]

Each of these women had distinct reasons for rebelling against religious orthodoxy. Child was particularly motivated by its constraint of her educational ambitions. After attending a college preparatory academy, her brother Convers went on to Harvard, an education that groomed him for social advancement. Lydia, meanwhile, received an education common for girls from middling New England families of this time: two years at a town school and another in the "hardly more stimulating regime" of Miss Swan's Female Academy. At this point, her recently widowed father, alarmed by this twelve-year-old girl's "increasing fondness for books," sent her to live with her married older sister, Mary, in Norridgewock, Maine, in order to eradicate her intellectual notions and prepare her to become a wife and homemaker.[19]

Child's move to Maine was the first stop in a twelve-year migration. After leaving her sister's house, she moved to a nearby town, where she taught school. Then she returned to Massachusetts, staying first at her brother Convers's parsonage in Watertown, then moving to Boston for another teaching position, and finally returning to Watertown for another teaching assignment. Like Willis, she sharpened her ideals about social authority during this nomadic phase of her maturation; and as with her educational experiences, gender was a determinative factor. Her time in Maine had exposed her to the mistreatment of Indian communities, and her subsequent wanderings provided further evidence of the restrictions that respectable white societies were placing on ambitious women. These experiences reinforced her sense that orthodox patriarchy was a source of

social injustice. What remains unclear, however, is how she became convinced that the market economy might provide a viable way to counteract
these inequities. Faith in economic opportunity was pervasive in the new
nation, but Americans generally assumed that such opportunities were limited to men. By the 1820s, ambitious young women could become teachers;
and Child, like other young women of her generation, tried to work the
educational marketplace to her advantage by jumping from one position
to another. Yet such changes offered no long-standing solution to her economic or social dilemmas.[20]

Child's rationale for turning to novel writing as an avenue toward economic independence or respectability is also unclear: the practice was
somewhat disreputable and rarely remunerative for authors of either gender.
Perhaps earlier female authors such as Catharine Sedgwick and Susanna
Rowson had inspired her, or perhaps the process was spontaneous, as she
suggests in both the preface to her first novel and later correspondence.[21]
Whatever her motivation, she achieved early literary success, which fueled
her confidence in the market economy as a tool for personal advancement.
At the age of twenty-two, she anonymously published *Hobomok: A Tale
of Early Times,* based on stories she had heard in Maine. In the preface,
her male narrator describes the book as "a New England novel," not only
linking her book to Sedgwick's successful *A New-England Tale* (which had
appeared two years earlier) but also connecting her to an ambitious, mostly
male company seeking to forge a distinctly American literature—a bond
emphasized by her male narrative persona.[22] The book received largely favorable reviews from Boston's literary establishment, although those readers
uniformly described her plot, in which a respectable young white woman
elopes with her Indian lover, as "in very bad taste, to say the least."[23]

Hobomok was initially a financial loss. However, the secret of Child's
authorship soon emerged, and her publishers quickly offered her the opportunity to produce another book, *Evenings in New England: Intended for
Juvenile Amusement and Instruction,* which moved her from the typically
male domain of historical fiction into a more acceptably feminine genre
of writing for children. She capitalized on those gendered expectations
and intertwined them with the nationalistic motivations already evident in
Hobomok. Adopting the pseudonym "An American Lady," Child used patriotism to legitimize her literary endeavor. "To write books for children, after
Miss Edgeworth and Mrs. Barbauld have written, is indeed presumptu-
ous," she declared but justified herself by calling on her desire to introduce
"American scenes and characters" into an "emphatically English" genre.[24]

She replaced Barbauld's narratives about kings and aristocracy with stories about Plymouth Rock, Indian tribes, and the American Revolution, and exchanged concerns about how to navigate the British class system with exhortations to maintain republican simplicity. By continuing to emphasize patriotism, Child was able to move into a more culturally acceptable forum while diminishing neither her ambition nor her confidence.

Evenings in New England also provided the first public indications of Child's pedagogical philosophies. As her introduction had promised, Child followed Barbauld and Edgeworth's instructional models, employing "conversations" between children and adults (in this case, "Aunt Maria," a character whom Child later revived in the *Miscellany*) to engage children's interest in academic subjects and, as she later stated, "to bring the moral emotions into *activity;* such emotions as tenderness toward the aged, kindness toward animals, compassion for the poor and suffering, [and] brotherly feeling towards all races of men."[25] This final goal figured prominently in *Evenings;* the book included several stories that criticized the subjugation of Indians and slaves in the United States.[26]

Evenings was a resounding success. Child wrote to her sister that it had received "much more unqualified approbation" than *Hobomok* had. The *North American Review* proclaimed, "The book cannot fail to amuse children, it cannot fail to instruct them and make them better." As Child's biographer notes, in less than a year, critics had transformed her from an author whose work was "revolting ... to every feeling of delicacy in man or woman" to one cheered for "nourishing the plant of virtue at its tenderest age, and protecting the blossom of innocence at a time, when it may so easily be withered and destroyed by the rude assaults to which it is exposed."[27] In comparing the responses to *Hobomok* and *Evenings,* Child seems to have learned she could succeed in promoting her reformist impulses to respectable audiences as long as she directed them to the socially sanctioned end of raising genteel children.

Her immediate response to this success, however, was to use it as a means of generating renewed support for *Hobomok.* The acclaim she received emboldened her to asked her brother's friend, Harvard professor and "literary kingmaker" George Ticknor, to advocate publicly for her novel. Ticknor agreed; he paid her debt for publishing costs, encouraged a friend at the *North American Review* to publish a second, more favorable assessment of the novel, and invited Child to gatherings at his personal literary salon. Her exotic status as a poor young woman in the city's literary community made her an object of curiosity and delight among fashionable society, procuring her invitations to grand events such as the public reception celebrating the Marquis de Lafayette on the fiftieth anniversary of the American Revolution.[28]

These successes inspired her to begin a new historical novel, a story of "Boston before the Revolution" called *The Rebels*. Given that *Evenings* had sold better and received more acclaim than *Hobomok* had, this decision suggests that Child's thirst for literary reputation surpassed her desire for economic stability. In the meantime, as she worked on *The Rebels*—and continued to teach school—she received an offer from the firm of George Ticknor's cousin William to edit a new children's magazine, the *Juvenile Miscellany*, modeled on *Evenings in New England*. The publisher's motivations for introducing the *Miscellany* are unclear; children's magazines were a new and relatively unproven genre at the time, although the success of the *Youth's Friend* and *Evenings* offered hope of financial success. The timing of the *Miscellany*'s debut—just four months after Reverend Beecher's arrival in Boston—also hints at religious and political reasons for the decision. Yet Child was not a member of any Unitarian congregation: though supportive of Unitarianism's liberal ideals, she was apparently dissatisfied with its spiritual practices.[29]

Child hesitated to accept the offer, not for religious reasons but because she feared that this responsibility, along with her teaching obligations, would prevent her from making progress on her novel. Ultimately, however, pressure from her social circle convinced her to take the position, and she quickly realized the benefits of this new opportunity. Like *Evenings*, the *Miscellany* was an immediate success. Child wrote to her sister Mary, "Valuable gifts, jewels, beautiful dresses pour in upon me, invitations beyond acceptance, admiring letters from all parts of the country."[30] The editorial position brought her relative financial stability as well as fame: she earned an annual income of three hundred dollars—not enough to allow her to quit her teaching position but enough to keep her economically independent.[31] Four months after the *Miscellany* debuted, she wrote to Mary, "Children's books are more profitable than any others, and I am American enough to prefer money to fame."[32] Now that her books and her magazine were achieving critical and commercial success, Child had every reason to be confident about the elevating power of the market economy. She was accomplishing goals that, a decade earlier, any woman—never mind one with limited education, financial means, and social status—would never have dreamed of, and she was doing so with the public support of Boston's genteel elites.

CHILD REVELED in her success but also recognized her vulnerable position in this community. She later described herself as "a butterfly under a gilded glass tumbler"; even at the time she recognized that her celebrity, in conjunction with her controversial opinions, was alienating members of her social circle. She told Mary that "just in proportion to my conspicuousness I have had enemies as well as friends—and I have deserved them both."[33]

In the *Miscellany* she also acknowledged her vulnerability. Balancing her ideals against her need to uphold her audience's genteel expectations meant expanding children's cultural parameters without threatening parents' sense of protecting young readers from the hazards of modern society. To do so, Child created what one scholar has called "the first children's magazine in America that was . . . really childlike."[34] Unlike the *Companion,* which was printed on broadsheets in imitation of the adult newspapers of the day, the *Miscellany* looked like a book for children. Its three-by-six-inch chapbook size mirrored the small-volume format that publishers had been using to produce children's literature for much of the previous two centuries. Yet the magazine was more extensive and lavish than most books of this type, an indication that the publisher was trying to reach an elite audience. It was 104 pages long with three or four illustrations per bimonthly issue, in contrast to the *Companion*'s four weekly pages and the *Youth's Friend*'s sixteen pages and one illustration per month. The *Miscellany* also included riddles and puzzles at the end of each issue, giving children the type of entertainment that orthodox publishers eschewed and simultaneously adding a marketing benefit: Child published answers to these games in the next issue.

What made the *Miscellany* really "childlike," though, was the editor's focus on young readers' interests as well as their obligations. Child's opening editorial told children:

> Though I have great affection for you, and the kindest interest in your welfare and improvement, perhaps I may not always be able to afford you amusement and instruction. I have, in some measure, forgotten what pleased me, when I was a child, and it is difficult for me to imagine how I should think or feel, if I were as young as you now are. You, my dear young friends, shall be my critics. What you find neither affords you amusement nor does you good, I shall find badly written.[35]

This admission was remarkable not for its self-deprecation, which was a standard practice for authors of the era, but because it addressed such humility to children. For two centuries, New Englanders had viewed children's deference to their elders as an essential element of a stable social hierarchy.

Child's willingness to suggest that young readers should exert a degree of control over their magazine's content reflected a degree of confidence in their moral and intellectual capacities that genteel Bostonians increasingly favored over orthodox beliefs in youthful depravity.

The content of the *Miscellany* indicates that Child's dedication to children's interests was not merely puffery. She encouraged her young readers to develop their characters and intellects but also offered them stories of adventure and wonder unlike any material in the *Companion* or the *Youth's Friend*. In addition to "Adventure in the Woods" (the story that opened this chapter), the first issue included a biography of explorer John Ledyard, with an accompanying illustration of a top-hatted man sitting in a sledge pulled by reindeer; a funny "Letter from Summer to Winter: Written Between the Tropics"; a lesson on "Ruined Cities"; a story called "The Dwarf"; and a play titled "The Little Rebels," which displayed Revolutionary-era Boston boys standing up to the British soldiers who had destroyed their skating pond.[36]

Child balanced these examples of exoticism and youthful empowerment with a moralistic story about gratitude and sharing, conversations about effort and attentiveness, and a comparison between "The Tulip and the Tri-Colored Violet" that offered "young ladies" the moral of learning "to prize those qualities, which will make them useful and cheerful companions, in preference to those, which fit them only to be the gay flutterers of an evening."[37] Even the exciting material imparted lessons; for instance, the biographer of Ledyard told young readers, "We should never read accounts of great or good men, without learning some profitable lesson. If we cannot, like Ledyard, defend Gibralter [*sic*], sail round the world with Captain Cook; project trading voyages to the North-West coast; study Egyptian Hieroglyphics; and traverse the dreary northern zone, on foot; we can, at least, learn from him the important lesson of *perseverance.*"[38] Yet these didactic elements did not diminish young readers' enthusiasm for a magazine that treated them as more than Sunday school students. One subscriber later recalled that "children sat on the stone steps of their house doors all the way up and down Chestnut Street in Boston, waiting for the carrier. He used to cross the street, going from door to door in a zigzag fashion; and the fortunate possessor of the first copy found a crowd of little ones hanging over her shoulder from the steps above . . . How forlorn we were if the carrier was late!"[39]

Parents shared their children's enthusiasm. Child told her sister, "It seems as if the public was resolved to give me a flourish of trumpets, let me write what I will."[40] Yet her editorial practices in the magazine suggest a less naïve perspective. She carefully modulated the *Miscellany*'s content to produce a cohesive message that remained mostly within the parameters of genteel sensibilities. For instance, after the first issue, Child curtailed narratives that thrust children into public or unsupervised environments. Subsequent examples of this genre generally featured poor and nonwhite children and resulted in nearly catastrophic consequences for those exposed youths (although, in contrast to the *Companion,* the *Miscellany* rarely showed children who died or were injured due to misbehavior).[41] Thus, while she continued to deliver stories about distant places and exotic subjects, she indicated to young genteel readers that such experiences were not yet appropriate for them.

Child also calibrated her treatment of gender in the *Miscellany*. She avoided representations of the severe male ministers and Sunday school teachers favored by the *Youth's Friend* and the *Companion.* Instead, she introduced strong female narrators such as "Aunt Maria," the character from *Evenings in New England* who guided children in a strict but gentle manner. In the *Miscellany,* Aunt Maria is revealed as intelligent enough to teach children a variety of academic subjects and often chooses topics that defy gender conventions. Using Edgeworth's and Barbauld's conversational models, she advocates a diverse education for both boys and girls. Aunt Maria's nephew James prefers natural science and modern history, while her niece Sophia favors archaeology and ancient history. Yet when James tells her he does not enjoy poetry as Sophia does and would rather read *Robinson Crusoe,* she replies, "That is because you have paid no attention to the cultivation of your imagination." He protests that he does not believe that the cultivation of "fancy ... [is] of so much consequence as many other things." Aunt Maria rejoins, "Neither do I, my dear nephew; but in forming your character you should neglect nothing." She also tells him not to laugh at Sophia's efforts to learn to throw a ball, any more than Sophia should mock his stumbling interpretations of poetry:

> What I wish to impress upon you, is the importance of bringing *all* your faculties to the greatest possible perfection. Sophia sees everything with so fanciful an eye, that I am afraid she will not be able to judge, to compare, and to reason for herself, hereafter. You, on the other hand, have neglected imagination so much, that half the beauties of nature, half the charming fictions of genius, will seem like a blank book to you. Either of these extremes, is better than cultivating the memory alone, I acknowledge; but all of them should be avoided.[42]

The "Aunt Maria" pieces were dialogues rather than lectures, and in Barbauldian fashion, Child always let the child have the last word. Yet she guided her readers toward more gender-neutral and wide-ranging educational experiences, thus challenging expectations that boys were more physical and rational, girls more passive and emotional.

The same was not true of her presentation of adults in the *Miscellany*. As Child acknowledged, men and women inhabited different realms of American society. She included women characters who were capable academic, spiritual, and moral instructors and regularly featured selections from prominent American female authors such as Sigourney, Sedgwick, Hale, and Eliza Leslie.[43] She also portrayed women as children's primary caregivers. In contrast to the *Youth's Friend* and the *Companion,* the *Miscellany* rarely featured men in domestic scenes; and when it did, the narrative results were often disastrous. For example, in "Maria and Frances, or, the Birthday Present," Maria's father leaves her alone in London, where she is arrested under a false accusation of theft. He pays for a prominent attorney and more comfortable prison quarters for the child but cannot prevent her conviction and five-year prison sentence. Only when a female witness (who turns out to be the long-lost mother of Maria's adopted sister, Frances) confesses her own guilt at the last minute does the child go free. Thus, even a corrupted mother, who has abandoned her child and must spend the rest of her life in prison, proves to be a more capable caretaker than a father is.[44]

Yet even as she celebrated women's capabilities, Child presented few public outlets for these skills. In the magazine, the caring and educated women characters who preside over children's instruction do not have the professional opportunities that Child herself had garnered. As with her portrayal of children, women who worked outside the home were generally poor and nonwhite.[45] In the *Miscellany,* genteel public life belonged to men. When Child wanted to introduce non-domestic scenes, she often turned to biographies of American and British heroes such as Ledyard, Sir Isaac Newton, and particularly Benjamin Franklin, a recurring figure in the magazine. These profiles emphasized the public value of the men's work (she noted that "few individuals have been as useful to mankind as Benjamin Franklin") but also encouraged the cultivation of skills that children could apply at home. For instance, asking her readers to learn from Newton's "habits of close observation and active thought," Child suggested:

> If the laugh of the gay and fashionable, should ever make industry and economy appear like contemptible virtues; let them remember that Benjamin Franklin, a poor, hard-working mechanic, became, by means of these very

virtues, a philosopher, whose discoveries were useful and celebrated throughout Europe. If they grow weary of application, and despise frugality; let them
think of a dirty, printer boy, eating his roll of dry bread, in the streets of
Philadelphia, afterwards ambassador to the Court of France; welcome to the
most splendid of Parisian saloons; and his grey hairs crowned with a wreath
of laurel, by the young and fair of that enthusiastic nation.[46]

The passage exhibits the balance that Child sought to sustain between
the possibilities of the outside world and the domestic virtues that her
genteel audience expected from children's literature. The *Miscellany* generally presented opportunities to venture beyond the home as rewards for
practicing habits of thrift, perseverance, and education in the household.[47]
Although Franklin's success was surprisingly non-republican, it paralleled
on an international scale Child's experiences among Boston's "fashionables"
and reflected her faith in the democratizing possibilities of a society shaped
by the values of the market economy.

Child's biographer identifies the contradictions of this approach, arguing
that the *Miscellany*'s egalitarian ideals consistently conflict with the inferior
position of women, the poor, and people of color in the magazine. She also
believes that Child's presentation of poverty as a condition that hard work
and frugality can overcome is undercut by her repeated resort to *deus ex
machina* characters who suggest that such habits are insufficient to guaran-
tee upward mobility.[48] Her assessments are accurate yet overlook the fact
that the young editor herself had experienced such an intervention when
George Ticknor decided to champion her work. Moreover, Child's private
correspondence indicates that her success with Ticknor and other elites
had given her the confidence to believe that skills and determination could
transcend the restrictions of gender or poverty. To maintain a readership,
Miscellany stories did compromise Child's ideals, but they also reveal how
her experiences and the increased tolerance in genteel 1820s New England
society temporarily aligned her views with those of her audience.

THE ISSUE that destroyed that alignment was race. Before 1830, the *Miscellany* regularly presented characters from a variety of ethnic and racial
backgrounds: Chinese, Turks, South Sea islanders, Eskimos, and Africans
as well as American Indians and African Americans. In her stories, Child
both exoticized and humanized these characters—for instance, Lariboo, a
"Negro girl . . . reckoned quite a belle" by her Tibboo community: "I don't
think you would have thought her very good looking, if you could have
seen the oil streaming over her face, the coral stuck through her nose, and
the great brass rings on her arms and ancles [*sic*]. But Lariboo thought she

dressed beautifully; and I don't think she was a bit sillier than the ladies here, who pride themselves on feathers and gauze."[49] When describing Euric, a Laplander, she balanced foreign details, such as his skill at hunting reindeer and the community tradition of having a groom serve his bride's father for four years after marriage, with descriptions of him as a man with "a good reputation for industry, fidelity, generosity and courage," qualities that genteel families would have appreciated in their own culture.[50]

These stories exemplify the *Miscellany*'s pattern of evaluating nonwhite, non-Protestant peoples according to genteel conventions. This practice occurred most frequently in stories about Indians, who were New Englanders' most proximate and, by this time, most unthreatening foreign population. In "The Indian Boy," a young Penobscot child develops into a skilled weaver and "the best hunter in his tribe." Yet the story focuses on his faithfulness in delivering his earnings to his grandmother, an act that marks him as successful even though "[he does] not know every thing that has been taught us ... [and] has never been to any school." Another story introduces "Pol Sosef. The Indian Artist," who goes to study with an artist in Bangor, Maine: "It is yet uncertain how far the experiment will succeed . . . but should he prove to have real genius, how the world will stare at the INDIAN ARTIST!" Not only does this description of the protagonist draw an implicit comparison with Child herself, who became the toast of Boston society as the GIRL WRITER, but it also indicates that the only judgment of his work that matters is white society's.[51]

Child called on readers to accept Indians' humanity and offered (for the time) nuanced interpretations of both friendly and exploitative relationships between whites and Indians. Yet she did not comment on contemporary white-Indian conflicts in the nation's southern and western regions, a decision that reflected the emerging genteel convention of shielding young children from political controversy. Initially, she was even more circumspect on the issue of slavery. Before 1830, it is mentioned only once in the *Miscellany*, when the author concludes, "It is much regretted that such a thing as slavery exists; but so far as concerns the situation of slaves at the South, I think New England prejudices have been violent and unreasonable."[52]

In contrast to her engagement with Indians during her time in Maine, Child appears to have had little interaction with blacks during her early life. Like many liberal Bostonians of her era, she supported the cause of colonization during the 1820s, but she did not display the passion that she did for Indians' plight or women's status. Yet as she developed her voice on those issues, slavery increasingly attracted her attention. In 1829, the same year she addressed the mistreatment of Indians in *The First Settlers of New England*, she publicly suggested that blacks could assimilate into American society through intermarriage. Then, after a June 1830 meeting with abolitionist William Lloyd Garrison, she began to introduce the topic of slavery into the *Miscellany*.

Initially, as with other controversial subjects, Child avoided attacks on U.S. slavery, focusing instead on atrocities practiced by slaveholders in Brazil and Cuba.[53] She also inserted the issue of racism into articles on seemingly unrelated subjects. For example, a review of an arithmetic primer mentions an abolitionist's discovery of the "mental dexterity" of Africans who performed complicated calculations "*in their heads*" in a manner "surpassing . . . the European method" of solving such problems on paper. She used this example to refute the argument that Africans are "a baser race than whites" and to tell "all good little readers that it is very rash, and must be offensive in the sight of God, whose children we all are, for any portion of the human family to arrogate to themselves a superiority over others."[54] In "William Peterson, the Brave and Good Boy," she describes the hero's rescue of skaters who have fallen into the ice, mentioning only at the end that William is "a colored boy" and the children he rescued "all white boys." This revelation leads to her "*true* anecdote": "I believe no generous-minded white children, will be tempted to speak unkindly, or uncivilly, to people whom God has made of a color different from their own."[55]

She had already used this sentimental humanizing approach in promoting the interests of Indians and the poor, and she returned to it in January 1831 when she expanded her abolitionist message to directly criticize slavery in the United States. The story "Jumbo and Zairee" focuses on the experience of "two pretty negro children" kidnapped into slavery in Africa. After establishing the similarities between these victims and her young readers, Child explains that the two children love stories and are very attached to each other and to adults who treat them kindly. She then highlights the atrocities that the children have experienced. They were "put in a dark hole with a great many other wretched negroes" and shipped across the ocean in horrifying conditions, where they watched sailors throw overboard those who had died on the passage to the Americas. They were "driven to the market-place to be sold" in this foreign land, separated from their families, and beaten by "brutal overseers." Now, having established her emotional case against slavery, Child for the first time castigates the United States for its involvement in this practice: "'Shame on my country—everlasting shame.' History blushes as she writes the page of American slavery."[56]

The *Miscellany*'s circulation numbers appear to have begun to decline after the publication of "Jumbo and Zairee." As early as January 1833, nine months before her *Appeal* to end slavery was published, rumors circulated that "Mrs. Child . . . is about to give up the editorship" of the magazine. By the time her final abolitionist story in the *Miscellany*, "Mary French and Susan Easton," appeared in May 1834, she had recognized the fragility of her social and economic position. The backlash against her abolitionist message was swift and pervasive: Ticknor and his friends dropped her, and even her brother Convers failed to support her position. Child seems to have known that her removal was imminent, for she abandoned her previous restraint, arguing that slavery had become so poisonous to the nation that no one—slave or free, black or white—could escape its malevolence.

The story "Mary French and Susan Easton" is set in an unnamed free territory west of the Mississippi. The Frenches, a white homesteading family, and the Eastons, a free black family, are neighbors, and their girls are friends. The two are kidnapped from a field near their homes by a man who stains Mary's skin dark and sells them, separately, into slavery. Each scene reinforces Child's argument that slavery creates a moral callousness that damages all Americans: the Frenches are unable to conceive that a slave trader has kidnapped their daughter; a witness provides no information because he fails to take interest in children whom he believes to be slaves. Mary is ultimately released when her master discovers her whiteness, and she pleads with her father to search for her friend. But the story ends with Susan's location still unknown, even though "the only difference between Mary French and Susan Easton is, that the black color could be rubbed off from Mary's skin, while from Susan's it could not."[57]

"Mary French and Susan Easton" was the product of a disillusioned author who no longer believed that American society's inequalities could be overcome within the existing parameters of genteel society. She left the *Miscellany* three months later, telling her audience only that she was "compelled to bid a reluctant and most affectionate farewell to my little readers" and that she intended "hereafter to write other books for your amusement and instruction."[58] She did write more books, but her greatest influence on the children's magazine industry was the model she offered for how—and how not—to address children.

CHILD WAS a member of the first generation of commercially oriented American authors for children. The most successful of these writers—including Samuel Goodrich (author of the Peter Parley books and editor of *Parley's Magazine* and *Merry's Museum*, two popular antebellum children's magazines) and Jacob Abbott (author of the Rollo books and other series for children)—followed her practice of introducing young readers to the wonders of the world outside the home. Yet few children's books and no other commercially successful children's periodicals of the era chose her course of directly engaging young readers in discussions of slavery or other controversial topics in modern society. According to one study of the era's children's literature, publishers generally supported reform only when it promoted what they perceived to be desirable patriotic characteristics.[59] Thus, the near-universal avoidance of antislavery positions was unsurprising, for they did not fit the individualistic framework or benefit populations that white Protestants viewed as American.

Children's magazines, which needed to procure repeat audiences, were particularly conservative in their approach to the issue. A historian examining antebellum children's literature believes that "Mary French and Susan Easton" is the only story in a commercially successful children's periodical to directly attack slavery in the United States. Goodrich, an abolitionist sympathizer, adopted a moderate position in his 1830 book *The Tales of Peter Parley about Africa:* "I do not . . . mean to blame every person who keeps slaves. But slavery is a bad system; it always brings great evils along with it. Instead, therefore, of defending slavery every good person should condemn it, and use his efforts, on all proper occasions, to hasten the time when there shall be no slavery in the land."[60] Yet his magazines largely ignored the issue. In both publications, I found only a satirical poem that implicitly condemned South Carolina congressman Preston Brooks's brutal beating of Massachusetts senator Charles Sumner while suggesting that young readers should avoid the shameful conflicts of politics altogether:

> And let me not be hypercritical
> I scorn to speak of things political
> Of such poor trash as freeman's brains
> Revolvers gutta-percha canes,
> Of insults, ribaldry, abuse
> Such as in Congress they let loose
> Who, paid enormous sums for ruling
> Waste time and money all in fooling;
> Who, whatsoever, the laws they're making
> Know less of honoring than of breaking
> And who, if laws should have their due
> Would hang. But what is that to you?[61]

The *Youth's Companion* was equally conservative. Willis publicly supported colonization of slaves during the 1820s and addressed the topic in a

series of 1828 editorials about Abduhl Rahhahman, a kidnapped Moorish
prince who was returned to his homeland through the efforts of the
American Colonization Society.

> No doubt the feelings of our readers are much interested in the fate of this
> poor old man, who has suffered so much from the hands of our country-
> men, and whose children still remain in unrighteous bondage. But Abduhl
> Rahhahman is not the only African who has claims upon our sympathies.—
> There are at this moment many hundreds of thousands of Africans in our
> country who are slaves to white men, and have no prospect of becoming free.
> There may not be any among them who were *princes* in Africa; but they are
> all *human beings,* who were torn from their country, from their homes, from
> their parents and neighbors and friends and sold into cruel bondage.

Willis's lingering animosity toward the aristocratic privilege that had freed
Rahhahman mingled with his antislavery beliefs, but he also displayed res-
ervations about abolition's consequences:

> All the pious people in the land, and a great many others, now wish to make
> the slaves free; and are very sorry that their fathers ever put the yoke of
> bondage on them. But it is not easy to set them free. They are unfit to take
> care of themselves and their families; many of them are very wicked; and if
> one and a half million should be made their own masters at once, it would
> produce great confusion and misery in the country. Strange as it must seem,
> no doubt it is true, that mercy to the colored people themselves requires, that
> they should *for the present* continue as they are.

The next week he concluded with the cautious argument that "much has
been done for the blacks, and a still brighter prospect is opening upon
them for future years and generations . . . The way is evidently preparing,
for removing this great evil from our country, though it will not be fully
done in our day."[62]

This gradualist rhetoric aligned with public opinion in 1820s Boston,
but Willis generally retreated from addressing slavery after the abolitionist movement emerged in the 1830s. Only widely accepted positions such
as condemnation of slave auctions appeared in his publications, and his
omission of the topic from both his publications drew criticism from abolitionists.[63] In a letter to William Lloyd Garrison, a correspondent asked,
"Has not the editor of the *Recorder* yet gone forward to the conclusion that
guiltless men cannot be converted into mere property? He writes as if this
point has not been fixed among the established convictions of his mind."
According to another contemporary, Willis's approach was "not such as a
Christian editor should pursue—it seems to be such as is sometimes in

politics said to be 'twistical or so.'"[64] In 1850, however, a southern subscriber wrote to thank him: "In these times of political feverishness, it is no small satisfaction to perceive that those subjects which are calculated to stir up strife and to embitter sectional jealousies are most judiciously excluded from your columns."[65] Willis printed this message in the "Letters to the Editor" department in the *Companion* but offered no response to the abolitionists' criticism, which suggests that neutrality was serving his economic interests, even as Boston was becoming increasingly hostile to slavery.

Like other antebellum authors and publishers for children, Willis acceded to the expectations of his genteel audience. Goodrich and Abbott sought to open the world beyond the home to their young readers, offering informational and inspirational travelogues, biographies, and stories of nature. Nevertheless, even though the Peter Parley and Rollo books were pleasant, upstanding, and even broadening, they did little to challenge their readers' understandings of childhood and children's place in the world. Child's experience at the *Miscellany* had restrained the reformist impulses that liberal Protestant authors were training on the nation's children. It would take another generation of economic expansion, and eventually the cultural transformations of the Civil War, to challenge that approach.

PART II

Commercializing Children's Magazines

1857–1873

IN OCTOBER 1871, THE *YOUTH'S COMPANION* PUBLISHED "A TRUE
Story," the tale of Ned and Charley, two bright young men living in a small
western town just before the Civil War. They are best friends and part of
a group of young salesmen, clerks, and students of law and medicine who
represent "the town's brightest hopes." One night at a supper with their
peers, both boys, despite initially resisting the pressure of their friends, become drunk on champagne and began to fight over a girl. Charley strikes
Ned "full in the face" and knocks him down several times, until Ned, with
"a dangerous gleam in his eyes that frighten[s] the boys" and a "white foam"
dribbling from his lips, retaliates with a blow that bangs Charley's head
against a rock, killing him instantly. As a friend attempts to help him escape, Ned, distressed by the pain his actions will inflict on his mother, asks
him to "tell the boys it was the liquor. Don't let it ruin their lives as it has
mine." Then he draws out a pistol and commits suicide.[1]

Two years later, a new magazine called *St. Nicholas* offered the first installment of a serial story, "What Might Have Been Expected." The hero,
Harry Loudon, is determined to provide financial support for Aunt Matilda,
an elderly freedwoman who has befriended him and his sister Kate. He
begins by hunting small game to feed her and gathering sumac to sell for
her other needs but gradually expands his efforts "to go into business in a
regular way." He devises a "grand scheme": he will create a corporation for
the purpose of laying a telegraph line across the local swamp that separates
his town from a mining business. His venture becomes so successful that
the mining business pays paid him 1,000 dollars to purchase the rights to

his telegraph, a sum that enables Harry to support Aunt Matilda for the rest of her days.[2]

Despite their contrasting perspectives and outcomes, these two stories share a number of features that exemplify the changes occurring in the children's magazine industry between the *Companion*'s change of ownership in 1857 and the founding of *St. Nicholas* in 1873. Both narratives are fiction, a genre that became more integral to the industry during this period. "What Might Have Been Expected" particularly exemplifies this trend, for by the early 1870s serial stories had become a prime marketing tool for these magazines. Both narratives also feature active male protagonists, a departure from the predominantly passive child characters in antebellum children's magazines and an indication of the growing gender divide in the industry's approaches to young readers. The emphasis on "true" details in both stories highlights the move away from allegory and toward tales grounded in the actual experiences of young readers, a shift that aligned children's magazines with broader trends toward literary realism during this period. These changes, along with the dramatic, exaggerated outcomes of both tales, reflect the industry's heightened efforts to entertain as well as instruct juvenile audiences.

Indeed, the predominant shared characteristic of this generation of children's magazines was their effort to cultivate more direct commercial relationships with young readers. Building on the practices of earlier authors such as Lydia Maria Child and Samuel Goodrich, they strived to generate stories that appealed to children, especially boys, as well as to adult subscribers. They also introduced other attractions, ranging from reader clubs to premium programs, intended to deepen children's connection—and thus loyalty—to the magazines.

There were multiple reasons for this shift during the third quarter of the nineteenth century, many of which were linked to the continuing expansion of the U.S. economy. Children's magazines between the 1820s and the 1840s had proven to be sustainable products in the urbanizing and increasingly market-driven communities of the northeastern United States; but difficulties of production, distribution, and culture limited the reach of these publications to regional audiences of 5,000 to 10,000 subscribers. By 1857, technological improvements had made printing periodicals cheaper and embellishments such as large illustrations more affordable. Railroads connected most northern cities, creating a new scale of possibilities for the size of a periodical's audience. By 1850 the *National Police Gazette* claimed a circulation of 40,000 and *Harper's New Monthly Magazine* more than

50,000. Four years later, *Merry's Museum*, a children's magazine started by Goodrich, also claimed to have reached 50,000 customers.[3]

The Civil War increased Americans' connectivity and in the process broke down many of the barriers that genteel American families had erected to protect children from outside influences. As fathers, brothers, and sons left home to join the Union forces, families hungered for information about what was happening on distant battlefields and in faraway cities. Wartime industrial expansion helped to satisfy these demands but also altered genteel standards regarding the relationship between children and the marketplace. As news of the conflict flowed into nearly every northern home, often through commercial products such as newspapers and magazines, the antebellum practice of isolating respectable children from public events and controversies became increasingly inconsequential.

As access to such products continued to expand after the war, adults searched for upstanding publications that might keep children's attention away from disreputable reading materials such as the penny press and story papers. This growing demand, combined with the technological advances that enabled publishers to meet it, transformed children's magazines into a big business attracting financially and culturally ambitious entrepreneurs and institutions. The *Companion*'s new editor, Daniel Sharp Ford, was already running one of the most successful religious magazines in New England when he and his partner purchased the struggling children's magazine late in 1856. A decade later, after the end of the war, publishing houses and entrepreneurs across the Northeast and Midwest had launched an unprecedented wave of well-funded, well-networked children's periodicals.

Despite their significant resources, these publications initially found commercial success elusive. Editors labored to construct formulas that would entertain young readers and sustain conservative, parent-approved social values. As a narrative, "A True Story" was more than a decade in the making, as Ford and his adult subscribers struggled to integrate sensational content with orthodox doctrines. Other magazines, despite impressive pedigrees, proved unsustainable. *Our Young Folks*, created by New England's elite publishing house Ticknor and Fields and featuring a roster of contributors that included Charles Dickens and Harriet Beecher Stowe, lasted for only eight years. *The Riverside Magazine for Young People*, produced by a rising young editor named Horace Scudder and offering original stories by Hans Christian Andersen as well as work by soon-to-be-famous writers and artists such as Sarah Orne Jewett and Winslow Homer, survived for only four years.

As these setbacks reveal, increased access to American families both created and solved difficulties for the editors of mid-nineteenth-century children's magazines. Urban growth, and its accompanying explosion of print, forced genteel American adults to accept some role for children as more active consumers, but the nature of that role remained contested. Ford believed that, under certain conditions, such an expansion could be both a spiritual and a commercial boon. He embraced young readers as business partners, providing them with more entertainment and offering them presents for helping to increase the circulation of the magazine. Yet even as he enhanced his commercial relationship with his readers, he maintained patriarchal control over the content of the magazine. He rarely offered children opportunities to contribute to the *Companion* through letters, stories, or artwork, nor did he seek to develop reader loyalty by nurturing communities connected by their consumption of his magazine. For Ford, the benefit of linking commerce and orthodox religion was that both practices guided children toward the development of self-reliance as Christians, American citizens, and consumers.

While Ford's *Companion* used tales such as "A True Story" to highlight the dangers of immersion in peer groups and other organizations, liberal Protestant magazines sought to integrate young Americans into intellectual and emotional communities that would elevate their minds and spirits. Flushed with the success of the Union army and concerned more about the vapidity of children's literature's than its immorality, the editors of *Our Young Folks* and the *Riverside* welcomed children's literary and artistic contributions as a means of stimulating their imaginations and created clubs that intensified young Americans' connections to each other and their publications. The editors, however, refused to accede to children's commercial tastes in literature, which they perceived as too mundane to fulfill the magazines' uplifting mission. Mistrustful of market cultures in a way that Ford was not, they sought to shape rather than cater to young consumers' tastes, improving them by way of a higher-quality brand of children's magazine.

The struggles of these magazines with the commercial and pedagogical aspects of gentility reflect the fluidity of respectable thinking about the child consumer during this period. The challenges to Ford's editorial strategies at the *Companion* and the demise of *Our Young Folks* and the *Riverside* also suggest that, despite the expansion of the children's magazine industry into big business, genteel audiences retained substantial power to shape the content of these products. Consumer authority within those audiences was changing: the combination of urban growth and wartime social breakdowns had enabled children to gain more influence over the content of their magazines. But this only meant that editors now needed to accommodate the demands of two constituencies to achieve commercial success. Ford's magazine flourished in part because he was more willing to satisfy the consumer demands of children than were his liberal Protestant counterparts. *St. Nicholas* prospered in the wake of the failures of *Our Young Folks* and the *Riverside* because editor Mary Mapes Dodge placed more faith in her young readers' commercial tastes than did her predecessors. Even so, her magazine, which continued to strive to produce a higher quality of literature for children, reached an audience that was only a fraction of the size of the *Companion*'s.

Meeting the expectations of adult subscribers in this cultural environment required changes that counterbalanced the magazines' catering to youthful tastes. In particular, the push for more entertainment for children instigated the magazines to join the broader cultural trend toward subdividing the nation's children based on gender and age. Most children's magazines of this era were eager to gain the attention of older boy readers, a demographic perceived as particularly resistant to the appeal of traditional children's literature. Stories such as Ford's sensational narratives, the tales in *Our Young Folks* and *Riverside* about mischievous "bad boys," and *St. Nicholas*'s industrial fantasies such as "What Might Have Been Expected" emphasized the distinct experiences of boys and girls to an extent uncommon in earlier American children's books and magazines. Furthermore, to legitimize the decision to market some parts of their magazines more directly to young audiences, editors delineated these new types of stories as products for older youths, most often by adding distinct departments for younger readers elsewhere in each issue.

Such strategies allowed mid-nineteenth-century children's magazine editors more freedom than their predecessors had to implement their visions for safely expanding young readers' roles in the nation's growing consumer cultures. Yet the continuing tensions between commerce and ideology in these publications also ensured that such visions primarily reinforced the existing social order. In the face of massive economic growth, demographic shifts, and wartime cultural transformations, child readers' desires for more entertainment had to be balanced with adult subscribers' demands that such amusements limit the disruptive impact of urbanization and industrialization.

CHAPTER 3

Perry Mason and Sensational Gentility

*

A SIXTY-FOOT hollow wicker man towers over the religious ceremony of the "Fejee Islanders." Men, women, and children are forced inside the figure and covered with "combustible materials" in preparation for being burned alive. On the margins of this scene, elders select victims for the sacrifice while young men spear those who resist. Other islanders hang their heads or writhe on the ground, grieving the impending loss of their loved ones.

This scene appeared on the front page of the *Youth's Companion* on January 1, 1857. Below the picture, a brief article condemned the "Fejee" culture as "ignorant, superstitious and cruel," and the anonymous author distinguished such acts from behaviors in the Protestant world of *Companion* readers. Yet the story also belabored the horrors, noting that the islanders "consider it a part of their most solemn and most obligatory religion to put men to death; and to feed on their dead bodies they esteem most wholesome."[1]

"Fejee Islanders" was the first of a wave of cover stories combining exotic illustrations and moralistic messages that appeared during the first three months of editor Daniel Sharp Ford's tenure at the *Companion*. The stories featured pearl divers in Ceylon and Japan who were "destroyed by sharks," professional murderers in India who strangled their victims with handkerchiefs, and men practicing *bastinado,* a Turkish method of torture.[2] The illustrations focused on clothing (or the lack of it), landscape, and architecture to highlight the distance in space and time between the subjects and the lives of genteel Americans, and the articles provided compelling details that made these foreign scenes seem more realistic than the allegorical tales that had predominated in Willis's *Companion*.

73

The Islanders filling a wicker image with human victims and combustible materials.

Fejee Islanders practice human sacrifice. From *Youth's Companion*, 1857. Courtesy of the Rare
Books and Manuscripts Department, Boston Public Library.

Using exotic material to attract young readers was not a new practice
in American children's magazines. Earlier editors such as Lydia Maria
Child and Samuel Goodrich had amused and instructed children with
articles about natural phenomena such as "red snow" and the explosion of
Mount Vesuvius and humorous adventure stories in which the "go-ahead"
of American youth bested the savage impulses of non-Christian societies.[3]
The *Companion*'s illustrations and stories, however, introduced an unprecedented level of violence and moral didacticism into the genre, a combination that has led me to describe Ford's formula as *genteel sensationalism*.

These genteel sensational stories were an integral part of the new editor's effort to transform the declining magazine from a "religious and public
school supplement" into a commercially appealing publication for young
people that also maintained its traditional ideals.[4] Ford shared his predecessor's orthodox Protestant beliefs and artisanal background but not his
prevailing concerns about the dangers of market cultures. A publicly modest man who hid his identity as publisher of the *Companion* behind the
pseudonym "Perry Mason," he nonetheless harbored substantial financial

ambitions and a belief that commerce could facilitate moral progress.[5] He strived to imprint the *Companion* with this ideology by engaging young readers as consumers, a practice that departed from Willis's begrudging integration of children into the market economy.

Ford borrowed his strategy from the sensational entertainments that had emerged in northern cities during the 1830s and 1840s. These products, including the penny press and story papers as well as theatrical amusements such as Bowery B'hoy comedy and blackface minstrelsy, fixated on unusual events and people both in and outside American society. In doing so, they reinforced distinctions between white Protestants and others at a time when controversies in the United States over immigration, slavery, and territorial expansion threatened to blur those boundaries.[6] Sensational amusements emerged from, and served as leisure products for, the nation's growing populations of white, urban workingmen and women. By the 1850s, such entertainments had become particularly linked to the non-genteel sporting cultures flourishing among men of these cities.[7]

The reconstructed *Companion*'s reliance on elements of this sensational formula, and the fact that most of the prominent figures in its early cover stories were male, suggest that one of Ford's commercial goals was to attract more boys to the magazine. This strategy was becoming increasingly common among publishers for children, who feared that boys—who often had greater physical freedoms than did their female peers and thus, in urban settings, more access to consumer goods outside the home—would dismiss juvenile books and magazines as too genteel for their tastes.[8] The approach also had ideological benefits for Ford because producing stories clearly intended for older children (particularly for young men on the cusp of adulthood) and balancing them with more traditional sentimental children's tales for the rest of his audience could mitigate the social threat that genteel audiences perceived in marketing directly to young consumers.

Ford appealed to boys through these genteel sensational stories by presenting a martial, aggressive ideal of manhood that contrasted with the more sentimental, maternal perspective of masculinity featured in Willis's *Companion*. The stories romanticized these aggressive male behaviors even as they implicitly condemned them as antithetical to the *Companion*'s traditional social values. Through this balancing act, Ford sought to attract boys (and girls) who preferred the novels of Sir Walter Scott and James Fenimore Cooper—or, less reputably, the crime stories of the *National Police Gazette*—to the parables of Sunday school magazines.

Initially, this plan did not work. Ford's original genteel sensational template lasted for only three months. By April 1857, the *Companion*'s front page had returned to a more traditional genre of domestic fiction. No known evidence explains this editorial shift, but the reversal suggests that the magazine's adult subscribers were hesitant to accept this expansion of children's entertainment options.[9] That hesitation reflected a widespread public concern among mid-nineteenth-century genteel Americans that the nation's rapid economic growth posed a threat to their cultural authority.[10] Boston, the *Companion*'s hometown, was struck particularly hard by these concerns, as Catholic immigrants increasingly contested Brahmin leadership during the 1850s.[11] An economic panic exacerbated Protestant anxieties in 1857, the year that Ford assumed control over the *Companion,* and the city became a center for the national wave of religious revivals known as the Great Awakening or Businessman's Revival of 1857–58.[12] This name suggests the pressure that the downturn placed on commercial men to show that piety as well as profit was shaping their business decisions.

Yet even under these unsettled conditions, Ford's evangelical faith and personal economic ascent inspired him to persist in his belief that a growing connection to the market economy could facilitate the development of American children's moral character. Though his initial setback chastened him, he spent four years continuing to experiment with genteel sensationalism as a means of promoting this mutually beneficial relationship, until the outbreak of the Civil War led him to temporarily abandon his efforts. In his work on the inside pages of the magazine, he shifted toward a less ostentatious but potentially more radical approach of setting sensational stories in mundane rather than exotic environments. These narratives examined settings that more closely resembled those in which the *Companion*'s readers lived and derived their excitement from the possible moral and physical threats awaiting young Americans just outside their homes.

Ford's wave of genteel sensational stories continued to deliver a socially conservative message. Like his earliest pieces, the tales modeled how market products might be able to reinforce existing standards of respectable conduct: they enticed young readers' attention through entertainment and then capitalized on their interest to instill traditional values. Genteel sensationalism was just part of Ford's plan to strengthen the *Companion*'s commercial relationship with its young readers. He also redesigned the masthead to make it more child-centered, introduced long domestic stories that featured children as protagonists, and even started a premiums program that gave children prizes for selling subscriptions to the *Companion.* Yet it was the genteel sensational stories that most directly linked the magazine's commercialization to its continuing efforts to sustain genteel Protestant values.

Despite some stumbles (like the first genteel sensational stories, the premiums program quickly disappeared, only to reemerge after the Civil War), Ford's cumulative efforts increased the magazine's readership. A lack of records makes it difficult to assess the timing of this improvement; but the *Companion's* circulation, which was approximately 4,500 when Ford and Reverend John W. Olmstead purchased the magazine in late 1856, increased to roughly ten times that number by the end of the Civil War in 1865.[13] The continuing expansion of the market economy fueled this success. Improved transportation made the magazine available to a broader audience, and urbanization and cheaper production facilitated the proliferation of other commercial entertainment options, which in turn increased demand for a reputable children's magazine, even among audiences that did not fully share Ford's confidence in the benefits of exposing children to market cultures. Yet the new editor's persistent endeavors to convert that audience to his pedagogical perspective shaped the methods by which the industry haltingly and intermittently expanded children's roles as consumers.

DURING THE last six weeks of Nathaniel Willis's tenure as editor of the *Youth's Companion,* the magazine's lead stories alternated between Bible tales such as "Young Samuel, A Servant of God" and moralistic vignettes such as "Emma Winifred; or, The Little Girl Who Was Punished for Sabbath Breaking."[14] The masthead retained the slogan "No Sectarianism, No Controversy," which Willis had introduced in the midst of the Unitarian Controversy of the 1820s. He had built a small, consistent audience by blending religious orthodoxy with sentimental imagery and rhetoric but had not adapted his formula significantly for nearly two decades. By 1856, the *Companion* offered little to distinguish itself from a Sunday school magazine, and its stagnant circulation and declining revenues indicated its limited appeal to the growing audience for children's magazines.[15]

In late 1856, Willis, by this time in his mid-seventies, sold the struggling magazine to Olmstead and Company, a partnership of Reverend Olmstead and his thirty-four-year-old associate, Ford, who assumed editorial control.[16] The new owners introduced themselves in the January 1, 1857, issue; and although they retained Willis's name on the masthead as senior editor, the *Companion* underwent an immediate and dramatic transformation.

For readers, the most striking feature of Ford's first issue must have been the "Fejee Islanders" illustration, which was more dramatic than any previous image in the magazine. Yet other aspects were also noticeably different. Ford increased the size of the *Companion's* pages, already fifteen inches high, "by about a quarter part"without raising the price. Using larger sheets enabled him to add another column of print to each page and increase the size of the typeset.[17] He transformed the masthead, eliminating Willis's slogan and replacing the original picture (a mother watching her children read the magazine) with three images of children reading the *Companion* by themselves.[18]

The back page of this issue featured another significant change: the addition of advertising. Willis had repeatedly told his readers, "No advertisements, and nothing sectarian or controversial are admitted into the *Youth's Companion*" because such items had "a tendency to injure public morals, or to wound private feelings."[19] Ford, in contrast, introduced a column of ads on the back page and, in future numbers, expanded their presence as needed.[20]

Another new feature was a premiums program. Ford explained this concept in an editorial in the first issue: "We have no doubt it is your wish to get good from your reading, and also to impart good to others . . . You will consequently, we trust, make an effort to introduce the *Companion* to your friends, say a kind word for it, and induce them to take it. You will thus do good, and . . . entitle yourself to some one or more of the pretty and useful premium presents we have already offered you."[21] These presents were small tokens, such as roller skates and slingshots, which children earned by selling subscriptions to the *Companion*.

Collectively, these changes reveal the complexity and ambition of Ford's efforts to broaden the audience for his magazine. Some of his editorial policies, such as the decision to include advertising, were directed toward adults. During the first six months of 1858, the publishing industry placed almost 45 percent of the ads in the *Companion*, patent medicines 20 percent, and clothing slightly less than 10 percent. Some of these products, such as a book titled *The Fourteen Pet Goslings* and a microscope, might have appealed to children; but ads for Grover and Baker sewing machines, Radway's Ready Relief medicine ("Cold, Cough, Consumption—Death"), and Mrs. S. A. Allen's World's Hair Restorer clearly focused on adult consumers.[22]

Ford redesigned other parts of the *Companion* (for instance, adding genteel sensational stories) to broaden the magazine's appeal to both younger and older readers. Its new size and expanded illustrations further distinguished the *Companion* from the chapbook format of evangelical children's magazines of the era, making it look more like Boston's popular story papers. These changes, along with the addition of a distinct "Children's Department," indicate that Ford was working to transform the *Companion* into "a family paper." This goal became even clearer in 1867 when, after severing his partnership with Olmstead, he added the subtitle "A *Companion for the Whole Family*" to the masthead.[23]

The new editor directed a specific group of changes—notably, the masthead's new pictures and the premiums program—at younger readers. Rewards of skates and slingshots suggest that he wanted boys in particular to actively market the magazine. By engaging children as commercial agents, he was attempting to link their moral development to the magazine's growth. In the editorial that introduced the premiums program, Ford promised children he would produce a magazine to "best promote the good in your minds and hearts," and he linked that goal to making "the *Companion* one of the very neatest, most interesting and best papers in the land . . . It will be no fault of ours if its coming to a yet larger company than now, does not meet with greater pleasure than ever."[24]

This connection between morality and economics seems to have come from Ford alone. Because Olmstead opposed the addition of sensational stories, advertising, and the premiums program, their implementation lagged until he left the magazine in 1867.[25] Many contemporary editors shared Olmstead's fear of commercial influences. A few, especially producers of widely read publications, such as James Gordon Bennett of the *New York Herald*, "scoffed" at those "who warned of the negative consequences that often resulted from economic success."[26] Almost none of them, however, particularly among those producing publications for children, advocated Ford's position that exposure to commercial cultures could improve Americans' moral character.

His unique perspective derived from a confluence of his economic and religious experiences. Like many writers and editors of children's magazines during this period, Ford was not raised in a prosperous family. Born in Cambridge, Massachusetts, in 1822, he grew up in straitened economic circumstances after his father, a wallpaper manufacturer, died when he was six months old. Despite this disadvantage, however, he rose quickly to economic prosperity. He began his career as printer's apprentice, probably at Olmstead's *Christian Watchman* magazine. At some point between the age of twenty-two and thirty, he purchased an interest in the *Watchman*, which led to the creation of Olmstead and Company.[27] Because the *Watchman* was a commercial success, he entered the field of children's magazines in a more prosperous financial position than many of his competitors did.

Ford was an orthodox Protestant who was working in a field dominated by liberals. Evangelical magazines had been important to the founding of the industry; yet by the 1850s the most popular writers for children (including Samuel Goodrich, Jacob Abbott, Grace Greenwood, and William

Taylor Adams) viewed children as inherently moral and thus in need of idealized behavioral models. Ford's skepticism about human nature compelled him instead to instigate the unconverted toward the path of Christian righteousness, and his own success seems to have inspired him to view market cultures as a valuable instrument for such spiritual motivation.

His willingness to challenge prevailing beliefs about the market economy was probably facilitated by his outsider status. As a Baptist artisan, he was doubly excluded from Boston's cultural establishment.[28] Moreover, in 1856, when he took over the *Companion,* that establishment's stronghold over Boston society appeared to be vulnerable. Even before the national economic collapse known as the Panic of 1857, cracks in the Brahmins' authority had begun to create a crisis for the city's elites. A decade-long decline in the shipping, textiles, railroad, and finance industries had already reduced their incomes. The splintering of the Whig party had loosened their control over government offices; and challenges to their authority emerged at Harvard, Massachusetts General Hospital, and several other of the bedrock institutions they had founded or led for decades. Spiritually, the evangelical revivals of the winter of 1857–58 confirmed that the elites' Unitarian beliefs were not as dominant among Boston's middling and poor inhabitants, and the city's large influx of Irish Catholic immigrants was weakening the cultural authority of all forms of Protestantism.[29]

Yet even at this moment of elite vulnerability, Ford did not use the *Companion* to oppose that establishment, as Willis initially had done. Instead, he attempted to expand the boundaries of genteel respectability to reach the largest possible audience. Lacking reputable models for that effort, he sought to legitimize a source that shared many of his beliefs and concerns: the sensational literature emerging from the city's flourishing penny press and story papers.

IN OCTOBER 1848, *Flag of Our Union,* a Boston-based story paper, posted story guidelines as part of a prize competition announcement for aspiring authors:

> We wish for such contributions as shall be strictly moral in their tone, highly interesting in their plot, replete throughout with incident, well filled with exciting yet truthful description, and, in short, highly readable and entertaining. Domestic stories, so-called, are not exactly of the class we desire; but tales— of the sea and land—of the stirring times of the revolution—or of dates still farther back, are more in accordance with our wishes.[30]

These criteria corresponded to the prominent features of the *Companion*'s genteel sensational narratives a decade later. In fact, the *Companion* borrowed not only story elements from its neighbor (the *Flag*'s office on Winter Street was only a few blocks from Ford's shop on School Street) but also much of its look: the size, layout, masthead, and print style of the two periodicals' front pages are strikingly similar.

Flag of Our Union was part of a wave of cheap and popular publications produced by working-class printers and entrepreneurs in northern cities (particularly Boston, New York, and Philadelphia) during the 1830s and 1840s. Their growth was spurred by the same causes—increasing urban populations and literacy rates, improved printing technologies and transportation networks, cheap postage—that made the *Companion*'s increased circulation possible two decades later. Their appearance sparked an immediate and sustained growth in the number of American periodical readers. Before the 1833 appearance of the *New York Sun* (the prototype for the penny press), the total circulation of that city's eleven daily newspapers was 26,500. Two years later its three top penny papers alone had a circulation of 44,000, and by the 1850s the five top dailies combined to reach nearly 200,000 customers. Nationally, the number of daily publications increased from 65 to 138 between 1830 and 1840, and their circulation doubled to nearly 300,000.[31] Weekly story papers, which focused predominantly on fiction, began to appear near the end of the "newspaper revolution" of the 1830s. These publications first appeared in Boston, and *Flag of Our Union*, the most successful of this group, reached a circulation of more than 100,000 by the mid-1850s.[32]

In contrast to their "sixpenny" predecessors, which catered to the interests of the political and mercantile elite, these publications produced content for workingmen and women: a mix of news and fiction that concentrated heavily on crime, romance, and humor. Their popularity generated a backlash from more reputable authors and journals, fueled by genteel Americans' long-standing mistrust of fiction and desire to control the information circulating in the nation's burgeoning cities.[33] Edwin Whipple, a prominent genteel critic from Boston, described such stories as "The Romance of Rascality," complaining that they "exhibit[ed] criminals as proper objects of esteem and moral approbation." An anonymous Chicago physician described them as "public poison" that "subvert[s] the purity of our Republican institutions, destroy[s] the elective franchise and foster[s] elements of revolution, which, if we neglect to elevate the masses' through healthy moral literature, will crush us in the might and majesty of our fancied security."[34]

Journalist Lambert Wilmer focused particularly on the damage these publications did to the nation's children, arguing that their content meant that "no narrative of human depravity or crime can shock or horrify the American reader. He has studied every phase of profligacy and flagrant villainy in his early childhood." Narratives about "notorious highwaymen, burglars and pickpockets" and life in New York's "resorts of prostitution and infamy" were the most profitable books on the market, which, in Wilmer's view, indicated that the popular press emitted "the thickest of all darkness" through which young readers learned "atheism, obscenity, contempt and defiance of the law, the arts of the seducer, the mysteries of brothels, the practice of pugilism."[35]

Ford avoided some of the practices that distressed these critics. He eliminated most of the story papers' sexual content and initially presented his genteel sensational narratives in nonfiction form to avoid lingering orthodox concerns about the impact of imaginative literature on children's moral development. Yet even in modified form, he chose to integrate the publications' combination of exoticism, violence, and drama into his formula for revitalizing the *Companion*, despite vehement attacks and broader genteel anxieties about threatening commercial influences. His willingness to do so reflects his ideological distance from the prevailing trends of his industry. The Chicago physician's desire, for example, to "elevate the masses through healthy moral literature" mirrored the practice of most popular mid-nineteenth-century genteel writers. Jacob Abbott, Harriet Beecher Stowe, Susan Warner, and other authors created idealized child characters who rarely strayed from the path of Protestant virtue (Abbott's Rollo, Stowe's Eva St. Claire, Warner's Ellen Montgomery) to inspire empathy and piety in child and adult readers.[36] Previous generations of Americans, however, particularly those who grew up in evangelical families such as Ford's, had consumed religious publications designed to frighten audiences toward religious conversion. Many midcentury writers and editors who were exposed to these religious stories as children (particularly women such as Lydia Maria Child and Sara Willis Parton) rebelled against that patriarchal method, but Ford's preference for *Companion* stories that exemplified sensational literature's predilection for (in the anonymous critic's words) "vice unmasked" rather than "virtue portrayed" suggests that he still adhered to a traditional evangelical approach.[37]

Additionally, the physician critic's fear that such literature would subvert "republican institutions" and foment "revolution" clashed with Ford's perspectives on class and the market economy. The editor exhibited little despair about this issue, unlike both the critic and Willis, who like other workingmen of the 1820s had feared the destruction of the republic from above if wealth and power were concentrated with the elites. Indeed, Ford's personal economic ascent through the publishing industry suggested that the expansion of the popular press, including its sensational publications, offered an opportunity for ambitious young Americans to capitalize on the nation's exponential growth. Moreover, his subsequent work at the *Companion*, along with his lifelong philanthropic efforts to provide religious education for Boston's working classes, illustrated his belief that this expansion could have the conservative cultural effect of inculcating genteel beliefs and standards of behavior into a broader segment of the nation's white Protestant families.[38]

These beliefs help to explain why Ford embraced not only the popular press's content but also its marketing strategies. Sensationalist entrepreneurs such as James Gordon Bennett and P. T. Barnum were seeking to shape as well as cater to the desires of their consumers, in part by trumpeting the economic value of their products. Story papers were participating in escalating rhetorical battles over which publication offered readers the best bargain. The *Universal Yankee Nation*, for example, promised "to present the great WORLD OF UNIVERSAL KNOWLEDGE in a cheap and portable form" in "The Mammoth of all the Mammoths! . . . The largest newspaper . . . ever published in this or any other country." The *New World* proclaimed an unlimited ability to garner information for its readers: "No pent up CONTINENT contracts our powers: The whole boundless UNIVERSE is Ours."[39] The *Companion* did not match this degree of puffery, but Ford did constantly reiterate the economic value his magazine offered. Like many of his marketing strategies, this practice became more pronounced after Olmstead's departure; an 1868 advertising supplement claimed that the *Companion* was "the cheapest youth's publication in the world—it will give for one dollar and fifty cents, more reading than any three Youth's Magazines."[40]

Borrowing strategies from his peers in the sensational press helped to further Ford's commercial and ideological agendas for the *Companion*, but he did have to adapt their approach to fit the needs of his audience. Tales set in brothels and on pirate ships and filled with love affairs, murders, and suicides were too lascivious for young readers and risked not only alienating his genteel audience but also thwarting his evangelical aims. Thus, after the collapse of his initial wave of genteel sensational stories, Ford spent much of the next four years experimenting with formulas that might allow him to convince his adult audience of the pedagogical value of marketing the *Companion* more directly to children. By moving the settings of his genteel sensational genre closer to home, he emphasized how expanding, market-centered cultures were already dissipating boundaries that reputable families sought to construct between private and public life.

SINCE THE industry's founding in the 1820s, the relationship between private and public realms of society had been an inherent element of children's magazines, which delivered commercial products for children into tens of thousands of American homes. Willis had dealt with this concern by offering young readers only a limited public role as consumers. He believed they should receive the *Companion* in their own names and, if possible, pay for it with their own money. However, he offered them no role in shaping the magazine's content, restricting that privilege to his adult subscribers, who largely shared his desire to limit the magazine's worldview to children's domestic environments. Child, in contrast, had embraced children as "critics" of the *Juvenile Miscellany* and sought to illuminate the larger world for them through lessons in history, geography, and science and discussions of controversial subjects such as poverty, Indian rights, and slavery.

Ford initially sought to incorporate some elements of Child's approach to exposing young readers to the wider world, although he emphasized its dangers rather than its wonders. In addition to cataloging the violent and cruel practices of the "Fejee Islanders," early issues of the *Companion* highlighted the horrors of Turkish punishments and used "The Grape Harvest in Syria" to emphasize the "ignorant . . . superstitious, and degraded . . . customs" of that society.[41] These stories allowed Ford to introduce novel and dramatic subjects into the magazine while reinforcing its evangelical principles and the genteel message that children needed to remain cloistered at home to ensure their proper moral and physical development. But after three months, he moved away from this strategy, finding (as Child had) that adult subscribers were reluctant to introduce young readers to controversial subjects from the world outside the home. Yet he did not return immediately to domestic stories. Instead, he gradually moved his genteel sensational genre into settings closer to home.

An early example was "Moral Tale: Setting Up for a Gentleman," which appeared on the front page of the April 16, 1857, issue. The story's protagonist is Barney Cragin, an Irish Catholic youth who abandons his parents and migrates to "Ameriky," where he lives in New York and participates in cockfighting, boxing, and drinking, the types of disreputable activities regularly covered in the sporting newspapers of the time.[42] Barney ends up dying in a New York prison, thus linking the story to the cautionary narratives that Nathaniel Willis had produced in the *Companion* for three decades. Unlike those narratives, however, this long cover story offers detailed descriptions of the rakish characters Barney encounters and features an illustration of him standing in dandyish attire next to his father, an old, decrepit farmer hoeing a furrow, representing a scene in which Barney refuses to help till the land because he does not want to soil his fancy clothes.

Like the stories published during Willis's tenure, "Setting Up for a Gentleman" was didactic, moralistic, and allegorical; but Ford eliminated his predecessor's generalized messages in favor of specific, compelling details and contemporary historical contexts. The tale was a thinly veiled attack on the values of the Catholic immigrants who had converged on Boston during the 1840s. At the same time, it shifted the genteel sensational genre into a modern American setting so that Ford could address issues that were directly affecting the lives of his young readers. Neither a Protestant American nor a South Pacific cannibal nor a Middle Eastern grape harvester, Barney Cragin was an intermediate figure, standing between the distant, exotic characters who had populated the genre's earliest stories and the youthful American protagonists of subsequent tales. Moreover, the story of Barney's migration from farm to city was relevant to the experiences of young male readers, foreshadowing Ford's strategy of using the moral and physical dangers of such a move to entertain and instruct his juvenile audience.

Less than two months later, Ford published "Wanted—A Boy From the Country," in which a naïve rural youth is financially exploited by an unscrupulous urban employer.[43] Now that he had removed all hints of foreignness from his narrative, he could focus on the message that would predominate in his genteel sensational genre for the next four years: the belief that the barriers that genteel Americans had constructed between private and public societies were increasingly insufficient to protect the nation's children from the corrupting influences of commercial cultures. This perspective contradicted Willis's claim that young men could develop a moral character that would allow them to choose to separate themselves from such hazards. In the 1847 story "Self-Denial, or, the Two Cousins," which I discussed in chapter 1, the hero Charles grows up under the supervision of his devoted widowed mother, who successfully strives "to fulfil [sic] the arduous task of moulding [his] young mind into perfect moral beauty." Meanwhile, his cousin William is raised in a wealthy family that indulges his every wish but neglects his ethical development.[44] Likewise, Lydia Sigourney's "The Farmer and the Soldier," which appeared in the Companion in 1846 as the nation stood on the brink of the Mexican-American War, attempted to drain the romance from military life, celebrating the young men who

bravely chose a quiet domestic existence rather than the exciting but corrupting experiences of war or urban life.[45]

Both the influential mother in "Self-Denial" and the famous female author behind "The Farmer and the Soldier" (Sigourney was one of the few
writers to receive a byline during Willis's tenure) link the ability to make
such upstanding choices to the influence of feminine domestic culture. By
the time Ford took over the *Companion,* however, the publishing industry's
growing pursuit of a young male audience was making this domesticized
version of masculinity increasingly anachronistic. Instigated by the success
of Boston novelist William Taylor Adams's *The Boat Club; or, The Bunkers
of Rippleton: A Tale for Boys* (1855) and British novelist Thomas Hughes's
Tom Brown's Schooldays (1857), the industry introduced a new genre of male-
authored "boys' books" in which protagonists ventured out of the domestic
realm to engage in the challenges of modern society.[46] Adams (writing
under the pseudonym "Oliver Optic") particularly capitalized on this template, publishing a series of *Boat Club* sequels and accepting an editor's position at the children's magazine the *Student and Schoolmate,* where he spent
fifteen years cultivating the genre through his own work as well as through
the writings of younger novelists such as Horatio Alger.[47]

The *Companion* adopted this gendered approach in both its original and
revised genteel sensational formulas, but here again Ford tailored the tactic
to suit his theological agenda. Unlike the works of Adams and Hughes,
which celebrated the successes of boys who ventured out of the home to
test their characters, the *Companion's* stories featured young men (and occasionally young women) who nearly always failed to transcend the challenges of public life. In "Frank Norton, or, The Unheeded Admonition,"
the protagonist, despite his mother's wishes, is unable to resist the pressure
of classmates who urge him to smoke. His capitulation leads to his association with an immoral group of classmates and ultimately a life of crime.[48]
In "Deception," a young debutante, unable to ignore the immoral rituals
of fashion and flirtation, mistreats a respectable suitor and pursues a flashy
but irresolute young man, destroying her reputation and dooming herself
to life as a spinster.[49]

These stories' emphasis on peer-centered environments reflected real
changes in the lives of American youth. By the late 1850s, many boys and
girls living in or near cities went out of their homes more often than their
parents had done a generation earlier. Young men sought commercial clerk-
ships instead of working at the family farm or trade, and children of both
genders generally spent more days in school. By 1860, 75 percent of children
ages ten to fourteen were attending school, although the length of their

terms and the number of years they spent in school still varied widely based on class, region, and race.[50] In Boston, home of the nation's first public school system and the center of most of the *Companion*'s readership during this period, the percentage was probably higher, particularly among the prosperous classes that constituted the majority of the magazine's subscribers.

Yet even as Ford recognized these changes, he was accentuating their extremes for ideological and commercial purposes. Not every young business clerk worked for an immoral employer, nor was every suitor a shiftless cad. Moreover, his stories exaggerated the breadth of the threat that emerging urban environments and peer-oriented situations posed for the *Companion*'s young readers during the late antebellum era. While children's access to potentially hazardous surroundings had increased, the United States, even in New England, was still predominantly a rural nation in 1857; and parents of white, Protestant, genteel families still dominated the upbringing of their offspring.[51]

By making the need for respectable influences outside the home seem more acute, Ford dramatized his commercial and ideological agendas. An emphasis on the inevitability of the dangers that older youths faced not only legitimized his decision to present more sensational content but allowed him to subdivide his approach to young readers based on gender and age. Thus, by adopting the incipient industry trend of targeting specific juvenile groups, he could maintain the *Companion*'s traditional values, appease the concerns of his genteel adult subscribers, and provide more exciting entertainment for young readers.[52]

Ford's strategy involved more than making sure that his genteel sensational tales about older boys (and occasionally girls) engaging with the outside world conveyed conservative social messages. It also meant continuing to publish sentimental tales about younger children who remained closer to home. These stories reinforced the ideals of the *Companion*'s sensational narratives by affirming the belief that female-dominated domestic environments could mitigate the corrupting influences of male-controlled realms of commerce. Ford's sentimental template idealized small children, girls, and women who remained cloistered at home, delineating them as purveyors of sympathy and spiritual relief for men and boys who were struggling to advance in the larger world.

In his first issue, Ford established this position by means of "The Swiss Basket Maker," the story of a small boy and his younger sister who convince the impoverished title character to attend church after learning he knows "nothing of Jesus." This act inspires their pastor to preach on the text "Out of the mouths of babes and sucklings hast thou ordained strength" (Psalms 8:2).[53] Similarly, "The Good Deed in Season" introduces a girl whose kindness sustains a poor boy as he struggles to live a life of respectability. Years later, when they meet again, the young man tells the young woman, "Twelve years ago you placed the bright flowers in my hand, and they made me a new boy—aye, and they have made a man of me, too. Your face has been a light, ma'am, all along the dark hours of my life, and this day that little beggar boy can stand in the old place and say to you, though he's a humble and hard-working man yet, thank God, he's an honest one."[54] This story grounds the girl's feminine appeal in empathy rather than sexuality, linking her to the *Companion*'s many maternal characters who keep young men faithful to the moral foundations of gentility.

Such characters were a constant presence in Ford's *Companion,* and their love was often portrayed as the most important catalyst for the development of a young boy's good character. In "Mother's Apron Strings" we learn that "Satan . . . knows he can never make 'anything great' of the children he seeks to ruin, till he has persuaded them to 'break loose' from a mother's influence. Till the first step is taken his power is feeble, for nothing guards a boy from sin and danger, like the prayers and counsel of a pious loving mother."[55] Conversely, children without mothers are exceptionally vulnerable to spiritual peril. A poem titled "The Motherless" describes such a youth as a "stricken, bleeding dove," while a story called "James Miller" claims that an orphan raised for too long without a mother may, even after he is restored to a properly nurturing domestic environment, lead other children to physical harm.[56]

The *Companion*'s homage to mothers had commercial as well as ideological motivations. Because women wielded primary moral authority over children's upbringing among the families from which the magazine drew its audience, Ford had expanded Willis's efforts to cultivate their approval and interest. Acknowledging their preeminence in childrearing matters, he changed Willis's weekly parenting column into a "Mother's Department," which offered examples of maternal devotion and courage designed to appeal to adult readers. In "A Mother's Love," for example, an elderly woman dies in her son's arms, content that he has returned home after two decades away as a soldier—a "striking illustration of the permanency and depth of a mother's love."[57] Ford also carried over a series of articles on "Women in the Revolution" from the last year of Willis's editorship. These pieces recounted the contributions of female patriots, from the "masculine courage" displayed by Flora McDonald when caught in the midst of a naval battle to the emotional and intellectual support offered by the wives of heroes such

as Ethan Allen and William Livingston.[58] These stories paid little attention to children and, despite their backdrop of war, offered few thrills and
little melodrama for young readers. Instead, they seem primarily intended
to appeal to women who subscribed to the *Companion* for their children.

The revolutionary stories were in some ways anomalous, both in their
target audience and in the active roles that some of these women characters
assumed. Most mothers in the *Companion* provided comfort to boys and
men through their inherent spirituality and sympathy rather than their
actions, a pattern of passivity that linked them to girls and small children
as domesticated members of society too pure for public life. Yet the revolution narratives also fit Ford's broad argument about the dissipating divide
between private and public life. The women in these stories, like other females and young children in the magazine's sentimental fiction, facilitated
both individual and community success through their domestic values of
devotion, piety, and courage.

The story "Grace Darling," which appeared twice in the *Companion*—
once during Willis's tenure, once during Ford's—exemplifies this approach.
In 1855, Willis published his version of a widely publicized true story about
a lighthouse keeper's daughter, whose determination to save shipwreck
victims spurs her father into action. Willis's narrative focused on Grace's
moral virtue in risking her own and her father's life in order to rescue a
group of strangers. In 1857, Ford published a second version of the story. Although he retained Willis's message, he added details—information about
the Darling family, their life in the Farne Islands, the names of the ship
(the *Forfarshire*) and the victims (among them, Mrs. Dawson, who clung to
her two dead children)—which added dramatic and didactic weight. Both
editors presented Grace as a model of genteel behavior, but Ford's sensationalized version transformed her story into a source of entertainment that
could produce both consumer satisfaction and moral growth.[59]

Ford's recognition that public and private lives were entwined with commerce and morality drove his antebellum editorial policy at the *Companion*.
If children could no longer be protected from the outside world, then market products needed to prepare them for the world's moral challenges. His
editorial mix of genteel sensationalism and sentimentality was designed to
teach through entertainment in a way that would maximize both profits
and young readers' development. While it is difficult to measure the success
of his early efforts, there is no question that the Civil War both complicated
and facilitated his plan.

CHAPTER 4

The *Youth's Companion* and the Civil War

WILLIAM WALKER, the hero of "William Walker, A Story of the War," represents the "hopes" of his mother's "many years of widowhood and toil." He has completed his education with honors and has the opportunity to enter either the ministry or his neighbor's business. Yet the month after his graduation, following a period of intense self-examination, the young man decides to forgo these prospects and enlist in the Union army. His mother accepts his decision while his sisters protest against it, but "Willy" remains determined to do "what I think right." A few months later, his mother and sisters receive a letter notifying them that William has been killed in his first battle "while cheering on his men. Shot in the breast and died instantly."[1]

This story appeared on the front page of the *Youth's Companion* on December 19, 1861, eight months after the start of the U.S. Civil War. It was the first time the magazine had featured the conflict so prominently. Like most other children's magazines, the *Companion* had remained relatively silent about the war throughout most of that year. When editor Daniel Sharp Ford did begin to address the conflict, he initially emphasized it as a tragedy that was victimizing young Americans—an approach that also paralleled his competitors' prevailing attitude in 1861. Yet "William Walker" portends the differences that emerged between Ford's war coverage and that of other children's books and magazines. Much wartime children's literature was more patriotic than ethical, but "William Walker," with its dilemma of whether a young man should stay home and care for his family or enlist in the great national cause, exemplifies how the *Companion's* war-related stories focused predominantly on personal, moral challenges raised by the conflict.[2] This emphasis meant that while other children's books and magazines romanticized the possibility of boys and girls serving as drummer boys, nurses, and even soldiers for the Union, the *Companion* more often suggested that a young reader could "prove . . . a better patriot by staying at home."[3]

Ford's wartime editorial policies contrasted with the approach he had taken during his first four years at the *Companion*, when he had exposed young readers to dramatic, often violent stories to heighten interest in the magazine. Initially, his impulse to revert to more a traditionally genteel pattern of sheltering children from the outside world may have been part of a broader cultural response to the war's horrors. Yet as the *Companion*'s policy diverged from the rest of the industry's, Ford's choices reflected the persistence of the theological and class divisions that distinguished his magazine from most of its competitors.

Publications that embraced fuller integration of children into the Union war effort generally shared the liberal Protestant values of New England's commercial and intellectual elites. These communities vigorously directed their optimistic faith toward the unprecedented collective effort to save the Union. Their men volunteered for the army in disproportionate numbers, their civilian leaders established Union leagues and produced sanitary fairs, and their public voices promoted cooperative action throughout the North as a means of cultivating loyalty to the national cause.[4]

Ford, although unreserved in his support for the Union, retained an orthodox skepticism about human nature that left him uncomfortable with this collectivist approach. He also maintained, despite his personal economic success, a workingman's discomfort with elite methods and values. Yet commercial relevance and moral responsibility demanded that the *Companion* produce a response to the national crisis, so Ford refashioned its editorial formula to politicize the magazine's traditional focus on individual responsibility. When addressing adult participation in the war, the *Companion* usually presented Union successes as products of individual dedication rather than cooperative work. When speaking to young readers, whom his competitors sought to inspire with patriotism through stories about the war's great events, Ford suggested turning inward. He told them their primary responsibility as citizens was to develop moral characters that made them effective advocates for the Union cause.[5]

This focus on individual responsibility fulfilled the *Companion*'s patriotic responsibility and sustained its religious heritage. It also left Ford well situated after the war to capitalize on his ambition of expanding children's roles as consumers. The war dissipated genteel boundaries between private and public life that had hampered Ford's antebellum efforts to commercialize his magazine. The conflict's reach into nearly every American home made protecting women and children from the outside world almost impossible. Heightened patriotism furthered weakened these boundaries by encouraging all Americans to remain informed about and engaged with the northern war effort. Wartime chaos and displacement also left many northern children with less adult supervision, allowing them greater access to commercial amusements—now more available because of the expanded Union transportation network—that had often been forbidden before the war.

One product that indicated how the *Companion* might benefit from these changes was the dime novel, a new literary format with a perspective similar to that of Ford's magazine. Dime novels became popular with soldiers during the early years of the war and then trickled down to the boys who idolized these men, to the point that youngsters' fascination with the books became a cultural phenomenon—one noted but not yet disparaged by the nation's literary elite.[6] Sharing Ford's preferred template, which featured individual male heroes whose dramatic adventures both entertained and instructed readers, the publications achieved a level of commercial success that revealed a growing audience for the sensational yet socially conservative formula that the *Companion* had used to attract young consumers.

Given the success of dime novels, Ford felt able to gradually reinstate his genteel sensational formula into the *Companion*, using an editorial framework that continued to emphasize the perpetuation of existing social hierarchies. Wartime sensational stories were patriotic and appeared without pictures on the magazine's inside pages. When the war ended, he immediately expanded the genre by reintroducing dramatic illustrations and adventure stories to the front page; but these narratives retained the gender and age distinctions his antebellum stories had employed to mitigate the social consequences of children's expanding commercial roles.

His strategy, which had achieved limited success during the antebellum period, flourished after the war. The *Companion*'s circulation climbed from approximately 45,000 in 1865 to 263,000 in 1882; and by 1885 it had the highest circulation of any magazine in the United States.[7] The war made these numbers possible, both by improving northern capacities for producing and distributing goods and by instigating cultural changes that aligned a wide segment of American families with Ford's belief in the moral value of exposing children to carefully managed commercial influences. In doing so, the conflict expanded the nation's genteel standards for children's reading and transformed the *Companion* from an industry outlier into the model of a profitable and respectable children's magazine.

I_N A_{PRIL} 1861, a week after Confederate guns fired on Fort Sumter, the *Companion* opened an issue with a tale called "The Counterfeit Quarter," and its editorial column discussed "Good Friday in Brazil."[8] The issue that appeared after the first battle of Bull Run led with a story called "The Suicide," and its editorial considered "The Notches in the Osiers."[9] These issues exemplify the *Companion*'s pattern of ignoring the Civil War, an approach that prevailed for much of 1861. Although Ford had spent four years struggling to develop a method for respectably expanding his young readers' integration into the nation's growing commercial cultures, the war triggered a retreat into his magazine's traditional practice of sheltering children from current events and controversies.

His decision contrasted with the war fever that gripped much of the North in the months after the bombardment of Fort Sumter. New England's genteel society was particularly excited by the moral opportunities and physical challenges provided by the war. Anecdotal evidence suggests that many northern parents sought to imbue their children with patriotic spirit by encouraging them to play war games and dress in uniforms with guns and swords.[10] Yet the *Companion* was not unique in its reluctance to transform that martial energy into print. Until editors realized that the war would not end quickly, most children's magazines refrained from incorporating the conflict into their content.

Ford did not articulate the reasons for his policies, but his editorial practices throughout 1861 suggest a belief that war and its consequences were inappropriate subjects for children. During that chaotic year, he halted efforts to expand his readers' worldview, returning instead to his predecessor Nathaniel Willis's policy of isolating children from public life. Cover stories such as "Russell's Paint-Box," which highlights a boy's shame when he spends a friend's quarter, and "Susie's Mistake," which teaches the value of offering compassion, even to a tormentor, followed the *Companion*'s traditional practice of publishing moralistic narratives that fenced children's lives into narrowly constructed small-town settings without geographic or historical context.[11] For Willis, this approach had reinforced his orthodox message that unconverted children needed protection from the temptations of modern, market-driven cultures. For Ford, the policy had the added benefit of shielding young readers from the increased moral and physical hazards of a nation at war.

Ford did not wholly adopt his predecessor's approach, for by 1861 changing social circumstances made Willis's methods both unrealistic and increasingly inappropriate. Rapidly expanding communication networks meant that information was circulating much more quickly throughout the United States than it was when Willis had introduced these policies in the 1820s. This expansion made it more difficult to isolate children from public life, particularly those who were members of the *Companion*'s genteel urban audience. The unparalleled scale of the Union war effort, which brought news to and took men from even the most rural regions of the North, exacerbated this situation.[12] Moreover, as the war lengthened, its effects became more pervasive in northern society, and efforts to insulate children seemed not only futile but an abdication of the *Companion*'s responsibility as a moral advisor to its young readers.

Ford had recognized the anachronistic nature of Willis's editorial policy when he assumed control of the magazine in 1857. Although he shared his predecessor's evangelical views, he had altered the *Companion*'s message to reflect his belief that properly managed market cultures could facilitate children's moral development. At the end of 1861, Ford gradually began to reassert this philosophy in the *Companion,* ending his near-silence on the war in order to address concerns that the conflict had created for and about American youth.

"William Walker" established the template for how the magazine's war coverage would proceed. Rather than focusing on external threats to young Americans, as Ford's antebellum genteel sensational tales had done, this story concentrates on the home environment and concerns about internal moral dilemmas in ways that are characteristic of the magazine's traditional evangelical, domestic fiction. The narrative centers on the fatherless protagonist's private debate over whether to enlist in the Union army or stay home and provide for his mother and sisters. His death, the one dramatic event that might have connected the story to Ford's genteel sensational genre, occurs offstage: it is conveyed only through a letter to William's mother. Unlike the *Companion*'s antebellum cover stories, this one has no accompanying dramatic illustrations because the piece's preeminent concern involves neither entertainment nor politics. (The author never mentions the Union or the United States.) Instead, it focuses on the family's process of discovering its Christian duties:

> The great hearts o' all times are those which rise above the thoughts of personal interests, and feel that wrong must be put down and right vindicated at any cost ... And is it worth all this? ... Yes it *is* worth it, and the mother felt so, in all her grief and desolation, or rather she felt that this is a time when we must not stop to count the cost; when we have nothing to do but go straight forward and leave everything to God.[13]

This emphasis on modeling responses to young Americans' wartime moral dilemmas remained the primary focus of the *Companion*'s coverage for the duration of the conflict. Thus, as the war persisted, Ford remained circumspect about exposing his young readers to emerging patriotic cultures in the North. Other books and magazines incorporated entertainments, ranging from stories to songs to panoramas, intended to sweep children into a collective nationalist spirit by emphasizing the martial excitement and glory of the Union cause. In contrast, Ford largely avoided such enthusiasms by keeping his magazine's focus upon individual experiences of the war.[14] While his competitors encouraged participation in patriotic organizations and communities, he emphasized that children could best aid the cause by improving the propriety of their own conduct. Beginning with the story of William Walker's resolution to enlist in the Union army and ending with an editorial on President Lincoln's choice to attend the theater on the night of his assassination, Ford persistently reminded his audience of the power that individual decisions could have for a family, a community, and a nation.[15]

This message aligned with the magazine's traditional evangelical emphasis on the spiritual and social importance of personal responsibility. The *Companion*'s war-related content built on this tradition as it sought to delineate young Americans' moral obligations to the Union. Those responsibilities included contributing to the war effort, and some of the magazine's earliest war-related editorials requested that children send money, books, clothing, and letters to the men at the front or wear their old clothes for another year and forward the money saved to buy supplies for the army.[16] However, the *Companion*'s emphasis remained on individual decision making and the need to maintain one's own moral bearings in a time of chaos rather than on the power and solace of community building. In "The Patriot Boy," a boy too young to join the army takes a job as a bookkeeper and relegates his studies to the evening hours so that he can help support soldiers' families. Although his decision clearly has social benefits for those families and the local community, the author focuses on it as evidence of strength of character, ending the story with "We shall hear of him yet. A boy like that will surely develop into a good and great man."[17] In "Myself or My Country?" a young girl realizes that she has no right to prevent her father from enlisting. Rather that seeing this realization as a sacrifice to the public good, the author characterizes it as a "strange comfort" because the girl has passed a test of her personal faith and morality.[18]

Such individual challenges proliferated during the war, and the *Companion* sought not only to help children confront these tasks but also to counsel them regarding which ones they should avoid. For example, although he wavered on the subject, Ford inclined toward the belief that boys on the cusp of manhood should not yet join the military. "William Walker" implies that the protagonist has made the right decision when he chooses to enlist, but the story does not follow him out of the domestic realm to relate his experiences as a soldier. William dies almost immediately upon entering the service—as a spectator rather than a combatant—and the audience learns of his death only through the letter read at home. The author's response to this death further confuses the message: "But why not do it some other way? Why must men maim and murder each other like wild beasts? Why not settle their differences like rational beings? These are hard questions, too. We only know that every war and every change among the nations is helping to work out God's great plan for the redemption of the world." This ambiguous conclusion highlighted Ford's ethical concerns about young people's proper place in a society at war and further distinguished the *Companion*'s message from the unquestioning patriotism that predominated in other publications and entertainments offered to children during this era.[19]

The magazine maintained this ambiguity for much of the war. On the one hand, the *Companion* occasionally participated in the trend of heroic drummer boy stories that became popular across the North. For instance, "The Michigan Drummer Boy" glorifies the "spunk" of the title character who, after having his drum "blown to atoms" by a shell, recovers to capture a Rebel soldier single-handedly. On the other hand, "The Boy Soldier" warns readers not to become enamored of the supposed glory and romance of military service because "this is not your place. You are too young for that."[20] Ultimately, the latter perspective came to dominate *Companion* stories during the second half of the war. After publishing "The Michigan Drummer Boy," Ford never again supported, even in ambiguous "William Walker" form, young men's decision to participate directly in the fighting.

Instead, the *Companion*'s war stories sought to channel young readers' patriotic impulses away from the battleground and toward the duty of shaping their own moral characters. Narratives about Union generals tied the nation's success to such individual efforts, focusing on the childhood experiences that had prepared these men for their important positions. In "Gen. Mitchel and the News-boys," for example, a division commander reminisces about the persistence he had learned from selling newspapers. "General Grant's Boyhood" links national success with individual decision making as it offers advice about boys' propensity for fighting. In the story, Grant's father forgives this normally forbidden behavior after the boy defends the reputation of George Washington. He tells his wife, "He does not deserve to be punished. He has only stood up for his country, and the boy who will fight in defence of the honor and integrity of the name of Washington will rise, if God spares his life, to be a man, and a Christian, too."[21]

Other articles played on children's fascination with the military to reinforce the connection between individual choices and national success. In "The Brother's Letter," a soldier writes to his mischievous younger brother to convince him that the best thing he can do for the Union is to mind his parents. "Army Life," presented as a chaplain's story, suggests that "if some boys and girls were put under strict drill and temperate diet, and made like the soldiers to keep within certain limits of territory, neither they nor society would be losers."[22]

These tales of youthful misbehavior hint at the broader social concerns fueling Ford's wartime editorial decisions. By 1863, displacement and separation of families were instigating national concerns about the spread of juvenile dissipation and delinquency. Commentators blamed the absence of fathers and older brothers for unleashing a "tide of disobedience and incipient crime" among northern children. Newspapers described juvenile gangs prowling urban streets and a "wave" of new offenders entering reform schools.[23] Such fears seemed to confirm the *Companion*'s long-standing message about the dangers of freeing boys and girls from adult supervision. In this context, Ford's decision to protect young readers by restricting their access to thrilling but potentially destabilizing wartime propaganda and to emphasize their patriotic responsibilities at home reinforced his magazine's credo that individual choices can serve the national interest.

THE *COMPANION*'s approach to the war contrasted with the strategies of most other producers of children's books and magazines. While Ford attempted to isolate young readers from the crisis, other publications sought to inspire children by making them feel as if they were part of the northern war effort. This integration of children into the Union cause largely started with the true story of a drummer boy. When twelve-year-old Clarence McKenzie was accidentally shot and killed in a Maryland army camp in June 1861, the tale of that tragedy circulated widely in the northern press. Even the *Companion* covered the story—in a brief notice on the magazine's back page—as an example of how Christian youth should live and die: Clarence was "a faithful Sunday-school scholar . . . exerting an influence for good among [the troops]"; and "when the sorrowing soldiers took up the dying boy, . . . they found in his pocket the Bible which had been to him so constant and loved a companion."[24]

This story fit a trope of the good child's death that was widely popular in antebellum American literature, and employing this framework allowed the press to celebrate the boy's Christian sacrifice for the Union cause while minimizing the risk of enticing young Americans into the military.[25] However, its popularity spawned a genre of drummer boy stories that veered from the formula and purpose that the press had originally imposed on the tragedy. Whereas the McKenzie narratives followed the sentimental practice of generating pathos and piety in response to the tragic victimization of a virtuous child, later stories focused on drummer boys as heroic military actors. For example, "The Drummer-Boy of Marblehead" celebrates young Albert Mansur who, in the midst of battle, "[slings] his drum over his shoulder, and seizing a rifle from a wounded man near, deal[s] true shots for his country" before he is killed.[26] "The Little Prisoner," a story about a twelve-year-old drummer boy wounded at the Battle of the Wilderness, shows the young hero resisting John Mosby's infamous Confederate raiders.[27] The boy is captured but lives through this and other travails; his survival is a further sign of the genre's movement away from the sentimental template and toward the more sensationalized formulas of popular adventure stories.

During 1863, this trend accelerated with the production of a wave of patriotic children's novels in which young protagonists participated in the Union military effort. In John Townsend Trowbridge's *The Drummer Boy: A Story of Burnside's Expedition,* the boy hero is transformed from a civilian who does not know how to hold a gun into a loyal and beloved officer. Horatio Alger's first novel, *Frank's Campaign; or, What Boys Can Do on the Farm for the Camp,* describes a young man who takes over the family farm when his father enlists; within months, his peers elect him captain of the local home guard unit. William Taylor Adams, writing as Oliver Optic, published the Army and Navy Stories, a series of novels featuring twin brothers who enter the Union forces as privates at seventeen and rise to become officers by the end of the war. One book even allowed a young heroine to join in the national adventure: in *Dora Darling: The Daughter of the Regiment,* author Jane Goodwin Austin introduces a southern Unionist who, after her mother's death, becomes an adopted member of the Twentieth Ohio, where she serves as a nurse.[28]

Wartime child heroes appeared as characters more often in books than in magazines, perhaps because the former required more dramatic conceits to stimulate sales. Yet children's periodicals used other means to engage readers in the war effort, including articles about army life, military-focused puzzles and trivia games, and appeals for young people to volunteer time and money. They also promoted collectivism by developing departments that encouraged young readers to see their consumption of the publication as a shared experience, albeit nurturing and domestic rather than military. The *Student and Schoolmate* offered editorials from "The Teacher's Desk"; *Forrester's Playmate* published "Chats with Readers and Correspondence"; and *Our Young Folks* printed guidance from a "wise, kindly, and cheerful" retired clergyman named Father Brighthopes and supplied games, plays, and puzzles to entertain the family "Round the Evening Lamp."[29]

Such community-building efforts highlighted most magazines' association with a liberal Protestant cultural establishment that, particularly during wartime, embraced collective action as a means for overcoming social ills. Adams and Trowbridge wrote and edited primarily for Boston publishing houses (Lee and Shepard and Ticknor and Fields, respectively) that had inherited the meritocratic, optimistic ideals of New England's Unitarian elite. Sara Lippincott, who edited the *Little Pilgrim* under the pseudonym "Grace Greenwood," was a Quaker who participated in the abolition and women's rights movements. Of the major children's magazines published during the war, only the *Companion* was not part of this establishment; and Ford's working-class background, evangelical faith, and confidence in the moral power of the marketplace combined to steer him away from this collective approach.

The division between these two approaches was not absolute. Just as the *Companion's* calls for reader contributions to the Union cause reflected the communal impulse that Ford generally avoided, the adventure stories of the literary establishment integrated elements of the individualistic sensibility he advocated. Much of the action in these stories takes place when the young protagonists are separated from their units, and Adams described his works as "narrative[s] of personal adventure" echoing the "perils and privations, the battles and marches" of thousands of brave soldiers in the Army of the Potomac.[30] The balance between celebrating individual achievement and recognizing the importance of collective action exemplified what one historian has described as a "synthetic nationalism" that emerged in the North during the war. This synthesis combined traditional beliefs in "liberal self-interest" and the "right to rise" with "notions of Christian charity, sacrifice, and redemption" that encouraged Americans to embrace national identity as part of their perception of themselves as individual citizens.[31] The patterns of content in wartime children's magazines suggest that audiences embraced this synthesis, but other publications indicate that the popularity of individualist ideals still persisted, particularly among nonelite audiences.

ONE OF the most successful examples of this persistence was the new genre of dime novels; more than 4 million copies of these adventure stories were sold during the war.[32] Originally intended for adult rather than juvenile audiences, dime novel publishers employed content and sales approaches that closely resembled those of the prewar *Companion,* and their success reveals another, more long-standing way in which the war altered genteel standards for children's reading.

In 1907, Edward S. Ellis, author of *Seth Jones,* the first great dime-novel success, recalled the 1860 advertising campaign for his book:

> All of a sudden all over the country there broke out a rush of posters, dodgers and painted inscriptions demanding to know, "Who is Seth Jones?" Everywhere you went this query . . . glared at you in staring letters on the sidewalks. It came fluttering in to you on little dodgers thrust by the handful into Broadway stages . . . In the country, the trees and rocks and the sides and roofs of barns all clamored with stentorian demands to know who Seth Jones was. It got to be a catchword and a joke of the day. The theatres and the traveling shows took it up and billed announcements that the identity of the mysterious Seth would be revealed to all the favored ones who attended their entertainments . . . And just when it had begun to be a weariness and one of the burdens of life, when the reaction set in and people began to say "Damn Seth Jones," then . . . a new rush of decorations broke out all over the country, . . . big and little posters bearing a lithographic portrait of a stalwart, heroic-looking hunter of the Fenimore Cooper type, coon-skin cap, rifle and all. And above or below this imposing figure in large type were the words: "I am Seth Jones."[33]

Ellis may have exaggerated the extent of the campaign, but he captured the nature of the advertising and the essence of what made dime novels successful.[34] Although they were largely formulaic and indistinct and derived their plots and characters from romance writers such as James Fenimore Cooper and Sir Walter Scott, the books offered exciting adventure stories with prototypically American heroes. They also benefited from the aggressive salesmanship that Ellis described: *Seth Jones,* for example, sold 60,000 copies in its first few weeks on the market and more than 400,000 by the turn of the century. In the wake of *Seth Jones*'s success, the standing order for the first editions of dime novels was 60,000 copies, an enormous number at a time when book sales were in significant decline nationally.[35]

One scholar has called these books "an early example of mass-market advertising," but Beadle and Adams, the first firm to popularize the dime-novel format, borrowed much of its marketing approach from antebellum purveyors of sensational literature. Story papers and other publications of the 1840s and 1850s (including Ford's *Companion*) often promoted the mass appeal and economic vitality of their products rather than their entertainment, intellectual, or moral value. Beadle and Adams continued this practice, reducing the common price for such books from twenty-five to ten cents and adopting the slogan "BOOKS FOR THE MILLION! A DOLLAR BOOK FOR A DIME!" The books' brightly colored, dramatically illustrated covers, which drew attention at stores and newsstands, were another marketing strategy appropriated from prewar publications. The firm's primary innovation was extending the advertising for their books beyond the pages of print commodities and into public spaces, a practice already adopted by other industries but not yet widely by publishers.[36]

In choosing the content of their novels, Beadle and Adams also borrowed from antebellum publications' methods. In fact, their first book, Ann S. Stephens's *Malaeska; the Indian Wife of the White Hunter*, reprinted a serial that had appeared in the *Ladies' Home Companion* in 1839. With *Malaeska*, they revealed their intention to follow the established practice of submerging sensational content beneath a veneer of (often) gender-driven respectability. According to the firm, it began with this story in part due to "the chaste character of its delineations" and because "it is American in all its features, pure in its tone, elevating in its sentiments; and may be referred to as a work representative of the series that is to follow." Through the series they hoped "to instill a pure and elevating sentiment in the hearts and minds of the people."[37] By choosing Stephens as its first author, the company initiated a pattern that predominated in the early volumes of the series: books written by respected female writers could be promoted as suitable for the entire family.[38] Indeed, the content of these novels was both moral and mild by contemporary sensational standards. Except for a few violent events (such as a scene in which Malaeska's son commits suicide by jumping off a cliff) or occasional disreputable practices (such as the use of a psychic to capture a villain), most of the narratives could have appeared on the inside pages of Ford's *Companion*.[39]

In fact, Ford and Erastus Beadle, the primary manager of Beadle and Adams, shared similar backgrounds and work experiences. Beadle came from an orthodox Protestant family, had trained as a printer, and had even produced a children's magazine, the *Youth's Casket*, which ran in Buffalo from 1851 until 1856.[40] Beadle also shared Ford's sensational entrepreneurial approach and his focus on promoting individualism. The heroes of Beadle and Adams's dime novels nearly always worked alone, though a sidekick sometimes served to confirm the protagonist's accomplishments. The elite mentality of community building and gentle nurture was as scarce in these books as it was in the *Companion*. Both editors emphasized self-reliance, personal responsibility, and strong moral character as the assets necessary for success in modern American society.

The most important difference between Ford's *Companion* and Beadle's early dime novels was their intended readership. The rhetoric of Beadle and Adams's early advertising, along with the firm's employment of so many respected female authors, suggests that it did not originally view boys as a primary audience. The company's strategies began to shift with the war's onset, when Beadle started marketing aggressively to soldiers. He shipped books to the Union army, donating enough to whet readers' appetites and ensuring that more were available for purchase.[41] One writer recalled, "Dime Novels . . . were the soldier's solace and comfort in camp and campaign, and contributed, in a wonderful degree, to ameliorate the trials and sufferings of army life."[42] Although scholars have suggested that this association between dime novels and soldiers may be apocryphal, wartime perceptions of the connection may have made the books more appealing to boys who idolized the men of the Union army.[43]

It is unclear how many children purchased or read dime novels during the 1860s, but a flood of recollections suggests that many northern boys consumed them voraciously. Memoirs describe boys running to "corn cribs, haylofts and attics" or reading "in barn lofts, down by the old swimming hole, under the house, up in trees and wherever the time without interruption could be had." According to one writer, angry fathers who caught their sons reading dime novels would take them "to the woodshed for a leather strapping." Another writer recalled that the last whipping he received in school "was for putting a copy of Buffalo Bill inside his large geography to read it during study hours."[44] An early twentieth-century piece in the *Atlantic Monthly* encapsulates this widespread nostalgia:

> What boy of the sixties can ever forget Beadle's novels! To the average youngster of that time the advent of each of those books seemed to be an event of world consequence. The day which gave him his first glimpse of each of them set itself apart forever from the roll of common days. How the boys swarmed . . . to buy copies as they came hot from the press! And the fortunate ones who got there before the supply gave out—how triumphantly they carried them off to the rendezvous, where eager groups awaited their arrival! What silver-tongued orator of any age ever had such sympathetic and enthusiastic audiences as did the happy youths at those trysting-places, who were detailed to read those wild deeds of forest, prairie, and mountain!

Though such rhapsodizing invites us to suspect a clouded memory or "ideological rewriting," other evidence suggests that these novels were pervasive in boys' lives.[45] In *The Adventures of Tom Sawyer*, Mark Twain selected the titles of real sensational novels as Tom's "favorite literature."[46] Even an elite journal, *North American Review*, noted dime novels' wartime popularity with boys.[47]

Unexpectedly, Beadle and Adams found themselves able entertain young audiences without conforming to traditional standards for children's reading materials. Although memoirists recalled parental disapproval, public opposition to young readers' consumption of dime novels remained muted during the war. The *North American Review* described the books as "unobjectionable morally," although "up-hill work" because of their lack of literary quality.[48] Reputable publishers sought to copy their success by producing children's books that offered more excitement. For instance, the war novels of Trowbridge, Optic, and Alger all follow the dime-novel template of sending heroes on improbable adventures and allowing them to succeed through a combination of skill, bravery, and fortuitous interventions of providence.

Children's magazines did not adopt this formula so overtly, but they, too, were influenced by dime novels' success. For instance, the *Companion*'s inside pages in 1863 and 1864 made both implicit and explicit references to this new genre. "A Story of the Backwoods" presents a character similar to Seth Jones: a man not quite fit for respectable society, "but the backwoodsmen can't get along without 'em . . . [He finds] the folks deer-meat and turkey—[can] turn his hand to almost anything—spen[ds] weeks in the woods alone with Indians, and [is] always ready to give a hand at anything 'cept work."[49] Ford also acknowledged boys' love of the sensational in "A Dead Man's Revenge," a moral tale given a "terrible title" at the request of the narrator's grandson, "a fine boy of nine."[50]

Dime novels influenced children's magazines more substantially through the increased competition they engendered. As the war ended and Beadle and Adams's books retained their popularity, publishers across the North increased their pursuit of the youth market, often through new periodicals. *Our Young Folks* and the *Little Corporal* appeared in 1865; *Demorest's Young America* and *Frank Leslie's Boys and Girls' Weekly* in 1866; and the *Riverside Magazine for Young People*, *Oliver Optic's Magazine*, and the *Nursery* in 1867. A second wave, including *St. Nicholas*, *Wide Awake*, and *Harper's Young People*, emerged in the 1870s, making the immediate postwar era one of the most prolific in the industry's history.[51] Yet among these magazines, only the *Companion* approached dime novels' commercial accomplishments.

Ford's path toward this success became clear during the second half of the war, when relaxed standards for children's reading allowed him to gradually reincorporate his genteel sensational formula. Although his war-related stories in this genre were tempered versions of his pre- and postwar narratives, they served his patriotic, commercial, and moral agendas while laying the groundwork for expanding his commercial relationship with young readers immediately after the war.

FORD'S RETURN to genteel sensationalism began in early 1863, in conjunction with the magazine's expanded war coverage. Like his pieces on children's wartime roles, these stories conflated patriotism with personal responsibility. In fact, they enhanced this message. By replacing the historically and geographically exotic locales of his original versions of the genre with the dramatic but contemporary and proximate environs of battlefields and southern plantations, he worked to contrast individual Unionists' skills and empathy with Confederates' ignorance and depravity. This shift further justified Ford's pedagogical reversion by emphasizing the immediacy of the crisis and thus the futility of sheltering young readers from it.

Ford followed the long-standing sensationalist formula of highlighting the socially conservative elements of his approach, particularly in the small group of stories in this genre that appeared on the magazine's cover during the war. These tales generally followed the magazine's template for domestic fiction by promoting the salutary effects of familial environments. They featured women, and occasionally children, as domesticated figures who mitigated wartime horrors for combatants on both sides of the conflict. Most dramatic action took place offstage (and none of it appeared in cover illustrations), while the author focused on the protagonists' moral development.[52] Yet sensational elements remained, particularly in the form of improbable plot resolutions, as a means of attracting readers to these traditional lessons.

"My Revenge" exemplifies Ford's formula. It opens with a pair of soldiers, one Union, one Confederate, who had been friends before the war. Now both are lying wounded on a battlefield. The Confederate begs the northerner for water, but the Union soldier refuses until a wounded drummer boy crawls into his lap to die and begins to recite the Lord's Prayer. This innocent action revives the soldier's compassion and motivates him to offer the enemy his canteen. Both men recover from their wounds; and the Confederate, inspired by this act of Christian charity, swears allegiance to the Union in order to fight "side by side along with his restored friend."[53]

"The Rebel Officer" also emphasizes the importance of maintaining empathy, this time by means of a heroine. When a Confederate officer enters a young northern woman's home, she tells him, "I hope you will never get back, but that your bones will strew the way, and bleach in the sun all the way from here to the Potomac." A few days later, she finds him lying wounded on a battlefield and repents, caring for him as he dies. The implausible outcome, in which she learns that the man was the husband of her long-lost sister, suggests that this story (like "My Revenge") is not trying to portray wartime society realistically. Instead, both narratives suggest that a domestic culture of sentimentality, as reflected through a child's piety or a woman's compassion, may be a salve—even a means of social regeneration—for a fractured and weary nation.[54]

This celebration of domesticity reinforced the importance of maintaining genteel expectations for women and young children, even in times of crisis. In contrast, the more political and violent stories inside the magazine predominantly focused on the conduct of men, offering individual examples of northern aptitude and southern degeneracy as proof of divine sanction for the Union cause. The stories rarely focused on men's physical capacities. Instead, they portrayed northern soldiers as brave, intelligent individuals who were able to trick southerners into surrender or death. In "Vermont Strategy," for instance, a "crafty, hard-working, rough-sinewed" young soldier creates a device that allows him to fire a gun from a distance. When the Confederate sentry stands up to attack the gun, the Vermonter shoots him in the side of the head. "The Way a Rebel Officer Was Trapped" introduces a Union soldier who is taking refuge in a ditch as he about to be overrun by a southern regiment. When a rebel officer "who had lagged behind his advancing regiment and who was very careful with his person" hides in the same place, the Yankee feigns death until the southern troops depart. Then he captures the officer and leads him back to the Union line.[55]

Other stories characterize southerners as war-weary and cowardly. "A Brave Woman" relates the story of a Kentucky mother who captures ten "secessionists" who invade her household. When Union soldiers mock the Confederates for surrendering to a woman, the rebels say "they had been wanting to get captured for sometime past, and were heartily sick of the war, and did not care how they got out of it."[56] Mingling sympathy with its traditional suspicion of elites, the *Companion* often attributed such cowardly behavior not to southerners' individual failings but to systemic flaws derived from planter-bred ignorance. "Vermont Strategy," for example, links the soldier's resourcefulness to his home state, whereas "A Southern

Boy's Idea of the Yankees" offers a contrasting view of southern capabilities. In the latter story, the title character learns to his astonishment that the Yankee soldiers invading his neighborhood do not have tails. The author concludes, "It seems incredible that any people in a civilized country could be so imposed upon as the 'poor whites' of the South have been by their slaveocratic lords."[57]

In his stories about slaveholders, Ford reinforced this message by sensationalizing their aristocratic villainy, which he attributed to the power they retained over other human beings. In "The Iron Yoke," a Union soldier discovers a runaway slave locked in a dungeon with a yoke fastened around her neck. After freeing the girl, he sends the collar to a northern exhibition so that "refined and cultivated women" (who represent the genteel society he is trying to protect) "may look upon this relic of barbarism, and feel that some good has been done by . . . sending their loved ones to deliver the oppressed from the hand of the cruel and tyrannical oppressor." Other stories provide horrifying details of slaveholder cruelty, from tying up slaves so that rats can eat their feet to whipping a woman and soaking her cuts in brine to prevent scarring.[58]

After decades of ignoring the issue of race, the *Companion* began to advocate for abolition and for civil rights for freed slaves, in part because of the support that black men and boys had offered to the Union cause. Stories such as "The Faithful Negro" create a contrast between the white southern elite's abdication of the genteel responsibilities of manhood and the exemplary conduct of male slaves. In this tale one black man offers so much assistance to northern soldiers as they escape from a Confederate prison camp that the narrator exclaims, "I could have embraced him as my father."[59] Such controversial stories reveal the degree to which the war had expanded boundaries of propriety for children's literature, but Ford continued to contain his narratives within the magazine's traditional moralistic framework. For example, the *Companion*'s editorial on the Lincoln assassination, rather than following prevailing trends of celebrating the martyred president or seeking to temper calls for vengeance, used the tragedy to reinforce lessons about the dangers of public entertainments and irresponsible personal choices:

> We are sorry that he should have received his death-wound in a theatre. For some reason it seems to be required of men of very high station, and much honored, that they should consent to receive some of their popular honors at the theatre, and probably Mr. Lincoln's education had not rendered him fully sensible of its wrong. But we are sorry he was there. The fearful op-

portunities for sin and crime afforded by the theatre have made it fatal for more than one.[60]

This piece also reveals how the *Companion's* editorial policy was transitioning as the war ended. Ford's eulogy of Lincoln as "so noble of soul, so tender of heart" employed well-established sentimental imagery and continued the magazine's association of the Union with moral superiority. Yet its focus on the tragic consequences of the president's theatergoing also foreshadowed the publication's postwar shift away from praising northerners' upstanding conduct and back toward its antebellum preference for cautionary tales that highlighted the dangers of less exemplary behaviors.

The cover of the issue that memorialized Lincoln epitomized this shift. An illustration of a boy sneaking out a bedroom window accompanied the story "The Runaway," written "for the *Companion*" by Mrs. M. A. Denison, a regular contributor to Beadle and Adams's dime-novel series. This image, along with a story by a popular dime novelist, emphasized the wartime dissipation of the protective power of domesticity. Now freed from the constraints of the national crisis, Ford constructed an editorial policy that addressed lingering genteel anxieties about the blurring of public and private cultures in genteel society and used sensationalism to promote traditional methods for reasserting the established social order.

IN THE *Companion's* wartime stories, children and women, genteel society's most domesticated populations, generally avoided mortal danger. Perhaps recognizing that his audience was weary of death and injury, Ford only sparingly exploited their sensational potential, and never in the context of the war.[61] Immediately after the surrender, however, he abandoned this policy, beginning with his return to dramatic cover illustrations. In 1865, front-page images included a man scaling down a cliff to rescue a young girl, an anguished woman pulling an infant out of roiling surf, and a shivering, meagerly clothed young girl gripping an iron gate and staring at a large, well-lit home on the other side.[62]

The sensational stories that followed reinforced this focus on endangered women and children. The prototype for the genre was "The Lighthouse on the Skeve Mhoil," a serial story about a mother and a son trapped in their island home with two burglars, one of whom has sworn revenge on the woman because she once spurned his marriage proposal. The son remains in hiding, undiscovered by the villains for most of the story, but his mother faces multiple hazards before her rescue, including being tied to a post and left to drown in the incoming tide.[63]

These examples marked a return to the *Companion*'s late antebellum practice of locating sensational threats in environments familiar to the magazine's genteel readers. Yet instead of focusing predominantly on nearby sites such as workplaces or schools, as the prewar stories had done, the postwar narratives highlighted the potential for suffering and corruption within the home. Ford intensified this threat by gradually converting his young characters from victims or observers into perpetrators of domestic acts of violence. Sometimes the magazine presented these acts as consequences of social inequities. In "Reclaimed," for example, a boy sets fire to the barns of local farmers because he "hates rich people . . . [who] have no mercy for poor folks."[64] Similarly, in "The Slave's Crime," a young man (fathered by his owner) and his adopted white sister fall in love. When the plantation mistress discovers the relationship, she sends the daughter away and has the slave whipped. With "crime in his heart," the young man retaliates by inducing a rattlesnake to kill the mistress in her bed.[65]

By the 1870s, these violent domestic stories would largely disappear from the *Companion*, perhaps because wartime anxieties about the sanctity of the home were fading. Yet a broader stream of dramatic stories in the magazine continued to display children and youth as both victims and instigators of physical and moral peril. At the same time, Ford returned to his antebellum practice of mitigating frightening but commercially appealing messages: he divided the way he handled youthful characters by their age and gender. The older the child, and the farther he or she ventured from home, the more extreme the hazards became. Thus, stories for and about young children who remained close to home suggested that their security was rarely in doubt. This comforting position even allowed Ford to diverge occasionally from the *Companion*'s traditional message—that misbehavior led to dire consequences—without fear of social repercussions. Tales about children who carelessly got caught in blizzards or who canoed over waterfalls now sometimes featured happy endings. Occasionally such reckless behavior even proved heroic, as with a girl who rescued an infant from a burning house.[66] These stories invested young children with unrealistic degrees of ability or luck previously reserved for less reputable forms of fiction.

Nonetheless, when older children moved beyond the protective realm of the home, postwar *Companion* stories laid out clearer moral guidelines and consequences. Many stories about this age group were set in schools, where young readers were spending increased amounts of time. Ford presented schools as places where children, away from parental oversight and subject to potentially dangerous peer influences, collectively succumbed to base instincts and strayed from proper standards of conduct. Schoolgirls

in these stories were "savage beings," a characterization that reinforced orthodox beliefs in youthful depravity. They planned secret rendezvous with
boys, gossiped inappropriately about their classmates, and generally treated
each other cruelly.[67] Schoolboys, released from the feminine influences of
the home, were thoughtless, violent pranksters whose tricks killed or dis-
membered their classmates.[68] One editorial attributed such behavior to
a biological stage that psychologists were just beginning to recognize as
adolescence and suggested that bringing such youths together in poorly or
unsupervised peer groups exacerbated such conduct and posed substantial
threats to their physical and moral health.[69]

The *Companion* did not argue that its readers should avoid school, but it
did seek to maximize domestic influences over maturing youths. The prominent minister Edward Everett Hale told young readers "not to let school
life sweep you away from the home," and an entire subgenre of sensational
stories highlighted the tragic ends of children taken from their parents to
become slaves or circus performers.[70] Ford also discouraged the magazine's
oldest readers from leaving familial environments for the dangers of the
city, a subject complicated by new cultural challenges that I will address
in chapter 7.

Ford presented the *Companion* as a source of reliable domestic influence, a tricky strategy that required balancing the genteel sensational stories designed to appeal to young male readers with respectable models of
femininity. Like Beadle, he procured regular contributions from prominent
female authors. The *Companion's* featured writers included Harriet Beecher
Stowe, Louisa May Alcott, and Rebecca Harding Davis; and Ford featured
them on the *Companion's* front page and advertised them prominently in
the magazine's annual prospectus, which targeted adult subscribers more
than young readers. Popular writers who engendered less critical respect,
such as Edward S. Ellis, the author of *Seth Jones*, appeared further down in
the prospectus, and their stories ran on the inside pages of the magazine.[71]
Most sensational writers in the *Companion* received even less publicity:
they published anonymously or had their attribution limited to initials or
pseudonyms.

By the early 1870s, such genteel balancing efforts permeated nearly every
aspect of the *Companion*, and Ford used them as a means of maximizing
the magazine's commercial and moral appeal. Thrilling front-page pictures
were juxtaposed with domestic stories by leading female authors. Page 2 offered an adventure story and perhaps a romance; page 3 featured nonfiction
pieces, often on mechanical science or natural history. When the magazine
expanded to eight pages in 1869, Ford added more didactic articles and

adventures stories as well as occasional nonpartisan articles about international affairs on page 4 or 5. Page 6 had moral and religious articles, and a "Children's Column" for the youngest members of the audience. Advertisements occupied page 7. The back page offered editorial comments and moralistic vignettes or human-interest stories. This balance of sensationalism and sentimentality, entertainment and orthodox morality attracted an enormous audience whose genteel sensibilities had been altered by the war's social upheavals; and the nation's major publishing houses needed to respond to Ford's model as they launched new children's magazines to compete in this burgeoning market.

CHAPTER 5

The Cultural Custodians

J ACK H AZARD begins John Townsend Trowbridge's story "Jack Hazard and His Fortunes" as a "ragged little wretch." A "vicious," barely educated, twelve-year-old orphan, he is a drinker and "the most profane little driver on the [Erie] canal."[1] With its focus on a young man's immoral behaviors, this story might have run in the *Youth's Companion*, except for one point: Jack gets better. After he is transported to the Chatford farm, three women—the devoted, maternal Mrs. Chatford; the sassy, sensible housekeeper Mrs. Pipkin; and the angelic schoolmistress Annie Felton—help him become a respectable youth. Yet even as he improves, Jack struggles to control his baser instincts, particularly when he returns to the male-dominated realms outside his new home.

"Jack Hazard and His Fortunes" was the first of three serial stories about Jack to appear in *Our Young Folks*, a children's magazine founded in 1865 by the prestigious Boston publishing firm Ticknor and Fields. Throughout these stories, Jack struggles to regulate himself in the face of selfish neighbors, unjust schoolmasters, and cruel peers. Unlike the *Companion*, *Our Young Folks* avoided attributing such struggles to the boy's sinful nature; even at his most depraved moments, Jack retains glimmers of benevolence, such as his kindness to canal horses and his dog Lion. Instead, his difficulties derive from his environment. Also unlike the *Companion*, *Our Young Folks* offered a formula for rescuing the boy. When Jack moves from the male-dominated, commercially driven culture of the canal to a pastoral, familial environment shaped by women, he transforms from an aimless youth into a steadily improving young man.

Between January 1871 and December 1873, a Jack Hazard story opened every issue of *Our Young Folks*, suggesting that Jack's coming-of-age experiences were popular with young readers and reinforced the magazine's perspectives about childrearing. That philosophy descended both ideologically and relationally from Lydia Maria Child's liberal Protestant magazine, the *Juvenile Miscellany*. William Ticknor's previous firm had published part of the *Miscellany*'s run, and Child was a muse for and celebrated contributor to the new magazine.[2] Yet *Our Young Folks*'s editors faced different challenges than Child had a generation earlier. A wartime cultural shift had led genteel families to accept an expanded role for children as participatory consumers in commercial cultures, and this change persisted into the postwar decade. As a result, children's magazines became more stable and potentially more lucrative. An unprecedented number of well-financed publications emerged during this period, creating what one scholar has described as "perhaps the richest [decade] in the history of American children's periodicals."[3] Competition among these publications, however, meant that postwar magazines needed to focus on engaging young readers as customers as well as spiritual and intellectual protégés.

In addition, the industry's postwar market had turned against liberal Protestant principles. Genteel antebellum readers had embraced the optimistic views of Child, Samuel Goodrich, and Jacob Abbott; but circulation numbers indicate that postwar audiences greatly preferred the thrilling but cautionary genteel sensational narratives of the *Youth's Companion* and dime novels, which promoted orthodox Protestant anxieties about the hazards awaiting young people in urbanizing and industrializing societies.[4] This trend compelled new liberal Protestant magazines such as *Our Young Folks* to expand their editorial approaches to remain financially viable.

The response to this challenge at *Our Young Folks* was a collaborative effort. The magazine's nominal editors were Trowbridge, Mary Abigail Dodge (no relation to the *St. Nicholas* editor), and Lucy Larcom. Yet of these three, only Larcom, a poet and former Lowell mill girl, participated in the publication's daily operations. Editorial decisions came from a group that included Larcom and James T. Fields, senior partner at the firm and editor of the *Atlantic Monthly*.[5] All nineteenth-century children's magazines were products of their time and place, but *Our Young Folks*, more than any other periodical examined in this book, offered the voice of a community.

That community was dominated by New England's intellectual elite, men and women who recognized the value of the market economy in disseminating their products but viewed their offerings as more high-minded than the commercial entertainments manufactured for general audiences. They viewed themselves as the conscience of the American reading public. Thomas Wentworth Higginson, a prominent minister and a regular contributor to *Our Young Folks* and the *Atlantic,* described them as "teachers, educators, and bringers of the light with a deep and affectionate feeling of obligation towards the young republic their fathers had brought into being. That New England was appointed to guide the nation, to civilize it, to humanize it, none of them doubted."[6] The *Atlantic,* as a historian of the magazine notes, was intended to be a "missionary agent" for "the propagation of high ethical, aesthetic, and intellectual values in the American republic."[7] *Our Young Folks,* which members of the community called "the little *Atlantic,*" was created to transmit these values to the next generation of American readers.

To fulfill this agenda, *Our Young Folks*—and its competitor, the *Riverside Magazine for Young People,* overseen by Horace Scudder, a future *Atlantic* editor—exposed young readers to a higher quality of literature and art than previous children's magazines had. Its editors believed that such access would elevate the tastes, and consequently the morals, of their audience. These publications were part of a group of cultural institutions, including the Museum of Fine Arts and the Boston Symphony Orchestra, through which New England elites undertook their educational mission during the last third of the nineteenth century. Artistically, the magazines succeeded in their quest: one historian has argued that, "as far as literary merit is concerned, the *Riverside* is arguably the most important children's magazine to be published in America," and critics generally agree that both publications substantially improved upon the quality of all previous American children's periodicals.[8] Yet whereas the other elite institutions flourished during this period, both the *Riverside* and *Our Young Folks* proved to be unsustainable, lasting only four and eight years, respectively. Other postwar magazines with a similar ideological bent, including *Oliver Optic's Magazine: Our Boys and Girls* and the *Little Corporal,* also failed by 1875. Their combined fate suggests that their paternalistic approach was unable to meet the challenges that liberal Protestant children's magazines faced in attracting a broad postwar audience.

The primary shortcoming of this approach was a reluctance to accept readers as participatory consumers. *Our Young Folks* and the *Riverside* wanted to entertain as well as instruct children. Indeed, they felt a responsibility to do so, for they believed that only through such entertainment could they convince children to move beyond formulaic fiction toward readings that stimulated their critical and imaginative faculties. Yet the editors' perception of themselves as custodians of American culture made them uneasy about entering into the types of reciprocal commercial relationships that genteel subscribers expected during the postwar decade. Seeking to shape rather than meet the demands of their audiences, the magazines' editorial policies kept their readership at unsustainable levels.

The magazines' ideological inconsistency reflected their producers' uneasy relationship with the market economy, particularly its connection to children. Both *Our Young Folks* and the *Riverside* continued to favor antebellum sentimental tropes about children's piety and innocence but also promoted new genres, including fairy tales and stories about mischievous boys, that undercut those conventions using the popular contemporary practices of literary and artistic realism. The introduction of those genres was both ideologically and commercially motivated. In particular, it reflected a broader industry strategy to pursue young male readers; for instance, none of the serials and few of the fairy tales in *Our Young Folks* featured a female protagonist. Yet here, too, the magazines displayed an ambivalence that harmed their efforts to attract a larger audience. Fairy tales and bad-boy stories broke new creative ground for American children's magazines, but they were also conservative formats that offered (unlike the stories in the *Companion* and the dime novels) no perspective on young people's roles in modern society. The simultaneous immersion of readers in new imaginative worlds and evasion of the central issue of contemporary American childhood—the role of children in an urbanizing, industrializing nation—reflected an intellectual noblesse oblige that was antithetical to the workings of the postwar children's magazine industry.

Although their methods proved to be incompatible with this commercial environment, *Our Young Folks* and the *Riverside*, like the *Juvenile Miscellany* before them, continued to influence children's magazines long after their own relatively short runs concluded. Their fiction, particularly the bad-boy stories, contributed to a lasting cultural nostalgia for the ideal of a carefree, mischievous childhood, which sparked the subsequent commercial success of novels such as *Little Women* and *The Adventures of Tom Sawyer*. The magazines' inclination toward literary realism also aligned children's literature with the broader intellectual currents of adult society. Spurred by their publishers' connections and their editors' discernment, they brought notable contributors such as Charles Dickens, Harriet Beecher Stowe, Louisa May Alcott, Hans Christian Andersen, and Winslow Homer into American children's magazines, establishing a trend that persisted in the industry for the rest of the century. Thus, even as the editors remained wary of commercial influences on their audiences, they adopted strategies that further blurred the line between adult and child customers and consequently accelerated the integration of young readers into the nation's commercial cultures.

THE STRUGGLES of *Our Young Folks* and the *Riverside* reflect the continuing tension in the industry between ideology and commerce. Yet as with other nineteenth-century children's magazines, these tensions did not align neatly with class expectations. The producers of *Our Young Folks* and the *Riverside* were elite in their sensibilities but not in their incomes or their ancestry, and their customers (based on numbers alone) were not the mass American audience of the *Companion* or Beadle's dime novels. Instead, they were from the more educated and prosperous segments of genteel American readers. Thus, the problem that felled these magazines was not an elite failure to entertain the masses but the inability of aspirational publishers to meet the demands of an established genteel audience for engagement with contemporary market cultures.

The experiences of James T. Fields, senior partner at Ticknor and Fields and editor of the *Atlantic Monthly*, exemplify the challenges that producers of liberal Protestant children's magazines faced in their relationships with both writers and audiences. Fields was the foremost architect of his firm's editorial approach, yet he was not born into elite society, and he struggled for much of his life to gain the acceptance of New England's literary lions. Indeed, he grew up in circumstances similar to those of *Companion* editor Daniel Sharp Ford. The two men were contemporaries—Fields was born in 1817, Ford in 1822; and although Ford spent his youth in Boston and Fields in New Hampshire, both came from respectable but financially straitened families in which the fathers died early. Each boy apprenticed with a Boston publisher during the 1830s, and both rose quickly, achieving partnerships in their respective firms before they were thirty years old and becoming editors of successful and influential magazines.[9]

The similarity of their experiences highlights both the fluid economic environment and the expanding diversity of avenues into genteel society for white Protestant northern men during the middle third of the nineteenth century. Ford pursued a more traditional course to prosperity: he learned the skilled trade of printing, earned enough to purchase a partnership, and then expanded the firm's holdings into related fields of business. In doing so, he followed the path of generations of ambitious publishers, including Benjamin Franklin, *Companion* founder Nathaniel Willis, and penny-press entrepreneur James Gordon Bennett.

Fields pursued a different course, one that reflected the emerging commercial trends of his time and place. He trained in sales rather than a craft, apprenticing with the booksellers Carter and Hendee at the Old Corner Bookstore, an establishment that he helped to transform into an intellectual center of Boston society. Having received only a rudimentary

education, he undertook a self-directed course of readings at the Boston
Mercantile Library, where he developed his literary judgment and formed
a network of publishing contacts. While building a minor reputation as a
poet, writer, and critic, he cultivated relationships with more talented authors; by 1840, for example, he had begun a lifelong correspondence with
Henry Wadsworth Longfellow. According to his biographer, his talents as
"a shrewd judge of literature as a commodity" emerged when he encouraged his new employer, William Ticknor, to publish books by Thomas De
Quincey, Alfred Tennyson, and John Greenleaf Whittier. The books of all
three sold well, and Ticknor invited the twenty-six-year-old Fields into
partnership in the new firm of William D. Ticknor & Co. Unlike Ford,
Fields had no money to put into the firm but received his position "in
consideration of his knowledge of the business."[10]

Although the reasons behind Fields's professional rise contrasted with
Ford's, both men subsequently faced similar challenges that revealed the
growing importance, among publishers, of gauging and shaping public
tastes. Because the two men approached magazines and books as commercial products rather than simply theological or artistic statements, they
faced substantial opposition from partners and colleagues, despite—or
because of—their financial successes. The choices they made in response
to those challenges and the distinct responses their decisions invoked illuminate the persistent religious and class divides in genteel New England
publishing that continued to shape the children's magazine industry as it
expanded from a regional into a national enterprise.

Fields received no public credit for editing *Our Young Folks*, his firm's
children's magazine, and the degree of his direct involvement in its editorial
decisions remains unclear. Yet his practices dominated the firm during this
period and are evident in the magazine's approach to its readers. Moreover, the unstable management situation at *Our Young Folks* suggests that
its publisher needed to assume an active supervisory role. Lucy Larcom,
one of the magazine's three named editors, was a poet of some reputation
among New England's intellectual elite. She initially undertook much of
the magazine's everyday work, with the assistance of Howard Ticknor, a
junior partner and son of the recently deceased William.[11] However, she
had had no previous editorial experience and little practice in the world of
professional authorship; before assuming her position at *Our Young Folks*,
she had never earned a living through literary work.[12] Then, in 1868, the
firm dismissed young Ticknor for misconduct, at which point Fields named
Larcom editor-in-chief of the magazine.[13] With such an unproven and (in
the case of Ticknor) apparently callow management team, the publisher

needed to closely monitor this major endeavor; and Fields, who had a reputation as an attentive supervisor, appears to have maintained final editorial
control over *Our Young Folks*.[14]

Beyond his editorial management, Fields shaped the magazine's message through his broader role of establishing Ticknor and Fields's intellectual culture. He approached this task as the primary public representative of a firm that had produced an astonishing roster of books over the
previous quarter-century. In addition to De Quincey, Tennyson, Whittier,
and Longfellow, its list of writers included Nathaniel Hawthorne, Ralph
Waldo Emerson, Harriet Beecher Stowe, Henry David Thoreau, William
Makepeace Thackeray, Robert Browning, and Matthew Arnold. Fields's
role expanded after his partner's unexpected death in 1864. As the firm's
newly unconstrained leader, he launched a wave of change that included
impressive new Boston offices, a satellite New York office, and the purchase
or founding of four magazines, including *Our Young Folks*. These endeavors
overextended the firm and probably caused some of the magazine's problems, but they also illustrated his belief that quality literature, when properly marketed, could appeal to a broad commercial audience.[15]

The previous two decades had tested this faith. Although Fields's endeavor was an inversion of Ford's effort to invest entertaining content with
moral value, it, too, blurred the line between amusement and instruction
in ways that inspired cultural resistance. In Fields's case, such opposition
emerged primarily from his firm's authors. These intellectually elite men
and women appreciated the profits that he produced but still largely perceived their work as highly individualized artistic and philosophical statements rather than categorizable commodities. Thus, they alternately celebrated and castigated him, depending on their immediate needs.

Fields's reputation for effectively cultivating and promoting authors'
work to appeal to larger audiences brought him some degree of loyalty.[16]
Oliver Wendell Holmes told him, "I was nothing but a roaring kangaroo
when you took me in hand ... and combed me down and put me in proper
shape." Hawthorne claimed that the publisher "smote the rock of public
sympathy on [his] behalf," and Emerson expressed gratitude to him as "the
guardian and maintainer of us all."[17] Yet such appreciation was sporadic.
In 1865, Emerson became disillusioned enough with Fields's editorship of
the *Atlantic* to celebrate the "superiority" of the New York–based *Nation*,
a new competitor, "to any other journal we have or have had."[18] Emerson's
fellow *Atlantic* founder, James Russell Lowell, who had served as the magazine's initial editor, attacked Fields more directly (though privately) when
Ticknor and Fields purchased his magazine. Learning that Fields would

replace him as editor, Lowell sniffed that the publisher would make a good "dining editor" who could "look after authors when they came to Boston and the like."[19]

Such commentary calls into question some historians' assessment of elite New England culture, particularly those who argue that it was "far more of a meritocracy than a hereditary gentry."[20] While the culture's expansion during the three decades before the Civil War did create new avenues for poor youths such as Fields to achieve economic and social success, it also produced tensions that led community members with more established educational pedigrees to treat newcomers with dismissive condescension. Lydia Maria Child had endured a similar experience, although her gender and the limitations of the 1820s market economy made her advances more limited and the backlash more extreme. Fields, in contrast, held a position of commercial power that made him both appealing to literary authors and more threatening to their ideals. The tensions between Fields and his authors, which seem to have emerged particularly in struggles over the *Atlantic*'s content, foreshadowed the firm's challenges in defining the content of *Our Young Folks*. Authors such as Emerson continually implored him to "defy the public" and guide rather than follow public taste, and to some degree the editor built his reputation on this advice.[21] Yet Fields's experience also led him to recognize the financial impracticality of overdoing this paternalistic approach, particularly in a periodical genre that relied so heavily on repeat customers.

In Ticknor and Fields's new children's magazine, the effort to balance ideological and commercial interests resulted in a variable blend of content that was often encapsulated in one of the magazine's favorite genres: the fairy tale. At least one fairy story appeared in every issue of *Our Young Folks* during the first year of its run. For its part, the *Riverside* scored its greatest coup when Scudder convinced Hans Christian Andersen to sell ten previously unpublished fairy tales to his magazine. These decisions broke from established practices of the children's magazine industry, which to this point had rarely published fairy stories because of audience concerns about their morality. Yet for these new postwar magazines, such stories offered a valuable means of simultaneously appealing to customers and promoting an ideological agenda of intellectual improvement.

During the first half of the nineteenth century, many Americans striving for gentility rejected fairy tales as insufficiently Christian or too irrational to be useful for children who were seeking to establish themselves in a changing world.[22] Samuel Griswold Goodrich, author of the Peter Parley stories, claimed that as a young reader he had been disturbed by "Little Red Riding Hood, Puss in Boots, Jack the Giant-killer, and some of the other tales of horror, commonly put into the hands of youth, as if for the express purpose of reconciling them to vice and crime."

> Some children, no doubt, have a ready appetite for these monstrosities, but to others they are revolting; until by repetition and familiarity the taste is sufficiently degraded to relish them . . . That such tales should be invented and circulated in a barbarous age, I can easily conceive; that they should even be acceptable to the coarse tastes and the rude feelings of society, where all around is a system of wrong, duplicity, and violence, is not a matter of surprise. But that they should be put into the hands of children, and by Christian parents . . . excites in me the utmost wonder. The common opinion, no doubt, is that they are at least amusing; that at the same time they are too improbable on the very face to carry with them any moral effect. This is a double mistake. The love of the horrible, the monstrous, the grotesque, is not indigenous to the youthful mind . . . Is it not leading children into fearful temptation to put such works as these into their hands?[23]

Given the fact that Goodrich himself had already published a book titled *Fairy Land, and Other Sketches for Youth,* his protestations seem at least in part an attempt to appease his audience. Even in *Fairy Land* he had hedged his bets as he equivocated about the audience's acceptance of such stories: "Peter Parley . . . seems to be no great favorite of the [Fairy] Queen, and not very deeply touched with her inspiration. There is not enough of fancy in him to make him dangerous!"[24] Yet his ambivalence reflected the American publishing industry's growing uncertainty about the genre. Disparaging fairy tales had few commercial consequences during the early nineteenth century, when most communities possessed few books for children beyond the *New England Primer* and the Bible. As the industry grew, however, it began looking for new ways to attract young readers, and leading publishers increasingly turned toward fairy tales. Harper and Brothers published *The Fairy Book* in 1836, and by 1849, James Fields, always astute about literary trends, wrote to his firm's English agent, asking for "£100 of Cundalls Juveniles . . . the rage is for 'Eng Juveniles' & very few to be had." Joseph Cundall was a London firm that "specialized in high-quality, illustrated children's books, . . . fairy tales, legends, nursery rhymes, ballads, folktales and other kinds of imaginative story books."[25] Two years later, Fields purchased Nathaniel Hawthorne's story collection, *A Wonder Book,* which the author described as "not . . . exclusively Fairy tales, but intermixed with stories of real life and classic myths, modernized and made funny, and all sorts of tomfoolery—The Child's Budget of Miscellaneous Nonsense."[26]

Hawthorne's book received praise from both children and the press and sold well enough for the firm to publish a sequel, *Tanglewood Tales*.[27]

Publishers justified these tales as a means of improving the quality of American children's literature, an argument that aligned with the view of New England antebellum cultural elites that literature should stimulate readers' intellectual and moral faculties rather than merely cater to their demands. Thus, *The Fairy Book* described most American children's reading as "something halfway between stupid story-books and bad school-books."[28] Similarly, a review of *Tanglewood Tales* argued that Hawthorne's tales were "to be rigidly distinguished from ordinary books for children. They have nothing of the book-making, hack-writing, soul-lacking character of job work, but are true products of imagination—of the literary artist as discriminated from the literary artisan."[29]

Hawthorne's timing in producing these books, however, implies that fairy tales were still marginalized in genteel society. He had written extensively for young readers (including ghostwriting for Goodrich) during the 1830s and 1840s and had long desired to invest children's books with more imagination. As far back as 1838, he had spoken to Longfellow about collaborating on the project that eventually became *A Wonder Book*. Hawthorne did not start to work on the tales until after the commercial and critical success of *The Scarlet Letter* and *The House of the Seven Gables*, but he was clearly anxious to do so: he began *A Wonder Book* less than two months after the publication of *Gables*.[30] This chronology suggests that he believed the genteel reading public would accept such stories only from an established literary author.

Criticism of fairy tales persisted through much of the nineteenth century, and often it came from liberal Protestant literary women. Maria Edgeworth had opposed the stories for a variety of articulated reasons, including their continental origins, lack of Protestant values, and absence of rationality.[31] Child stated her objections to the genre in an 1873 letter to Larcom: "In the juvenile literature of the present day, I decidedly think there is too great predominance of the *fairy* element. *Moral* influence is too much neglected."[32] Perhaps these women worried that such tales reinforced social patriarchies, as the fairy stories in *Our Young Folks* and the *Riverside* did by regularly—and seemingly paradoxically—linking the genre to the emerging ideals of literary realism.

These magazines, and their successor *St. Nicholas*, repeatedly emphasized the need for fairy tales to be "real" and "true." For instance, the narrator of "Thumbling," a story that appeared in the January 1865 debut issue of *Our Young Folks*, describes children's "most insatiate appetite for" and "most thorough appreciation of . . . real fairy stories," noting that young readers "turn up their little noses in contempt at the *moral* fairy stories, which some of their kind aunts have attempted to impose upon them."

> I myself have a secret dislike for those sham stories which deceive you into believing you are hearing about real fairies and giants, only to tell you, at the end, that the good fairy is no other than Cheerfulness, Industry, or some other sister virtue, and that the giant is Luxury, Ill-Temper, or some other kindred vice. Yet the children are severer critics than I. They will have nothing whatever to do with the good fairies who have no magical power and who live in their own little bodies; nor with the wicked giants who, they can see at once, have none of the attributes of the giants of old.[33]

Scudder pursued Andersen's tales for the *Riverside* at least in part because they had what the editor described as "the true fairy spirit." According to *St. Nicholas* editor Mary Mapes Dodge, who published a remembrance of Andersen when he died in 1875, "there was very little difference to him between a real story and a fairy-tale . . . as I once heard him say 'Every man's life is a fairy-tale written by God's finger.'"[34]

The magazines were inconsistent in their approach to this issue of literary realism and "the true fairy spirit." For example, the *Our Young Folks* story "Andy's Adventures; or, The World Bewitched" uses magical creatures to teach the title character to be kind to animals.[35] Yet the publications inclined toward linking fairy tales to the realist intellectual movement that flourished in elite genteel magazines after the Civil War. In children's magazines, the ideological ferment created by this movement extended beyond abstract concerns about the relationship between imagination and truth to include a reconsideration of gender roles, and particularly a reorientation of genteel conceptions of boyhood.

THE LIBERAL Protestant publications were not the only children's magazines concerned with finding truth in fiction during this period. In the introduction to part II of this book, I discussed "A True Story," an 1871 tale about the murder and suicide of two young men that demonstrates the *Youth's Companion's* concurrent fascination with the issue. Yet editor Daniel Sharp Ford knew which philosophical and pedagogical truths he wanted to convey in his magazine—or at least what his audience wanted to hear. In *Our Young Folks*, reality remained a contested subject, and the division emerged predominantly along gender lines.

Our Young Folks's first issue opened with "Hum, the Son of Buz," a Harriet Beecher Stowe sketch about a family's relationship with a hummingbird during their seaside vacation. The story displays many of the elements that William Dean Howells (then an *Atlantic* contributor and later its editor) would celebrate in his essay "Criticism and Fiction," which became a kind of manifesto for American realist fiction during the late nineteenth century. He called for portrayals of "the simple, the natural, the honest" in American life and for maintaining a standard of "fidelity to experience and probability of motive" necessary for a "great imaginative literature." Howells argued that "what is unpretentious and what is true is always beautiful and good, and nothing else is so."[36]

Stowe's detailed description of the hummingbird's habits and her focus on the family members' efforts to integrate the bird into their daily experiences make "Hum" a model of the realist literary ideal. At the same time, it exhibits the exaggerated pathos characteristic of the mid-nineteenth-century sentimental literary tradition in which she figured so prominently and which realists were rebelling against during the 1870s. The emotions stirred by the death of the bird, who goes "where other bright dreams go,—to the Land of the Hereafter," were reinforced by the next piece in the issue, Larcom's poem "The Volunteer's Thanksgiving." Describing a nineteen-year-old Union soldier's first holiday away from home, she transcribes his thoughts of his mother, who as she "wipes the platters bright, . . . [will] say 'I hope my baby doesn't lose his appetite,'" and of a girl whom he hopes isn't married. Larcom wanted her poem to inspire continued fidelity to the Union cause:

> For home and love and honor and freedom are at stake,
> And life may well be given for our dear Union's sake;
> So reads the Proclamation, and so the sermon ran;
> Do ministers and people feel it as soldiers can?[37]

The poem's focus on a young soldier's feelings for the women who inspired him links *Our Young Folks* to a feminized sentimental tradition, a connection that Larcom explicitly recognized and sought to reinforce. After Fields had hired her to edit the magazine, she solicited advice from Child, her girlhood muse; and according to Larcom's biographer, the two women agreed that "that a children's magazine needed a 'mother' in charge."[38] The mother in this case was metaphorical (neither woman had children), but it reflected a prevailing idea that women were uniquely qualified to nurture the moral and emotional development of the nation's children.

This idea had gained currency in the decades after the *Juvenile Miscellany* had folded. Child had not made such statements in her magazine, even though she had presented women as children's primary instructors and caretakers. In fact, such essentialist language contradicted the *Miscellany*'s message, which mirrored that of Child's contemporary (and successor at the *Miscellany*) Sarah Josepha Hale, who was also the editor of *Ladies' Magazine:* "There is no sex in talents, in genius."[39] By February 1857, however, Hale had undergone a conversion. In that month's issue of *Godey's Lady's Book,* which she now edited, she wrote, "The proposition 'Genius has no sex,' is preposterous as well as false."[40] This shift away from emphasizing men's and women's intellectual equality toward promoting their essential differences was in part a way for female writers and editors to gain cultural authority.[41] The popularity of the idea created a distinct commercial niche for women who were producing books and magazines for female, juvenile, or family audiences. By 1865, when *Our Young Folks* first appeared, it was nearly an industry requirement to include a female editor on the staff of such a magazine; and prominent women such as Stowe earned money lending their name to these publications even if they did little or no work for them.[42] Hiring women to actually produce the magazines benefited publishers in other ways. For instance, when James Fields handed Larcom control of the daily operations of *Our Young Folks,* he paid her half the salary he would give to Howells, a similarly inexperienced editor whom he hired a year later as assistant editor at the *Atlantic.*[43]

This belief in women's unique capacity to guide youthful development persisted throughout *Our Young Folks'* entire run. In the series of stories about Jack Hazard, it appears in the "calm voice and serene demeanor" of Mrs. Chatford and the "sweet, kind face" of Annie Felton, who observed the boy with both "awe and pity."[44] Feminized sentimentality was also linked to the magazine's intermittent presentation of innocent, pious children. For instance, Thomas Wentworth Higginson's story "The Baby of the Regiment" describes an infant girl whose mother brings her into a Union army camp to visit her father and whose presence has a salutary effect on the troops. The child becomes the "sunshine of the soldiers' lives," and thrives under the camp regime. Although she dies soon after returning home, Higginson stresses that her short life has been "a blessing to us all," giving the men "a perpetual image of serenity and sweetness, recalling the lovely atmosphere of far-off homes, and holding us by unsuspecting ties to whatsoever things were pure."[45]

Yet alongside this established formula, *Our Young Folks* and the *Riverside* were introducing alternative pedagogical approaches that the editors associated with boys and men. Fairy tales, nearly all of which had male protagonists, removed children from their homes and placed them in environments beyond parental control. The magazines' domestic fiction de-emphasized the importance of maternal guidance for boys, who in these years were increasingly freed from adult supervision, although they were still constrained within or just beyond the limits of small towns. Some serials, such as "Winning His Way" and the Jack Hazard stories, affirmed the traditional belief that such circumstances were dangerous, but other stories portrayed these conditions nostalgically.[46]

Perhaps because it lacked Ticknor and Fields's established audience, the *Riverside Magazine for Young People* turned to this approach before *Our Young Folks* did. In 1867, its first year of operation, editor Horace Scudder featured a series of boyhood stories written by Clarence Gordon under the pseudonym "Vieux Moustache." Scudder noted in his diary that he had selected these stories because of the way in which they represented "the freshness of boy life and the manly tone, the clear principle which I am eager to show in the magazine."[47] Although he did not elaborate on this explanation, the "freshness" of these stories appears to have derived primarily from their wistful and nostalgic perspective on boyhood. As Gordon wrote in "The Midnight Coast":

> The keen edge which life has in our youth—that intensity of thought, action, and feeling—tones down and rounds off as manhood has constantly to mow where weeds, nettles, and wire-grass grow among the grain . . . "I would I were a boy again" . . . is more than tune or song to us as . . . Our hearts unconsciously leave the possessions of the Present to stretch back again for the Romance of Boyhood,—its friendships, its chivalry, its ignorant and daring self-reliance.[48]

Gordon's stories did not ignore the shortcomings of such youthful enthusiasm, but they celebrated the untamed energy and unhurried enjoyment of boys' play, qualities that two previous generations of American children's authors had perceived as impediments to children's moral development.

Our Young Folks integrated this mentality more gradually, offering some indications in early stories that boyish mischief was not morally harmful.[49] The perspective emerged more fully in Thomas Bailey Aldrich's serial "Story of a Bad Boy," which opened each 1869 issue of the magazine. Aldrich satirized both cautionary melodramas and idealization of childhood virtue in the story's opening lines, which introduce "not such a very bad, but a pretty bad boy":

> Lest the title should mislead the reader, I hasten to assure him here that I have no dark confessions to make. I call my story the story of a bad boy, partly to distinguish myself from those faultless young gentlemen who generally figure in narratives of this kind, and partly because I really was not a cherub. I

may truthfully say I was an amiable, impulsive lad, blessed with fine digestive powers, and no hypocrite. I didn't want to be an angel and with the angels stand; I didn't think the missionary tracts presented to me by the Rev. Wibird Hawkins were half so nice as Robinson Crusoe; and I didn't send my little pocket-money to the natives of the Feejee Islands, but spent it royally in peppermint-drops and taffy candy. In short, I was a real human boy, such as you may meet anywhere in New England, and no more like the impossible boy in a storybook than a sound orange is like one that has been sucked dry.[50]

For Aldrich, chronicling a "real" boy (whose lack of a name suggests he is intended to represent his gender) meant describing his escapades with amusement and tolerance. A night watchman who catches the protagonist sneaking out of his bedroom window mutters, "Boys is boys," and lets the child slip through the gate. The protagonist and his friends destroy a carriage with firecrackers, ignite cannons on the bluff above town, and even fight in the schoolyard, yet the narrator presents their hijinks as morally and physically useful: "Daily contact with boys who had not been brought up as gently as I worked an immediate, and, in some respects, a beneficial change in my character . . . I became more manly and self-reliant. I discovered that the world was not created exclusively on my account."[51]

Aldrich's and Gordon's stories exemplified a postwar trend in children's literature toward nostalgia for the lives of boys growing up in antebellum America. These tales, which one scholar has described as "grandfather stories," included Mark Twain's *Tom Sawyer* and *Huckleberry Finn* and have been interpreted as part of an effort to reconstruct a unified vision of American boyhood after the Civil War.[52] Aldrich's story, which describes its protagonist as "a Northern man with Southern principles" and includes a mock battle between the "North End" and "South End" boys of Rivermouth, lends itself to this interpretation.[53]

Yet while postwar children's magazines did introduce a yearning for the allegedly innocent rambunctiousness of antebellum youth, their acceptance of youthful male aggression and independence reflected not just a desire for sectional reunion but also a belief that young men needed such characteristics to prosper in an industrializing capitalist society. When Aldrich's boys destroy the carriage, the narrator describes the vehicle as a "primitive mode of travel" that had been superseded by the railroad. One boy declares that "the old trundle-cart isn't worth twenty-five cents . . . and [owner] Ezra Wingate ought to thank us for getting the rubbish out of the way."[54] Thus, the act of destroying private property, although not sanctioned, is mitigated by the carriage's obsolescence. One of the narrator's main goals is to explain how this boyhood has prepared the protagonist (whom Aldrich later acknowledged to be a semi-autobiographical character) for adult life. Learning when to be aggressive and how to relate to technology transforms the boy from a callow child into a young man of character, who at the story's end leaves his small town to begin a business career in New York.[55]

These grandfather stories offered little corresponding advice for girls. Autobiographies from the period reveal that prepubescent genteel girls joined boys in active pursuits such as swimming, skating, and hunting, but there is no evidence of such propensities in these magazines.[56] They did emerge in contemporaneous novels such as Louisa May Alcott's *Little Women* (1868–69) and Susan Coolidge's *What Katy Did* (1872) and appeared slightly later in *St. Nicholas,* the first postwar magazine to be entirely managed by a woman. The absence of active girls in *Our Young Folks* and the *Riverside* suggests that the magazines were purposely directing realistic fiction toward young male readers. Moreover, the fact that nineteenth-century children's magazines managed by women generally paid more attention to girls' interests than *Our Young Folks* did suggests that Fields's influence on the magazine was more powerful than Larcom's was.

Both the *Riverside* and *Our Young Folks* were eager to placate a genteel audience that was anxious about the influences of economic transformation, and bad-boy stories served the genteel goal of expanding but containing the standards for boys' behavior. They were set in rural areas or small towns where the protagonists' mischief could do little harm, and editors kept a sharp eye on the implications of story content.[57] For instance, although Scudder conceded that he "may be thought overly fastidious for this comment," he asked Gordon to "to modify his text [in an unidentified story] so the comic side of drunkenness does not allow an audience of boys to overlook the degradation of the state."[58] Similarly, in an 1867 review of a book of poetry by Alice Cary, an editor at *Our Young Folks* praised a particular poem that "has a real *snap* to it, and will go straight to the heart of all the youngsters. But remember, it only asks that boys should be *boys,*—not hectors, or turbulent troublesome fellows. A great distinction there young gentlemen!"[59]

Thus, these stories, like the magazines' fairy tales (and much of the adult realist fiction of the era), were part an alternative literary approach that provided a strategy for imagining and managing the threats of social change.[60] They allowed the magazines to expand their content, a step that served the pedagogical purpose of offering children new imaginative worlds and the commercial goal of pleasing young consumers by giving them more active and independent child characters. At the same time the magazines could avoid focusing on the massive economic, political, and cultural changes that were occurring in the United States after the war.[61] Both *Our Young Folks* and the *Riverside* preferred to avoid the subject of these changes. Only when necessary did they adopt a critical stance toward these public shifts, and the resulting disparity between their editorial mindsets and the mentality of genteel audiences outside of New England contributed to their demise during the early 1870s.

NEITHER *OUR YOUNG FOLKS* nor the *Riverside* sought to replicate the practices of antebellum New England journals for adult readers such as the *North American Review* and the *Dial*, which prioritized intellectual and moral quality over commercial viability. Both children's magazines sought the largest audiences they could achieve reputably and went to significant lengths to accomplish this goal. Indeed, just as critics claimed that Fields had done at the *Atlantic, Our Young Folks* sometimes prioritized commercial appeal over quality, publishing serial stories from popular but formulaic authors such as Oliver Optic and Mayne Reid to please young readers.[62]

More often, however, the magazine pursued a genteel balance between intellectual quality and commercial popularity. Fields spent significant sums to procure regular contributions from reputable authors such as Longfellow and Stowe, and in 1868 he even contracted Charles Dickens—probably the most successful contemporary Anglo-American writer—to deliver the four-part story "Holiday Romance."[63] Scudder did not have the resources to match *Our Young Folks*'s prestigious authorial roster; but in addition to persuading Andersen to contribute to the *Riverside,* he identified rising literary figures such as Rebecca Harding Davis, Sarah Orne Jewett, Mary Mapes Dodge, and Frank Stockton and published their pieces in his magazine.

These literary writers contributed more often to *Our Young Folks* and the *Riverside* than to other children's magazines of the era. We do not know the comparative financial arrangements of each magazine, except to note that many of the most prestigious contributors had previous ties to Fields's firm. Yet it seems likely that writers were attracted to the magazines' willingness to break away from established tropes of American children's literature in an effort to deliver a higher-quality product to young readers. This approach may have alienated the larger genteel audience who preferred the more traditional *Companion*, but it did not necessarily doom the liberal Protestant magazines to financial failure. *Our Young Folks* had a circulation of approximately 75,000—nearly as many subscribers as *St. Nicholas*, its more flourishing successor, eventually reached.

The failure of these magazines was not entirely a consequence of their content. The *Riverside* was perennially underfunded, and *Our Young Folks* seems to have closed in response to Ticknor and Fields's financial situation rather than its own problems. Fields noted that the magazine "gave him no trouble." Instead, a series of misfortunes at the firm—his overextension of the firm's resources after Ticknor's death, his retirement, an 1872 fire that destroyed the firm's offices, and the subsequent national economic panic— pushed the firm into selling *Our Young Folks* to the publisher Charles Scribner and Sons in late 1873.[64] Yet even though other factors contributed to the magazines' downfall, their combined failure to sustain themselves at a time when orthodox approaches were thriving in the *Companion* and dime novels hints at the difficulty of using liberal Protestant ideals to reach a broad postwar family audience. *Our Young Folks* and the *Riverside* were not the only such children's magazines to fail: the *Little Pilgrim* ceased operations in 1868; *Demorest's Young America,* the *Little Corporal,* and *Oliver Optic's Magazine* closed down in 1875.

A comparison of the editorial formulas of *Our Young Folks* and the *Riverside* to the later and more successful *St. Nicholas* suggests that the most likely source of this disconnect was the earlier magazines' reluctance to embrace the changes in postwar society. Authors in *Our Young Folks* often equated technological advances, particularly the nation's rapidly expanding railroad network, with loss. Child's story "Grandfather's Chestnut Tree," which describes a family's four-generation connection with a tree on its property, decries the need to cut down the tree to make way for the railroad. In the course of that tale, a grandmother calls an impatient little girl a "steamboat." In another story, "Master Horsey's Excursion," author Gaston Fay tells his readers, "When you become a man, your present joyousness will depart, wrecked in the rush of crashing trains."[65]

Tales in both magazines, including the featured Jack Hazard serials, encourage children to use their developing skills in small towns or on farms rather than move to cities. Although the path of Aldrich's bad boy is more complicated (his move from New Orleans to Portsmouth, New Hampshire, reflects a shift from south to north as well as from urban to rural), he, too, flourishes in a small town. Both his childhood and his innocence end when he takes a job as clerk in his uncle's New York store.[66]

The author's choice to shift the bad boy from New England to New York is significant, especially in a Boston-based publication. Fields and Scudder, accustomed to Boston's long preeminence, opposed the pace of national urbanization and industrialization because they recognized that these changes were weakening their city's cultural influence. The publishing industry, long centered in Boston, was shifting toward New York; and Manhattan-based magazines such as the *Nation* and *Scribner's* were seeking to strip the *Atlantic* of its prestigious roster of New England writers. For decades, literary men such as Howells and Trowbridge had eschewed New York for Boston, but by the 1870s that course was beginning to reverse. In 1881, as soon as his novels were selling well enough to earn him an independent income, Howells himself left Boston—and his editorship at the *Atlantic*—for New York.[67]

At *Our Young Folks* and the *Riverside*, editors and writers responded to this shift by clinging to their region's history and values. Most of the contributors to *Our Young Folks* had been raised in New England's antebellum reform culture and retained its belief in moral certainty and its drive to improve American society. Fields, Larcom, and Trowbridge were all ardent abolitionists; and as the war ended, they were determined to preserve the mentality that they believed had conquered the South and redeemed American society. Thus, *Our Young Folks* focused on the Civil War longer than most of its competitors did and was also more stridently anti-Confederate. In contrast to the *Riverside*, which avoided discussing the war and sectional differences, and the *Companion*, which largely turned away from the subject after the surrender and Lincoln's assassination, *Our Young Folks* continued to celebrate the Union victory, denigrate southern heroes and belief systems, and promote the virtues of the freed slaves.[68] For instance, the 1865 story "The Boy of Chancellorsville" describes General Robert E. Lee as having "none of the smaller vices about him but all of the larger ones, for he deliberately, basely, and under circumstances of unparalleled meanness, betrayed his country, and, long after all hope of success was lost, carried on a murderous war against his own race and kindred."[69] *Our Young Folks* also introduced black characters far more frequently than did other nineteenth-century children's magazines and as late as 1872 was continuing to promote their intelligence, bravery, and piety.[70]

While *Our Young Folks* sought to preserve the legacy of New England's heroic past, *Riverside* editor Horace Scudder wrestled with the issue of how to maintain the region's high ideals and still remain commercially relevant. In a series of letters that he copied into his diary, he indicated an interest in finding the right author to teach his readers about politics, spoke of his "wish to make the element of adventure a prominent one," and "desire[d] to get strong, stirring scenes of a sort to produce a healthy sensation in a boy's mind." He wanted his magazine to "picture the world in which children live and yet constantly enlarge the boundaries of that world to them" and said "that there are few subjects interesting the old which will not interest the young." Yet he decried "what has sometimes struck me in looking at children's literature, a certain flavor ... of *worldliness*, using the word to express that spirit least akin to spirituality." Scudder thought that "one error to be avoided in conducting a child's magazine ... [is] the error of exalting the literary above the ethical," and "I should think my highest aim wholly missed, if the magazine should prove nothing more than a repertory of amusing and interesting articles; bright and lively I hope it may be, and I should like its very brightness to win children to purity and righteousness."[71]

Often, Scudder's solution was to return to the sentimental values of the antebellum New England community of his childhood. The *Riverside* displayed its discomfort with the changing world by avoiding most contemporary issues, and it demonstrated a prevailing impulse to remove children from the concerns of the modern world. Scudder was drawn to fairy tales, publishing more of them than any other periodical of the era, as well as to domestic stories about children at home.[72] Like the editors at *Our Young Folks,* he wanted to offer young readers a sense of timelessness that enabled them to maintain the inherent innocence, joy, and spirituality that he continued to believe were the best elements of youth.[73]

Many genteel postwar Americans shared this ideal, but they failed to extend that acceptance to *Our Young Folks* and the *Riverside* in sufficient numbers to keep the magazines alive. Part of the reason was economic: business partnerships such as Ticknor and Fields and the *Riverside's* publisher Hurd and Houghton had become increasingly anachronistic in the corporate world of American business. By the time the firms' owners had merged their interests and formed the publishing giant Houghton Mifflin to compete with large New York firms, the two magazines were long gone. Ironically, they had been absorbed into another conglomerate, the New York firm of Charles Scribner and Sons, which integrated them (along with three other publications) into *St. Nicholas,* a new magazine that sought to combine their high intellectual ideals and nostalgia for childhood with a more explicitly commercial and modern outlook.

CHAPTER 6

The Jack-in-the-Pulpit

*

WHEN JACK HAZARD made his final appearance in *Our Young Folks* in December 1873, author John Townsend Trowbridge was still portraying the character as a youth who struggled to control his selfish impulses. In the final chapters of the story "Doing His Best," Jack's experiences "severe . . . fits of jealousy" when his best friend Percy becomes engaged to Jack's beloved Annie Felton. After a long night of struggle with his emotions, Jack's "better nature" triumphs and "solace [comes] to him in the deep and unselfish love for his two dearest friends, and joy in their happiness, which well[s] up in his heart."[1] In the course of these chapters, Jack also solves a mystery, exposes a con man, and recovers stolen money, so the story remains as much an adventure tale as a moralistic one. Yet as he did in previous segments of the story, Trowbridge emphasizes the inconsistency of Jack's maturation process as the young man continues his efforts to regulate his passions.

In January 1874, Trowbridge brought Jack to a new magazine called *St. Nicholas*, where the character's internal battles vanished. In these new stories, the boy has a "bright, honest face, which expresses a good deal of quiet self-reliance and firmness of character." He is "cool and self possessed" and displays a "self mastery" that contrasts with his new friend George's "uncontrollable excitement" and "agitation" under pressure.[2] Even the story titles reflect Jack's transformed character. Whereas *Our Young Folks*'s "A Chance for Himself" and "Doing His Best" emphasize his striving, *St. Nicholas*'s "Fast Friends" and "The Young Surveyor" focus on his completed accomplishments.

Jack's success in *St. Nicholas* partially results from his willingness to supersede genteel standards of behavior. After the boys' pockets are picked as they board a boat to New York, Jack decides to earn money by performing

GEORGE WITH HIS FIFE, AND JACK WITH HIS HEELS

Jack Hazard dancing on the deck of a riverboat. His friend George plays flute in the background. From *St. Nicholas*, 1874. Courtesy of the Early Juvenile Literature Collection, Martha Blakeney Hodges Special Collections and University Archives, University Libraries, University of North Carolina at Greensboro.

for the passengers. George recoils at what he calls "a kind of beggary," but Jack, who had undertaken such work as a young canal boy, convinces him of the plan's propriety, given their precarious financial situation. The boys' flute playing and dancing earn them money and the admiration of the crowd. As they conclude their performance, one passenger proclaims of Jack, "That boy will make his way in the world!"[3]

Jack's conversion from a well meaning yet unsteady boy into a confident, successful young man exemplifies the ideological differences between *St. Nicholas* and its predecessors, *Our Young Folks* and the *Riverside Magazine for Young People*. Although the three magazines shared a liberal Protestant tradition of confidence in the moral and intellectual capacities of children, *St. Nicholas* distinguished itself by largely ignoring the earlier magazines' focus on protecting young Americans from commercial culture. Like the *Youth's Companion*, a publication that was otherwise its ideological and cultural foil, *St. Nicholas* promoted a belief that involvement in such cultures could facilitate moral and social progress. In contrast to the *Companion*, however, *St. Nicholas* embraced the market economy almost without reservation. Daniel Sharp Ford had submerged the *Companion*'s commercial impulses within a traditional broadsheet format and genteel sensational tales that presented modern society as a threat to young Americans' moral and physical development. *St. Nicholas* offered something new: a glossy, corporate children's magazine that produced industrial-era fantasy tales and welcomed young readers into the nation's growing consumer milieu.

St. Nicholas's recalibration of liberal Protestant ideology was largely the work of Mary Mapes Dodge, the magazine's editor from its inception in 1873 until her death in 1905. Since her early childhood in Manhattan, Dodge had been immersed in the genteel intellectual cultures of New England and New York. Within them, she rose to become an experienced writer and editor for adult magazines and the author of the popular children's novel *Hans Brinker; or, The Silver Skates,* before taking her position at *St. Nicholas.* Yet her path to success, like that of many other nineteenth-century children's magazine editors, included considerable economic and social tumult; and her use of the market economy to transcend those difficulties shaped the more optimistic perspective on commercial influences that she offered in her magazine.

Dodge's move away from her predecessors' anxieties about commerce was also a product of the city in which she grew up and worked. After the Civil War, the New York publishing industry began to emerge from the literary shadow of New England, gradually transforming the trade's traditional paternalistic approach to its audience into a corporate culture more devoted to fulfilling consumer demands and maximizing profits. Dodge and other writers of her generation, particularly those involved in the rapidly expanding magazine trade, adopted a similar, market-oriented perspective to their work. They viewed themselves as professionals and their work as commercial products, and they carefully negotiated prices and promotion and distribution strategies with publishers to maximize the financial and cultural benefits of their efforts. In such an environment, the idea of writing to satisfy readers' desires and of celebrating the impact of commerce and technology on American society had lost much of the stigma that older New England literati had attached to it.[4]

Dodge admired the work and culture of the New England elite and had professional relationships and friendships with several of its members, including Harriet Beecher Stowe and Horace Scudder, editor of the *Riverside* and later the *Atlantic Monthly.* Yet she also proudly celebrated her New York heritage, a feeling she expressed when she chose the name *St. Nicholas,* a tribute to an icon closely associated with the multiethnic tradition of her hometown. To distinguish her magazine from its predecessors in the *Atlantic* circle, she also worked to puncture the high seriousness (although not the ideological ambition) of those publications, incorporating satire and other humorously subversive strategies into *St. Nicholas*.

To a certain degree, these tendencies were a product of Dodge's gender, for her experiences as a female writer and editor in a male-dominated industry pushed her to both accept and contest cultural expectations. *St. Nicholas* was filled with examples of genteel sentimentality and maternalistic nurture, but Dodge also tweaked those standards, often through a character named Jack-in-the-Pulpit, a creature of indeterminate origin and gender who integrated nineteenth-century genteel concerns with play (as a jack-in-the box) and morality (as a preacher). During her first two decades at the magazine, Jack was her primary editorial voice; he offered a weekly advice department, composed vignettes, and responded to children's letters and became Dodge's vehicle for presenting ideas about society and children's place in it, even those that did not always align with her audience's prevailing views.

Dodge's careful balance between traditional and modern perspectives enabled her to maintain editorial authority at a time when the increasingly corporate nature of the publishing industry was diminishing opportunities for women in management. She presented *St. Nicholas* as a predominantly domestic magazine, which meant that her position remained culturally appropriate for a female editor. Although the publication celebrated the benefits of commerce, it mostly emphasized how consumer products (including her magazine) might enhance young people's domestic lives. Even its name, which invoked the newly popular image of grandfatherly Saint Nicholas distributing presents to homes around the world, affirmed that commercial expansion would reinforce rather than threaten the domestic ideals of genteel society.[5]

Yet this confidence in the continuing health of American home life allowed Dodge to coax both story characters and magazine readers out of cloistered domestic settings and safely integrate them into commercial society. Particularly in its featured serial stories, *St. Nicholas* displayed children (often boys) such as Jack Hazard, who transcended the difficulties of public, market-centered environments and frequently improved the adult communities into which they entered. Dodge also expanded on her liberal predecessors' practice of building participatory communities for children, creating new organizations such as the Bird-Defenders and the Agassiz Association that strengthened readers' bonds with each other and the magazine.

Dodge's trust in her young readers borrowed, whether consciously or not, from Lydia Maria Child's editing approach in the *Juvenile Miscel-*

lany almost half a century earlier. Yet just as Dodge's commercial instincts distinguished her magazine from *Our Young Folks* and the *Riverside,* her ideological agenda separated *St. Nicholas* from the *Miscellany.* Dodge's magazine regularly expressed concerns about social issues, but it was not an instrument for democratic reform. Indeed, her commercial relationship with *St. Nicholas* readers accelerated the industry's trend toward reinforcing existing social hierarchies. The expense of constructing what she described as a "pleasure ground" for children resulted in a magazine that cost three dollars a year, double the subscription price of *Our Young Folks* and the *Companion.*[6] Thus, the *St. Nicholas* audience was smaller and wealthier, an exclusivity that tempered the cultural reforms that Child, Larcom, Fields, and Scudder had pursued. Dodge established a new compromise between children's magazines and their readers that fueled the industry's growth for the next half-century: she accepted an optimistic view of genteel children's expanding role as active consumers while culturally separating them from the vast majority of their less fortunate peers.

MARY MAPES DODGE was no commercial mercenary. Like New England's cultural elites, she believed in challenging her readers intellectually rather than just deferring to public tastes. In its early years, *St. Nicholas* offered short narratives in German, French, and Latin so that children could practice translation.[7] Dodge encouraged her audience to read as much "classic" literature as they could and instituted a department called "The *St. Nicholas* Treasure Box of Literature" to facilitate this goal. The "Treasure Box" included short stories and poems by respected authors, most of whom were part of the *Atlantic* roster—among them, Hawthorne, Thackeray, Longfellow, and Elizabeth Browning—as well as nonfiction works such as Lincoln's Gettysburg Address.

Dodge wanted her audience to experience these texts at home rather than at school so that they would become "a mine of delight and satisfaction" rather than "a bugbear or a task-master." She told her readers, "We all require education . . . so that we may recognize the things, deeds and thoughts that are to delight and elevate us, and lead us in brotherhood to the Highest . . . Every time a true thought or feeling . . . enters *any* soul, it is sure to add to this beautiful power of recognition that forms the chief joy of life."[8] Such sentiments revealed the influence that elite New England ideals continued to exert on *St. Nicholas.* Yet Dodge also satirized those ideals. For instance, in a letter to Scudder, her close friend and mentor, she drew a cartoon of a giant Pilgrim sitting on Boston Common with his back against Plymouth Rock, fishing a group of New Yorkers out of the ocean with a rod and a reel. This self-deprecating yet acerbic assessment of New England's cultural importance recurred throughout her correspondence with him.[9]

Dodge's public writings were less overt but continued to deflate the pretensions largely associated with New England culture. "The Artist and the Newsboy," a story in her first collection of short fiction, chronicles the relationship between a painter and a street urchin. The boy agrees to sit for a portrait but takes the painter's advance and uses it to clean himself and get new clothes. The artist, dismayed because he wants to paint the boy in his "natural" state, decides to wait a few weeks until the boy returns to his more realistic (that is, dirty and tattered) condition.[10] Although the story does not identify the painter as a New Englander (in fact, it is set in New York), it punctures the hypocrisy of the realist movement linked to Boston's intellectual community—in particular, to the *Atlantic*—during the 1870s.[11]

Dodge did not limit her satirical wit to attacks on highbrow art. Her first published story, "My Mysterious Foe," mocks the conventions of melodramatic thrillers by revealing that a murderous stalker is really a squirrel.[12] Another story, "Cushamee," transforms a cautionary tale about the consequences of bad behavior into a horror story about an abused doll that comes alive to terrify its attacker.[13] Other stories take a more earnest, even derivative approach: "Po-no-kah: An Indian Tale," is a slightly altered version of "Adventure in the Woods," the Child story that opened the first issue of the *Juvenile Miscellany*.[14] Collectively, Dodge's stories reveal her as a pragmatic author who was not tied to an intellectual tradition and was willing to tweak audience expectations when that served her intellectual or commercial purposes.

Like the methods of other nineteenth-century children's magazine editors, Dodge's practical, and at times subversive, approach to publishing was a product of her upbringing. Born into a prominent New York family of English and Dutch heritage, Mary Elizabeth ("Lizzie") Mapes grew up listening to her grandmother's stories of dancing with General Lafayette at a ball in the city's Castle Garden. Her grandfather's best friend was DeWitt Clinton, U.S. senator and mayor of New York City. Her father, James, was a respected but unsuccessful writer and scientist who was intimate friends with the journalist Horace Greeley and the socialist educator Robert Dale Owen.[15]

Like her contemporary and friend Louisa May Alcott, Lizzie grew up in a home filled with girls. Despite their money struggles, both the Alcotts and the Mapeses engaged their daughters in constant discussions of science, philosophy, and literature, giving them a more extensive education than most of their female (or male) peers received.[16] Unlike the Alcotts, however, the Mapeses were, according to a biographer, "thoroughly an urban lot."[17] As a child in Manhattan during the 1830s and 1840s, Lizzie Mapes was a member of one of the first generations of American children raised in a rapidly expanding urban environment, which helps to explain her divergence from the prevailing genteel belief that cities offered young people only danger, squalor, and immoral temptations. It also situated her in a multiethnic community just beginning to assert its cultural authority on a national scale.

New York culture had many influences on Dodge's work. Her fascination with the Dutch traditions that surrounded her during childhood emerges in her novel *Hans Brinker,* which she set in Amsterdam and which, like many children's books of the era, blends fiction with information about the history, culture, and geography of its exotic location.[18] *Hans Brinker* also highlights her persistent interest in another unique facet of her New York childhood: the celebration of Christmas. Nineteenth-century New Yorkers transformed Christmas from a holiday rarely commemorated in the United States into a secularized festival celebrating family, domesticity, and consumption. The Dutch tradition of giving children gifts on Saint Nicholas Day (December 6) seeped into New Yorkers' Christmas festivities during Dodge's youth, a practice encouraged by the city's mercantile elite.

Beginning with Washington Irving and Clement Clark Moore early in the century and continuing through Thomas Nast in the 1860s, New York writers and artists gradually converted the icon of Saint Nicholas from a sly trickster into the jolly, rotund, grandfatherly figure of Santa Claus.[19] Dodge played a role in this process: her poem "Santa Claus" appeared on the front page of the December 1868 issue of *Hearth and Home,* accompanied by one of Nast's earliest published cartoons of the character.[20] She already had written repeatedly about the holiday and had promoted its emerging association with domestic consumerism. In addition to setting *Hans Brinker* during the Christmas season, she had mined her love of family games and puzzles for her 1867 *Riverside* article "Holiday Whispers Concerning Games and Toys."[21] Three years later she wrote "A Real Christmas" for the magazine *Hours at Home,* recalling a Christmas Eve when she and her siblings were failing in their efforts to "try to go right to sleep":

> "Remember what Ma said," cautioned Lou. "He doesn't go in houses where the children's awake. Go back to bed, Charley. You'd better."
>
> This sobered us. We punched our pillows, thoughtfully; disposed the distracted covers into something like their former condition, and squeezed our eyes as tightly shut as possible, while visions of sugar plums took toy partners and danced through our heads.

But even in the midst of the dance, we floated delightfully away—far, far—
"MERRY CHRISTMAS!"

O, those bursting stockings! And father and mother looking on as we
opened parcel after parcel in the early dawn! ... while the great blazing wood
fire crackled in the nursery fire-place. And then the letter from Santa Claus
himself, telling us to be good children always ...

Well, it's just a real Christmas, and that's all there is to be said.[22]

Explaining her decision to choose *St. Nicholas* as the name for her magazine, Dodge told an interviewer, "I never had a misgiving about it; it seemed
impossible that I should have thought of any other."[23]

New York's growth as a center of publishing during the 1870s facilitated
Dodge's success in creating this blend of liberal Protestant idealism, domesticity, and consumerism. Now that the city had become the nation's financial center, its leaders wanted to develop a cultural and intellectual prowess
that matched their economic power. As writers became disenchanted with
elite Boston firms' inclination to exclude non–New Englanders, New
York's publishers offered authors new opportunities in magazines such
as the *Nation* and *Scribner's Monthly* (eventually the parent magazine of
St. Nicholas).[24] For professional writers such as Dodge, whose motivations
were as much economic as ideological, these new openings—and the firms'
lack of Brahmin control—were fortuitous.

Dodge needed to write because a series of economic and personal setbacks had left her extended family financially dependent on her. After her
father moved the family to a New Jersey farm in 1847, his financial situation
had continued to decline. In 1850, Lizzie married William Dodge, a young
lawyer, and returned to Manhattan, where the couple soon had two sons.
Seven years later, however, her husband died suddenly; and in 1858, she and
the boys returned to the family farm, which her husband had bought in an
effort to ease her father's economic distress.[25] Dodge began her work life
here in 1861, writing and editing for her father's two struggling scientific
magazines, the *United States Journal* and *Working Farmer*.

From this starting point, Dodge built a career as an editor and author.
Along with her father's publications, she worked at the *Newark Daily Ad-
vertiser*, where she befriended Richard Watson Gilder, the future editor of
Scribner's. She then became associate editor of *Hearth and Home*, where she
oversaw daily operations for its nominal editor, Harriet Beecher Stowe.[26]
One of Dodge's responsibilities at *Hearth and Home* was to create a children's department, and in this space she and Frank Stockton, her future
associate editor, experimented with formulas they developed more fully
in *St. Nicholas*. They borrowed postwar children's magazines' participatory

strategies, inviting children to submit puzzle solutions, ideas for games and riddles, and letters. They addressed readers through the mouthpiece of personable recurring characters. Uncle Tim, an old sailor who dispensed both jokes and advice, resembled Peter Parley; and Our Sphinx was an imaginative creature that foreshadowed Dodge's *St. Nicholas* character, Jack-in-the-Pulpit. During their three years at the magazine, the two also improved the quality of illustrations in the children's department, an early indication that Dodge had recognized the importance of visual presentation in publications for young readers.

In *Hearth and Home,* Dodge and Stockton also published the types of didactic religious stories they later avoided in *St. Nicholas.* In John N. Dickie's "Bobby and the Demon," a devil stands on a young boy's shoulder—"one evil eye at the center of his forehead" and long, sharp ears "fastened together underneath his chin by means of a pin carved out of a piece of brimstone." The devil instigates the boy into hitting his sister and beating his dog.[27] Although Dodge and Stockton disliked such didacticism, the fact that they were able to produce such stories demonstrated their capacity for putting aside personal beliefs in order to produce content that satisfied their audience.

Dodge's ability to manipulate genres received its widest circulation in her 1865 novel *Hans Brinker,* which eventually became one of the century's bestselling children's books.[28] In addition to blending fiction, history, and geography, the novel intertwined sentimental optimism about the prospects of poor but virtuous children with a celebration of the mischievous, aggressive behaviors that became prevalent in the bad-boy fiction of postwar authors such as Thomas Bailey Aldrich and Mark Twain. Although the book did not achieve peak commercial success until Scribner's reissued it after *St. Nicholas*'s debut, *Hans Brinker*'s popularity, along with Dodge's editorial and magazine work, opened new opportunities for her in a publishing business that, by the early 1870s, was undergoing a significant transformation.

IN THE decade after the war, the United States experienced what one contemporary described as a "mania of magazine starting."[29] American periodicals were joining the corporate revolution that was transforming the nation's economy. Ticknor and Fields, publisher of the *Atlantic Monthly, Our Young Folks,* and much of the midcentury's most prestigious American and British literature, exemplified the industry's old business model. The firm functioned as a fluid partnership; and particularly after the 1864 death of its founder, William Ticknor, it operated on the "casual, freewheeling basis" that one historian believes was characteristic of mid-nineteenth-century

American commerce.[30] Ticknor and Fields's magazines, like those of its prominent competitor Harper and Brothers, existed primarily to promote the work of the house's authors. The firm's goal, beyond selling products, was to produce high-quality literature that elevated the intellectual and moral ethos of the nation.

Both *Hearth and Home* and the *Riverside* operated under similar conditions. However, *Scribner's Monthly,* Dodge's next employer, approached publishing from a new perspective. The magazine abandoned the partnership model for the joint-stock, or corporate, form of business that entrepreneurs in larger industries preferred during the late nineteenth century. Its publishers were predominantly members of an emerging managerial class, and they hoped to run more efficient business organizations than their competitors did. Charles Scribner was the industry expert. Roswell Smith was a respected lawyer with, according to a historian of the firm, "exceptional business acumen" and "deep pockets." Richard Watson Gilder, *Scribner's* assistant editor and Dodge's colleague and friend, shared her view of writing and editing as both commercial skills and instruments for promoting ideology. Only Josiah Holland, the magazine's first editor and a well-known writer of didactic poems and essays such as "Character, and What Comes of It," fit the older mold of moral custodian.[31]

These men did not see their magazine as an avenue for selling books. Smith pursued advertising as a primary source of revenue and adopted marketing techniques that made *Scribner's* a forerunner of mass-circulating 1890s periodicals such as *Munsey's* and *Cosmopolitan.* One of these techniques was departmentalization: the editors created distinct sections such as "Topics of the Times," Home and Society," and "Culture and Progress" that enabled *Scribner's* writers to specialize in attracting a particular segment of the magazine-reading public. Dodge and *Companion* editor Ford both borrowed this approach as they increasingly subdivided their audience by age and gender.[32]

This corporate mentality did not mean abdicating the traditional role of genteel magazines as cultural gatekeepers. Holland took the moral responsibilities of *Scribner's* particularly seriously; he and Gilder believed that departments such as "Culture and Progress" could move "the American middle class . . . to a higher plane of appreciation for literature and art," an improvement that "would impose morality on American public life, and would create a just, ordered, and gracious society."[33] *Scribner's* advocated for urban parks and cultural institutions such as museums, symphonies, and libraries, earning itself a reputation as "the most genteel of the popular monthlies."[34]

Yet even as they promoted this agenda, *Scribner's* management perceived their magazine's value in commercial as well as moral terms. Expanding on the antebellum and wartime advertising practices of sensational publications, they described their magazine as "the best reading that money can buy." After detailing the amount expended on the periodical during its first decade, they concluded that the audience "will realize . . . they obtain the results of a vast outlay of money and labor for a small consideration."[35] Unlike the *Atlantic,* which refused to publish illustrations or photographs, *Scribner's* also embraced the postwar reverence for facts and visuals.[36] Its editors paid for "the finest illustrations procurable here and abroad," offering an unprecedented number of images to satisfy "the hunger of its readers for visual knowledge of the many worlds that a well-illustrated magazine could open to them."[37]

Scribner's balanced these commercial and educational interests using an editorial formula that focused on both the nation's idealized rural past and its future as a model of industrial and technological progress.[38] While it persistently emphasized the sustaining power of domestic life, the magazine also displayed a fascination with scientific advances and methods, introducing readers to the typewriter, the motorized engine, and the electric light. It produced ethnographic reports about different regions of the country, which helped it attract a truly national audience.[39] This formula of combining ideology and commerce, science and domesticity, also became the editorial foundation of *Scribner's* children's magazine, *St. Nicholas.*

Holland, Smith, and Scribner developed the idea for a companion magazine early in their endeavor. In December 1870, just one month after the debut of *Scribner's,* they began buying rights to failing children's magazines, eventually purchasing five publications, including the *Riverside* and *Our Young Folks.*[40] This consolidation followed corporate cultural trends of this period and allowed *Scribner's* to reduce its competition for both readers and writers. In 1872, they began considering editorial candidates, and asked Dodge, whose *Scribner's* contributions were critically and commercially popular, to outline ideas for the new magazine.[41] Her response became the article "Children's Magazines," which they published in July 1873.

Dodge began the article by reiterating standard genteel concerns about the format: "Sometimes I feel like rushing through the world with two placards—one held aloft in my right hand, BEWARE OF CHILDREN'S MAGAZINES! The other flourished in my left, CHILD'S MAGAZINE WANTED! A good magazine for little ones was never so much needed, and such harm is done by nearly all that are published." Yet rather than lecturing to, shielding, or frightening children, her solution was to recognize their changing roles in industrial America and cater to their interests before their needs: "Let there be no sermonizing, . . . no rattling of the dry bones of history. A child's magazine is its pleasure ground . . . Most children of the present civilization attend school. Their little heads are strained and taxed with the days' lessons. They do not want to be bothered nor amused nor taught nor petted. They just want to have their own way over their own magazine." This approach did not mean abandoning "instruction and good moral teaching," but they must be accomplished "by hints dropped incidentally," for children were more likely to accept advice from a voice they trusted not to interfere with their amusements.[42]

Dodge's ideas combined the *Juvenile Miscellany*'s respect for young readers and *Our Young Folks*'s anxiety about the intellectual quality of their literature. In combination with this idealism, however, her work displayed a practical commercial sense that aligned with *Scribner's* editorial strategies. Smith offered her the editorial position even before he published the article. Yet she hesitated to accept the job. She had already received an offer to edit *Hearth and Home* and may have aspired to retire to write full time in order to spend more time with her sons.[43] Her hesitation may also have been a negotiating strategy that revealed her recognition of her worth.

Dodge saw writing as a profession rather than a calling. She worked for the explicit purpose of supporting her family; and as she gained prestige and profit, she fiercely protected her assets, battling with publishers over how to present and promote them.[44] In a June 19, 1876, letter to Charles Scribner regarding *Theophilus and Others,* a collection of her stories, she asked him to ensure that those receiving complimentary copies of the book not have to pay postage. Three days later, she sent another letter, requesting that he send a copy *"with my card"* to the "'Independent,' 'Appleton's Journal,' 'Harper,' 'Galaxy,' etc."[45]

Dodge's peers displayed a similar marketing savvy. Louisa May Alcott wrote to Dodge about her refusal to let publishers bully her about the British rights to her novel *Jack and Jill.*[46] John Townsend Trowbridge kept regular notes regarding the income he earned from each of his books and gave Dodge specific instructions about how his stories should look when they appeared in *St. Nicholas.*[47] All of these authors had grown up in financial hardship and were using their literary productions to gain financial stability and social respectability. Unlike the preceding generation of authors, they viewed the commercialization of their writings as an opportunity rather than a threat.[48]

In-demand writers such as Trowbridge and Alcott, who capitalized on ideological differences within the industry by crafting stories that met the distinct needs of multiple publications, displayed little inclination to take editorial opportunities seriously. Trowbridge's position at *Our Young Folks* was purely nominal, and Alcott abandoned her editorship at *Merry's Museum* as soon as she could support herself by writing.[49] Dodge, however, negotiated a remarkable deal with Roswell Smith for *St. Nicholas*'s editorial position. She was promised 5,000 dollars per year; in comparison, Lucy Larcom had earned a peak of 1,200 dollars per year at *Our Young Folks,* and Dodge herself had earned 9,000 dollars total during the fifteen years since her husband's death. She also began receiving that salary immediately, even though the new magazine did not debut for six months. In the meantime, the publishers sent her and her younger son Harry on a European tour at the company's expense to gather ideas for *St. Nicholas.* Dodge was given nearly complete editorial autonomy and a budget sufficient to attract the best writers and artists as contributors. While Larcom needed to seek publisher James Fields's approval for all expenses, Dodge later recounted that her employers repeatedly told her, "It is your magazine. Do what you think best."[50]

The Scribner group's decision to give Dodge control over its highly capitalized venture broke with industry trends. Publishers were abandoning the strategy of hiring prominent writers to serve largely ceremonial roles at their new periodicals. Titular editors such as Harriet Beecher Stowe at *Hearth and Home* (and, to a lesser extent, Holland at *Scribner's*) gradually disappeared; and professional managers such as Richard Watson Gilder, who assumed control of *Scribner's* in 1881, oversaw increasingly complex organizations. Dodge had the unusual benefit of having both name recognition and managerial experience, but her hiring conflicted with the pattern of diminishing opportunities for female editors. Whereas women such as Lydia Maria Child, Sarah Josepha Hale, Sara Jane Lippincott, and Louisa May Alcott had held executive positions at antebellum magazines, a shift toward consolidation and increased financial investment was convincing postwar publishers to hand control to men such as William Taylor Adams and Horace Scudder and to place female editors (such as Larcom and Ella Farman Pratt at *Wide Awake*) under male management. Dodge was the last woman to hold editorial authority over a prominent nineteenth-century American children's magazine.

The *Scribner's* team not only gave Dodge control but also celebrated *St. Nicholas* with a substantial promotional launch that repeated their successful marketing strategy for the parent magazine. Advertisements declared, "Wherever 'SCRIBNER' goes, 'ST. NICHOLAS' ought to go. They will be harmonious companions in the family, and the helpers of each other in the work of instruction, culture, and entertainment." They emphasized *St. Nicholas*'s economic value, trumpeting it as "SIX MAGAZINES IN ONE" and promising that, "with its great literary and Pictorial Attractions, and its beautiful Printing, it will be found to be THE CHEAPEST MAGAZINE IN THE WORLD." In a supplement titled "What Some Eminent Men Think of *St. Nicholas*," Trowbridge reiterated this theme: "It is a wonder to me how it can be afforded at the price." Other celebrated writers offered praise: John Greenleaf Whittier called it "the best child's periodical in the world," and Charles Dudley Warner claimed that it was "even more entertaining for grown people than some of the quarterlies . . . I do not see how it can be made any better, and if the children don't like it, I think it is time to change the kind of children in this country."[51]

The choice to promote the magazine entirely through the praise of men reflected *Scribner's* careful efforts to position *St. Nicholas* in the marketplace. Even as they were promoting it as the successor to *Our Young Folks*, the managers were de-emphasizing the largely feminized reputation of genteel children's magazines.[52] This strategy highlighted the now-standard goal of pursuing boy readers and also aligned with Dodge's harbored ambitions. She hoped not only, as a close friend indicated, "to gain a man's pay" but also to diverge from what a scholar has described as *Scribner's* "male-dominated and chauvinistic mindset" to create a magazine that would reexamine the industry's hardening gender conventions.[53]

DODGE CAREFULLY created a new kind of children's magazine that enabled her to pursue these ambitions. She and her publishers crafted *St. Nicholas* to appeal to a wealthier, more educated class of subscribers. With its glossy pages, unmatched quantity and quality of illustrations, and contributions from famous writers such as Alcott, Warner, Longfellow, William Cullen Bryant, and Lewis Carroll, it looked like no previous publication in the industry. While the *Companion* offered pianos or large cash payments as premiums, *St. Nicholas* enticed parents with trips to Europe and "a year's tuition at a first-class school."[54] As I have already discussed, the publishers also set an unprecedented price for their magazine, justifying it as "the best reading that money can buy" and emphasizing its intellectual quality over its commercial value.[55]

Yet when readers opened the inaugural issue, the first image they saw derived from half a century of romanticized representations of childhood. By 1873, the idea that children could improve their surroundings through their innocence was a well-worn sentimental trope that had appeared in magazines across the ideological spectrum, and Dodge chose to reinvoke it here. The picture, "Willy by the Brook," shows a cherubic boy lying in a meadow and playing a flute, one leg carelessly kicked into the air while ducks hover to listen. The accompanying poem begins: "Willy lay by the dimpling brook where the sun had laid before; And, strange to say, when its place he took the spot brightened just the more."[56]

Some of the magazine's early serial stories also borrowed heavily from the past. Alcott's "Eight Cousins," for example, recounts the story of a sickly, meek girl who becomes a thriving, useful young woman, largely because of the kindly but relentless mentoring of her uncle.[57] Alcott's pedagogy drew from Jean-Jacques Rousseau's text *Émile* as well as the ideas of her father, the educational theorist Bronson Alcott. Like the representation of children as cherubic innocents, this approach to juvenile instruction appeared regularly in *St. Nicholas* for the rest of the century.

These traditional perspectives on childhood produced some of the magazine's greatest successes, including Frances Hodgson Burnett's "Little Lord Fauntleroy," which became a national sensation when it appeared in *St. Nicholas* in 1885–86.[58] They also provided an ideological and commercial balance for Dodge's more contemporary ideas. Some of these ideas, such as the magazine's fascination with science and technology, aligned with the focus of *Scribner's*.[59] However, Dodge used them, particularly in the fiction she published, not just to celebrate industrial progress but also to highlight the social benefits that upstanding young Americans could derive from gaining access to advances in modern society. For instance, the magazine's first serial story, Frank Stockton's "What Might Have Been Expected" (discussed in the introduction to part II of this book), describes a boy who earns money to support an elderly neighborhood freedwoman by constructing a local telegraph line between his town and a local mine. Several of Trowbridge's early serials, including the Jack Hazard story "The Young Surveyor," made similar arguments.[60]

St. Nicholas displayed a confidence in young people's ability to harness these advances for reputable purposes, and this attitude was a byproduct of Dodge's faith in the salutary social effects of community. She worked to develop communal impulses among her audience in a variety of ways. Like its liberal Protestant predecessors, *St. Nicholas* offered riddles, games, and puzzles each month for its readers to share and solve together. In March 1874, she introduced "Letter Box," a correspondence department that for the next sixty years printed letters from children all over the world. Young people communicated with each other through the magazine, routinely responding to previous letters and columns in their own correspondence and sharing their experiences with other children who had little in common with them other than their love for *St. Nicholas*.[61]

Dodge also created clubs for her young audience. In *St. Nicholas*'s first issue, she introduced an organization devoted to protecting all kinds of small animals from the cruelty of heedless young children. Given the opportunity to name the club, readers chose "The Bird-Defenders," and the group became an immediate success, instigating follow-up articles and periodic reports about local chapters emerging across the nation. In 1880, Dodge founded the Agassiz Association, a national syndicate of natural history clubs administered through *St. Nicholas*. Response was so enthusiastic that by 1887 the Scribner group created a separate Agassiz Association magazine.

The success of these endeavors revealed children's thirst for creating new connections with the magazine and each other, and the content of *St. Nicholas* built on that desire. Nonfiction articles promoted philanthropic organizations to support the impoverished, infirm, and underprivileged, particularly celebrating the groups that helped children. Serial stories examined the alternative familial structures that young people formed so that they could thrive without adult oversight. In Noah Brooks's "The Boy Emigrants," for example, four young men travel together from Illinois to California to seek their fortunes. Gradually, they develop an organizational plan that enables them to survive internal and external conflicts. In particular, they learn to rotate responsibility for "demeaning" (that is, traditionally feminine) tasks such as cooking and maintaining their clothes and tools; each individual takes a turn sacrificing his personal interest for the group's benefit.[62] Likewise, in Trowbridge's serial "His Own Master," an orphan discovers the value of social networks, but in a different manner. Left on his own, he gradually develops the ability to assess others' trustworthiness, creating a reliable support group that facilitates his personal and professional growth.[63]

Dodge was confident that such communities were available to guide and protect modern children, and this belief allowed her to celebrate a variety of less reputable youthful behaviors without fear of social repercussions. For example, in his story "Being a Boy," Charles Dudley Warner lampoons overly obedient children. He contrasts Solomon, a "perfectly good boy" who "would rather split up kindling wood for his mother than go a-fishing"— and who is killed by his longing for green apples, which he refuses to eat because his parents have told him not to—with John, who often lives in a world of his own imagination and is "a very different boy from Solomon, not half so good, nor half so dead."[64] Such humor aligned with the editors' preferred methods of satirizing foolish cultural standards, and it remained a favored approach to social commentary throughout Dodge's tenure at *St. Nicholas*.[65]

Dodge's confidence also allowed *St. Nicholas* to counteract the hardening gender divisions in the children's magazine industry, which became more evident as postwar publishers reconsidered appropriate roles for American children. Dodge began by introducing female characters who assumed more active roles in boys' serial stories, though they still remained secondary. In Stockton's story "What Might Have Been Expected," the hero's sister Kate aids her brother's charity efforts by selling her handiwork, an activity her mother supports despite the neighbors' disapproval. Kate's facility for mathematics also gains her the position of bookkeeper when her brother Harry and his friends form their telegraph corporation.[66] In Trowbridge's "The Young Surveyor," a female character named Vinny supports Jack Hazard's efforts to reform a struggling family. As Jack inspires the men and boys to improve their work habits and business ethics, Vinny educates the children and teaches the women and girls to manage a household budget.[67]

St. Nicholas also expanded young women's roles in serial stories marketed to girls. Even though Alcott's "Eight Cousins" focused on a well established pedagogical approach, the serial offered unconventional ideas about feminine activities. By the story's end, Rose's uncle dispels her aunts' notion that she is too old to play with boys, replacing her medicines and restricted clothing with healthy food and comfortable outfits and involving her in coed amusements such as boating, gardening, riding horses, and playing football. He says that girls may add polish to their appearance later, but "no amount of gilding will be of use if the timbers are not sound."[68]

Other stories hinted at the potential fluidity of gender boundaries. In Charles Barnard's "Rebecca the Drummer," girls save a town during the American Revolution by dressing in patriot uniforms and playing a fife and drum to fool the enemy into thinking that American forces are arriving.[69] In Mary E. Bradley's "Mrs. Pomeroy's Page," boys dress as female beggars to incite sympathy from a feminine household.[70] Even in *St. Nicholas* such narratives remained exceptional; most stories continued to feature boys who were venturing out to explore the world while girls stayed close to home. Nonetheless, from the magazine's inception, Dodge worked to open the possibilities of modern society to both its female and male young readers.

The magazine's embrace of these possibilities distinguished *St. Nicholas* from its liberal Protestant predecessors as well as the conservative *Companion*.

Although it became the first liberal Protestant postwar children's magazine to develop a substantial and sustainable readership, its cost and ideals did limit its reach to an elite segment of the market that was roughly one-sixth the size of the *Companion*'s audience. The link that Dodge forged between children's economic class and their opportunities as consumers continued to expand during the last quarter of the nineteenth century, as industrialization and urbanization continued to challenge both her and *Companion* editor Ford's conceptions of modern American childhood.

PART III

Sustaining Children's Magazines
1873–1918

※

JONATHAN "JACK" REDMOND IS THE HERO OF MRS. FRANK LEE'S
"Redmond, of the 'Seventh,'" a serial published in the *Youth's Companion*
in 1888. He is a fifteen-year-old student at "Ninety," a New York public
school that houses close to 1,700 pupils, boys and girls, from "six-year-
old beginners to youths nearly ready for college." Many of them admire
Jack, a strong, independent, intelligent young man who ice skates down
the sidewalks of Manhattan and speaks in slang. His language is hardly
scandalous—when Jack makes a mistake, a friend tells him, "It's worse than
thirteen at table and a black cat!"—but it is exactly the sort of speech that
Companion editor Daniel Sharp Ford had castigated in earlier years. Nor,
in those earlier years, would Ford have approved of another male student
in the story, who somersaults into a girls' classroom to "make a favorable
impression on the ladies."[1]

Like many other boy characters in nineteenth-century American children's magazines, Jack struggles to regulate himself. Yet in contrast to earlier
heroes such as *Our Young Folks'*s Jack Hazard, this Jack is inherently competent and needs to curb his overconfidence rather than his corrupt impulses. His self-possession and determination occasionally spill over into
self-righteousness; his teacher Miss Allen compares him to "the boy in
Grimm's fairy tales, who didn't know how to shiver," even in front of the
stern headmaster, Mr. Haverhill. But with the assistance of Miss Allen
and a close friend, Jack gradually becomes more sympathetic, lenient, and
gentle. This combination of strength and empathy transforms him into a

hero who saves the headmaster's daughter during a school fire and helps him discover his calling as a "home missionary to the frontiers."[2]

Kate Douglas Wiggin's "Polly Oliver's Problem" was a *St. Nicholas* serial that ran from November 1892 through May 1893. Like Jack Redmond, sixteen-year-old Polly is "determined [and] ... impetuous, ... a person who feels matters rather strongly, and who is wont to state them in the strongest terms she knows." As she cares for her frail widowed mother, Polly searches for a profession so that she can support herself. She considers running a kindergarten but is stymied by a lack of funds. Then a wealthy patroness, struck by Polly's kindness, empathy, and imagination, pays her to tell stories to patients at San Francisco's Children's Hospital. The death of her mother diverts the young woman from this activity; but after receiving kind but firm adult counsel about the need to live rather than immerse herself in grief, Polly decides to become a professional storyteller. With her friends' help, she establishes a business plan and at the story's end is practicing her craft with great success.[3]

Both Jack and Polly need to develop self-control, which makes them similar to earlier characters in American children's magazines. Yet their proficiencies distinguish them from those predecessors. By the 1890s, fiction in both the *Companion* and *St. Nicholas* was portraying young Americans who were capable of succeeding in contemporary society. Nor were such successes limited to the insular small towns of previous stories. Boys and girls, with the assistance of adults and peer mentors, were presented as capable of navigating through complex modern social systems such as high schools and universities as well as mixed-class and multiethnic urban and business communities.

"Redmond" and "Polly" exemplified these magazines' efforts to update their formulas in order to remain relevant to young American readers of the late nineteenth century. The pressure to do so did not come from within the industry: by the mid-1870s the *Companion* and *St. Nicholas* were its unchallenged leaders, a status they retained through World War I. The *Companion's* circulation had reached half a million per week by 1890; and even though *St. Nicholas's* readership was much smaller, the magazine retained the loyalty of the nation's commercially and intellectually elite families. Nor did the publications perceive each other as competitors. The *Companion* praised *St. Nicholas* soon after it first appeared, but for the next four decades they generally ignored each other as they attended to distinct audiences.[4]

Despite this lack of industry competition, external pressures challenged Ford and *St. Nicholas* editor Mary Mapes Dodge as well as their successors. (They died in 1899 and 1905, respectively.) The period between *St. Nicholas's* debut in 1873 and the end of World War I in 1918 was a time of changing expectations for American children and their families. As the United States became more industrial and urban, genteel adults grew increasingly preoccupied with protecting and promoting the welfare of the nation's children. "Child savers" created organizations to prevent mistreatment of children and remove them from unhealthy living conditions. Social scientists studied children's maturation processes, leading to increased recognition of a distinct life stage known as adolescence as well as to efforts to reform children's educational, play, and home environments. The result, among other changes, was growing interest in athletic teams and scouting troops as activities for improving children's physical and moral characters.[5]

Reformers sought to prepare young Americans for modern citizenship by further segregating youth from the rest of society, particularly from urban, industrial environments. During these decades, childhood and adolescence extended longer than they had in previous periods of American history, particularly among genteel northern and western families who prioritized children's education over their labor. Between 1870 and 1915, the number of schoolchildren in the United States increased from 7 million to 20 million. By 1890, almost 80 percent of ten- to fourteen-year-old Americans spent some time in school during the year; that number was significantly higher in the North and West because fewer than half of all southern children were regular attendees.[6] The educational experience also extended to younger and older children as publicly financed kindergartens appeared and high school attendance exploded, rising by more than 700 percent (from 200,000 to 1.6 million) between 1890 and 1918.[7]

This segregation, however, did not necessarily have the effect of sheltering children—particularly older children—from public life. Significant increases in time spent among peer groups spurred their consumer demands, a process that accelerated as American businesses increased efforts to create and market products for children. Department stores opened children's sections that constructed elaborate fantasy worlds for young shoppers. Advertisers pitched products ranging from books to breakfast cereals directly to children rather than their parents. By 1914, even baseball card companies had replaced the tobacco that accompanied their cards with Cracker Jack.[8]

These reform and business interests in children tested the *Companion* and *St. Nicholas*'s continuing cultural relevance. Moral reformers of the 1870s and 1880s, whose crusade against sensational literature for children exemplified the anxiety that urbanization had stimulated among genteel Americans, forced the magazines to develop new editorial approaches that guided young readers toward respectable methods for surviving the perceived moral and physical threats of urban life. By the turn of the century, as children's maturation process in northern and midwestern towns and cities became more institutionalized through schools, extracurricular activities, and expert opinions on childrearing, Ford's and Dodge's successors had to reinforce the importance—and reconfigure the nature—of families as a source of social stability and of their own publications as mediators between those families and modern American society.

The manner in which the *Companion* and *St. Nicholas* addressed these issues reveals the changing status of gentility as a means of constructing social identities in the late nineteenth- and early twentieth-century United States. The magazines' traditional Protestant ideologies and formulas were effective in responding to moral reformers' concerns but became strained as the next generation of families adapted to the institutional shifts of contemporary childhood. The editors' expanded compartmentalization of children based on age, gender, and, increasingly, class aligned with modern childrearing trends, but their standards of genteel restraint were becoming anachronistic for young Americans as they became ever more immersed in a culture of consumer goods and leisure activities. One indication of that anachronism was the magazines'—particularly the *Companion*'s—increased focus on girls' public roles as students, athletes, and even professionals. By shifting their attention toward the interests of female and eventually working-class customers, Ford's successors ceded the vanguard of the youth market to new products less constrained by traditional standards of gentility.

By the 1910s, the *Companion* and *St. Nicholas* entered a long period of gradual decline. Ford's magazine began to lose circulation, and both publications struggled to procure regular contributions from prominent writers and artists.[9] Their diminishing influence amid a flood of new commercial entertainments for children was part of a broader dissipation of Americans' anxieties about commercial cultures that sapped gentility of much of its social authority during the early twentieth century. Ironically, during the previous four decades these magazines had laid the foundation for their own decline. By delineating genteel commercial roles for children in an urban industrial society, they mitigated the concerns of millions of ambitious American families regarding their offspring's potential for achieving both financial success and social respectability.

CHAPTER 7

Tales and the City

✳

IN THE AUGUST 1875 chapter of her *St. Nicholas* serial "Eight Cousins," Louisa May Alcott condemns a genre of fiction she describes as "sensation stories." Taking particular aim at the popular writer Oliver Optic (William Taylor Adams), the motherly Mrs. Jessie decries the "optical delusions" prevalent in these tales:

> Now, I put it to you, boys, is it natural for lads from fifteen to eighteen to command ships, defeat pirates, outwit smugglers, and so cover themselves with glory, that Admiral Farragut invites them to dinner, saying: "Noble boy, you are an honor to your country"? . . . Even if the hero is an honest boy trying to get his living, he is not permitted to do so in a natural way, by hard work and years of patient effort, but is suddenly adopted by a millionaire whose pocket-book he has returned; or a rich uncle appears from sea, just in the nick of time; or the remarkable boy earns a few dollars, speculates in pea-nuts or neckties, and grows rich so rapidly that Sinbad in the diamond valley is a pauper to him.

After Mrs. Jessie's son Will concedes that the boys in these books are "mighty lucky," she explains why she finds this type of book so harmful:

> It gives boys such wrong ideas of life and business; shows them so much evil and vulgarity that they need not know about, and makes the one success worth having a fortune, a lord's daughter, or some worldly honor, often not worth the time it takes to win. It does seem to me that some one might write . . . lively, natural, and helpful, tales in which the English should be good, the morals pure, and the characters such as we can love in spite of the faults that all may have. I can't bear to see such eager little fellows at the library reading such trash; weak, when it is not wicked, and totally unfit to feed the hungry minds that feast on it for want of something better.[1]

Alcott's diatribe was ironic, given her own history of writing sensational stories both anonymously and under pseudonyms.[2] It was also an unusual point of view for *St. Nicholas,* one that derived at least in part from a personal conflict between Alcott and Adams.[3] Yet if the extent of Alcott's complaint was atypical for the magazine, its core message—that such books left readers ill-prepared for life's actual challenges—was not. In monthly reviews of children's books, Mary Mapes Dodge accepted the reading of "adventure stories where the adventures are possible and the hero is honest and returns to his duties," but discouraged her audience from reading books

THE BOYS ENJOY THEMSELVES.

Mrs. Jessie's boys smoking cigars and reading sensation stories. *St. Nicholas,* 1875. Courtesy of the Early Juvenile Literature Collection, Martha Blakeney Hodges Special Collections and University Archives, University Libraries, University of North Carolina at Greensboro.

"you're ashamed of" or "with characters we would not meet in real life."
Overall, she preferred that young people "stick to the classics."[4]

The *Youth's Companion's* stance on such "sensation stories" was more
anxious and severe than that of its contemporary. Although he concurred
with Alcott's and Dodge's assessments of the dangers of such books, Daniel
Sharp Ford focused more on the sinister motives of their publishers and
the dire consequences that awaited readers than on the actual content of
the stories. He presented this "pernicious literature" as a "subtle and satanic"
influence that "poisoned minds and souls" and had led young men, including one "from a refined family and a graduate of a leading New England
college," to "the gallows."[5]

Like Alcott's argument, the *Companion's* position on these stories was
ironic, given the many genteel sensational tales Ford had published. Nevertheless, both stances were products of anxieties heightened during the 1870s
and 1880s by a national debate about children's reading. Arguments on this
subject often escalated into the type of frenzied rhetoric that Ford used in
the *Companion*. One librarian claimed that "many a girl's sentimentality or
foolish marriage, and many a boy's rash venture in cattle ranches or uneasiness in the harness of slight but regular salary, is owing to books that fed
early feeble indications of a tendency to future evil."[6] An author in *Scribner's*
believed that "the brutalizing and debasing power of [story papers] nullifies
parental culture and Sunday school instruction—they excite a craving for
bloody scenes, nourish the instincts of the savage and the bully, breed contempt for authority, and make that seem admirable and worthy of imitation
which is most reprehensible and heartily to be shunned."[7] An 1879 conference on the issue, attended by public figures such as former ambassador to
Great Britain (and son and grandson of presidents) Charles Francis Adams
and minister, abolitionist, and author Thomas Wentworth Higginson (the
lone published dissenter at the conference), reinforced the growing sense
that sensational children's literature should be a significant public concern.[8]

The foremost instigator of these discussions and a primary producer
of their fiery rhetoric was Anthony Comstock, a U.S. postal inspector and
anti-vice crusader whose beliefs and methods, like Ford's, were shaped by
orthodox evangelical Protestantism. Both men adopted rhetorical strategies borrowed from evangelical ministers of the eighteenth and early nineteenth centuries and refined by producers of the penny press, story papers,
and dime novels of the mid-nineteenth century. Indeed, the language that
both men used at the peak of this debate was strikingly similar; vehement references to "pernicious literature" and "satanic" influences appeared
in *Companion* editorials such as "Bad Books and What They Make" and

"Obscene Literature" as well as in Comstock's own books, particularly *Traps for the Young*.[9]

Because *St. Nicholas* retained its liberal Protestant confidence in children's innate benevolence and the progress of modern society, it was less inclined to follow Comstock's approach to warding off the dangers of sensational literature. Instead, Dodge maintained a more elite genteel tradition, seeking to nurture her audience's preference for more intellectually and imaginatively substantial stories. This endeavor occupied much more space in the magazine than did her efforts to caution young readers against inappropriate reading; she used recurring projects such as "The *St. Nicholas* Treasure-Box of Literature" to interest her audience in the writings of "gifted men and women [who] are the spokespeople for all others."[10]

The *Companion*'s and *St. Nicholas*'s respective methods for handling the sensational literature crisis exemplified their approach to the broader issue that had spawned these concerns: the social threat of urbanization. During the previous half-century, gentility had extended through the middling and wealthy populations of the United States as a method of coping with urban growth, but by the 1870s the size and diversity of city populations made genteel authority seem more tenuous than it had been during the antebellum and wartime periods. Both magazines' editors and contemporary reformers perceived this problem as particularly dire for children, who appeared to face a greater variety and degree of dangers than previous generations of American youth had.

Sensational literature became a subject of public controversy because it capitalized on these alarming changes. It was produced primarily in cities, and children could procure these publications in crowded urban commercial districts without adult knowledge. Late nineteenth-century genteel Americans particularly associated such freedom from supervision with children from poor and immigrant families who did not necessarily abide by respectable standards of conduct. Fears for and of these unguarded youths inspired a variety of ideologically diverse efforts to "save" children in American cities, including movements to protect children from not only sensational fiction but also excessive labor in factories and sweatshops, poor health in urban slums, and misdirected punishments by the justice system.[11]

During the 1870s and 1880s, responding to this urban crisis became a primary challenge for the newly hegemonic *Companion* and *St. Nicholas*. Although neither magazine faced accusations of distributing dangerous literature to children, Ford and Dodge had to adapt their editorial formulas to incorporate audience concerns about the maintenance of genteel control and to accommodate the demographic reality that more of their readers were living in cities. For both magazines, these adjustments served to reinforce rather than transform their approaches to child readers.

Before 1890, the editors had worked from the premise that cities represented a potential threat to the safety of young Americans. Their stories featured boys (and occasionally girls) who moved from rural or small-town communities into urban environments. Released from the supervision and guidance of respectable authority figures, these characters fell under the influences of morally unformed peers or, worse, disreputable adults who flirted, gambled, stole, drank, and otherwise violated genteel codes of behavior. The tales reflected a growing fear that, as Comstock stated, "thousands in our large cities . . . will do anything for money, catering to the lowest appetites in passions, there is no safety [for children] save in eternal vigilance."[12]

The *Companion*'s prescription for this problem extended beyond Comstock's call for vigilance. Ford sought to reaffirm traditional methods of social control by urging families to keep children out of the nation's cities. Using his genteel sensational formula, he highlighted the variety of horrible consequences that could result from even brief exposure to city life. Not until the early 1890s did the *Companion* begin to move away from this effort to keep young readers away from urban societies and shift its focus toward offering city residents guidance on moral and physical preservation.

Even as it acknowledged the dangers of urban environments and promoted the benefits of country living for the nation's youth, *St. Nicholas* developed a more ambivalent stance on the subject. This position reflected Dodge's skepticism about traditional moral and social authorities as well as her faith in the capacities of children and markets to create new solutions to the problem. It also reflected the wealth of her audience, which made such a position more palatable because *St. Nicholas* readers were better protected from urban dangers than their less affluent peers were. During the 1870s and especially the 1880s, *St. Nicholas* developed an optimistic message that young Americans could, with proper guidance, overcome these dangers. In addition to family members and the magazine, that guidance came from emerging networks of professionals who modeled respectable standards of urban genteel behavior for aspiring young men and women. By the early 1890s, *St. Nicholas* had extended its trust in the social expertise of these networks to embrace the "city beautiful" movement, an approach to urban planning that promoted the idea that attractive physical environments "could engender civic loyalty, thus guaranteeing . . . harmonious moral order."[13] The ideals of the "city beautiful" meshed with Dodge's vision for urban America because both promoted the city as a respectable environment for children under circumstances carefully managed by political, intellectual, and cultural elites.

At the turn of the century this view was a decidedly minority opinion. The extraordinary popularity of the *Companion,* which continued to offer warnings about the city's influence on American youth, suggests that many genteel families remained frightened of the heterogeneity, commercialism, and disorder of urban environments. Yet even as it created new challenges for Ford and Dodge, the topic affirmed their publications' didactic and commercial value as proponents of the existing social order. The *Companion's* genteel sensational stories and *St. Nicholas's* industrial fantasies both conveyed messages that asserted respectable Americans' capacity for maintaining control over their rapidly transforming nation. The magazines' ability to sustain this message and still appeal to children, even under the enhanced scrutiny of Gilded Age moral reformers, confirms the continuing relevance of gentility as a way to help middle-class and wealthy Americans adapt to, and limit the influence of, late nineteenth-century industrialization and urbanization.

FROM EVERY available venue during the late 1870s and 1880s, Anthony Comstock proclaimed the dangers of "pernicious literature" for children:

> After more than eleven years' experience contending for the moral purity of the children of the land, and seeking to prevent evils from being brought in contact with this ever-susceptible class, I have one clear conviction, viz., that *Satan lays the snare, and children are his victims.* There is a shameful recklessness in many homes as to what children read ... Sure fire traps [include] ... half-dime novels, five and ten-cent story papers, and low-priced pamphlets for boys and girls ... The finest fruits of civilization are consumed by these vermin ... [and] this evil is on the increase. These publications, like the fishes of the sea, spawn millions of seed, and each year these seeds germinate and spring up to a harvest of death.[14]

Elsewhere he called such books "worse than yellow fever or smallpox" and more dangerous to children than a mad dog. He decried their publishers as "midnight burglars," comparing them to "a highwayman who presents his revolver at a victim and demands your money or your life."[15]

Comstock did not limit his vehemence to the subject of cheap sensational fiction. In his crusade to eradicate sin, he also railed against pornography, gambling, liquor, and fraudulent advertising. What linked sensational stories to these more obvious social threats was a common connection to the rapidly changing, loosely regulated environments of the West as well as to Comstock's particular target, the nation's cities. Gambling and drinking were long-standing social problems, but during this period fear of their dangers was exacerbated by the presence of transient, anonymous populations in unstable urban environments. Pornography and fraudulent advertisements exemplified the corrupting power of an expanding form of amoral, unfettered capitalism.

To reformers such as Comstock, sensational fiction integrated both of these concerns and thus highlighted the diminution of genteel Protestant control over the stability and morals of industrializing communities. Such stories were produced by largely unknown publishers and sold by merchants who rarely had a social connection or obligation to the customer's family. They often circulated in peer environments beyond the supervision of responsible adults, and their plots romanticized the lives of unregulated young men living on or beyond the margins of respectability. One contemporaneous librarian linked the immorality of such stories to the speculative fever of the Gilded Age, blaming them for "many a boy's rash venture in cattle ranches or uneasiness in the harness of slight but regular salary."[16] Comstock also connected this genre to poor urban workers, whom many genteel Americans viewed as examples of the divide that industrialization was creating between respectable Protestants and other communities. His description of American children as a "class" hints at the connection he perceived between the values promoted by sensational literature and the increasingly violent clashes between the nation's workers and management. Similarly, his characterization of these books as "fire traps," a phrase used primarily to describe urban tenements, bonded this literature to the threat of social chaos triggered by poor and increasingly foreign-born urban populations.

Comstock's arguments, to the extent they survive in public memory, have acquired a taint of extremism. Much of this perspective derived from his overzealous and unsympathetic investigative and enforcement practices. He harassed and entrapped thousands of people whose most significant crime was to disagree with his moral standards. Comstock concocted elaborate fictions to entice mailings of what he deemed to be obscene materials and then arrested the senders for their actions. One woman was convicted for sending Comstock the pamphlet *The Wedding Night*, a sexual primer for newlyweds. Rather face a lengthy jail term, she, like several other Comstock targets, committed suicide. When confronted with her death, he shrugged it off as "a bloody ending to a bloody life."[17]

Yet his unattractive character obscures the fact that for much of the 1870s and 1880s his moral certainties aligned with prevailing views in genteel American society. His supporters included Vice President Schuyler Colfax and members of the U.S. Supreme Court. His New York Society for the Suppression of Vice was initially financed by the YMCA's board of directors, which included a number of well connected New York businessmen, several of whom had already convinced the state legislature to pass an 1868 law restricting obscene materials.[18] Other "child saver" organizations founded during the 1870s (for instance, the Society for the Prevention of Cruelty to Children and the Fresh Air Fund) exhibited similar zeal for Comstock's goal—if not his methods—of rescuing children from the physical and moral hazards of urban life.[19] The methodological distinctions between Comstock's approach and theirs paralleled the ideological and cultural differences between the *Companion* and *St. Nicholas*. Most child savers mirrored Dodge's perspective on child development; they had faith in children's capacity to flourish with proper guidance and control. Like Ford, however, Comstock was dubious about children's inherent nature and thus sought to restrict their access to the potentially corrupting influences of commerce. Both perspectives fit within the parameters of genteel society, and a surging collective interest in child saving fueled each side's efforts to delineate proper moral boundaries for children's periodicals.

In previous decades, discussions of such boundaries had inspired little vehemence or fear. For example, when Beadle and Adams's dime-novel series achieved commercial success among boys during the Civil War, the elite *North American Review* acknowledged that the publishers were "wielding an instrument of immense power" but mildly suggested that they should use their influence to develop a "correct public taste."[20] In the 1870s, however, these same novels were provoking a disparate group of critics to decry the dangers of such literature, sparking what one scholar describes as "the first major controversy in the history of American children's culture."[21]

Some of these complaints had a long history in Anglo-American culture. For instance, when a librarian at an 1879 conference on children's reading bemoaned the "desultory and careless mental habits engendered in pupils by this same inordinate consumption of story-books," including "inattention, want of application, distaste for study and unretentive memories," she was reasserting the traditional opposition to fiction as entertainment.[22] Yet other arguments display contemporary anxieties about class, particularly the potential for social disorder that was latent in poor urban neighborhoods. Another speaker at the conference claimed that sensational literature was particularly damaging to youths who did not have access to the new public libraries: "The library book is not found in the most wretched tenements nor in the market-boy's pocket, but you do find there some twenty or more papers which are sensational, detrimental, immoral, and some thirteen or fourteen which are flat, weak, [and] trashy."[23] Charles Francis Adams linked such reading to immorality among the working classes: "The taste for sensational and sentimental trash ... is a class distinction ... It has long been observed that a very small degree of book knowledge universally takes a depraved shape. The animal will come out. The man who can barely spell out his newspaper confines his labor in nine cases out of ten to those highly seasoned portions of it which relate to acts of violence, and especially to murders."[24] In fact, of all the conference's published speeches, only Thomas Wentworth Higginson's denied the importance of social distinctions in the choice of reading material for children. Correspondingly, he dismissed the dangers of sensational adventure stories, calling boys' love for them "the effort of the young mind to get outside its early limitations" and praising this propensity as the same spirit that had propelled the Anglo-American race to its greatest successes.[25]

THE DANGERS of sensational reading for working-class children received the greatest attention at the 1879 conference, and these same children were also the primary focus of the child-saving movement. Yet the publicity surrounding these causes instigated a correlative fear among genteel families, who worried that such reading would make their children unfit for respectable society.[26] This anxiety gave both Ford and Dodge an opportunity to confirm the value of their magazines to their particular audiences.

The *Companion* easily assimilated the issue into its existing ideological framework, and editorials illustrating the dire consequences of children's bad reading began appearing regularly by 1875. In keeping with the magazine's increasingly gendered approach, Ford focused much of this commentary on boys' reading, establishing a template that was only slightly different from the approach that he and his predecessor Nathaniel Willis had been using since the magazine's founding. "Bad Books," for example, describes "a young man from a refined family and a graduate of a leading New England college" who is hanged in the West as a bandit. Antebellum versions of this narrative had blamed such violent ends on drinking, gambling, or disobeying his parents. In this case, however, the convict "acknowledge[s] that his crimes were inspired by reading bad books." The author reflects that even prosperity and education cannot protect young men from the dangers of harmful reading, a statement suggesting that such hazards might also threaten the *Companion's* readers, not just poorer children.[27]

Misbehaving girls had appeared less frequently in the antebellum *Companion*, although during the 1850s Ford did criticize female readers who paid attention to fashion, declaring that it would lead them to make disastrous marriages.[28] After the Civil War, he also began warning girls about the sin of bad reading, with the dire consequence of such misconduct remaining the same. In "The Best of a Bad Bargain," for example, a middle-class girl becomes poor and prematurely old because romantic reading has led her to choose an inappropriate spouse.[29]

Ford also addressed this subject in the *Companion*'s newest front-page feature: serial stories. One of the earliest, Ruth Chesterfield's "A Boarding-School Romance," introduces Lillian Pope, a girl from a prosperous family whose "head has been a little turned by novel-reading." Her resulting fascination with a young itinerant, whom she imaginatively elevates into a European nobleman, leads her to instigate a secret courtship and engagement. Her father's timely intervention foils this potential tragedy, but the bad influence of her reading persists: a mortified Lillian proceeds to fake her own death.[30] In "The Jolly Rover," John Townsend Trowbridge describes the foolishness of a young man who is inspired by a "weekly paper filled with stories of astonishing boy-heroes" to leave a secure and comfortable life in search of adventure. After a series of miserable events and a prolonged illness, his "good angel"—a young girl who rescues him from ruin—contacts his mother, and together the domesticated females bring the abashed but wiser boy back home.[31] These front-page characters faced less serious consequences than did the tragic figures who appeared on the *Companion*'s inside pages, but their hardships were sufficient to convey the importance of avoiding poor reading choices.

As the *Companion* intensified its focus on the hazards of bad reading, Ford increased his internal policing of its fiction. He codified his expectations in the leaflet "The *Youth's Companion* Story," which he sent to every prospective new author. As Ray Stannard Baker later recalled, "few periodicals of the time ever set down their formula as explicitly in black and white as the *Youth's Companion* [did]."[32] The leaflet summarized the narrative elements that would fulfill the magazine's commercial and moral agendas and proscribed those that did not, including romance, slang, and protagonists' unsavory behavior.[33] Ford explained his motivations for these restraints in an 1875 letter to Louisa May Alcott, in which he asked her to tone down a dance scene in a submitted story:

> You have fully realized in the serial, all that I promised my readers as to its attractiveness . . . It is both genial and impressive, humorous and pathetic, and has your grace of expression that I always admire . . . But do you know that with the *Companion*, I have to be as "wise as a serpent and as harmless as a dove." Your whole plot turns upon a "ball" in the opening chapter, and the second chapter has such as charming presentation of dancing, that hundreds of readers of the *Companion* will turn up "pious eyes" lest their old "orthodox" paper should appear to countenance what seems to them

"dangerous pleasures." I am *orthodox,* you know—anyway I *am*—but still am sufficiently enlightened to accept things as they are, and to believe the good may "come out of Nazareth," but the old Puritan prejudices still linger among a large portion of our people, Now your good genius, I am sure, can relieve me from this dilemma. I want the story to please everybody, and to *influence* everybody—and there are stiff orthodox families, who "look upon the wine when it is red," as well as the delightful sinners who are outside the creed. It is sound morality when we want to win people, not to stir up prejudices to fight against our appeals. Now can you give the obnoxious word a sugar coating—calling the ball a sociable or something of the sort, and give the dancing of the second chapter somewhat less prominence?[34]

Ford's letter reveals the degree to which public pressure dictated the content of his publication. But either Alcott did not agree to his terms, or she edited the story beyond recognition, for the tale described in this letter never appeared in the *Companion.* Perhaps Ford's request had alienated one of his audience's favorite authors, or perhaps Alcott's budding friendship with Dodge was leading her to direct more of her work to *St. Nicholas.* Whatever the case, her contributions to the *Companion* diminished from about one story per month during the early 1870s to fewer than one per year by 1877. This outcome might have damaged another publication, but the *Companion* relied less on the quality of its literature than on the formulaic reinforcement of its messages. As its author leaflet explained, the magazine had created "the chart for sure-fire success; which is to be sedulously followed. Don't experiment. Don't originate; repeat!"[35]

Such an approach did not work at *St. Nicholas;* Dodge was too invested in the genteel elite's ethic of cultural custodianship to accept such a formula. Moreover, as her stance toward her own sons' reading reveals, she did not share Ford's concerns about the moral threat of sensational fiction. When she asked her son Harry what he liked to read best, he named Shakespeare and Mayne Reid's "Boy Hunters," a popular adventure story that was slightly disreputable according to the genteel standards of the day. His mother's response was "I did get an idea after all—and that is that some persons have queer children."[36] Meanwhile, her other son, Jamie, asked if he could subscribe to the sensational newspaper the *Police Gazette* yet "also took up Tennyson's Idyls [*sic*] of the King this winter [and] was perfectly fascinated with them." Dodge told *Riverside* editor Horace Scudder, "James is half butcher and half poet, and I really don't know which element I admire most in him."[37]

Despite her own lack of concern about the moral hazards of sensational fiction, Dodge recognized the need to address the subject in *St. Nicholas.* She adopted a less dramatic approach to the issue than the *Companion* did: no characters end up on the gallows or pine in solitude while their husbands serve prison terms. Yet occasionally *St. Nicholas* did take a strong stand against sensational reading, as Mrs. Jessie's conversation with her son reveals. (See the extract from Alcott's "Eight Cousins" that opens this chapter.) In a January 1874 editorial written for the third issue of the magazine, Dodge's character Jack-in-the-Pulpit tells young people "not to read what they [are] ashamed of": such books are "deadly poison" and these "poisoners should be punished like any other murderers, because they kill the soul (which is even worse)."[38] This attitude was an anomaly, however, and suggests that the pressures of her new job, which she had assumed in the midst of a public frenzy regarding the dangers of children's reading, may have pressed Dodge to temporarily adopt a more stringent position.

More often, *St. Nicholas* offered measured assessments of such literature. In Trowbridge's "Fast Friends," for example, the hero's attempt to write for a sensational magazine highlights how such publications financially exploited writers.[39] Even in Susan Coolidge's "The Fox and the Turkeys, or Charley and the Old Folks," which describes how the protagonist's love of "fancy foolish reading" has led him to run away to sea, the episode results only in a miserable day that convinces the boy to return home to his family.[40] These mild examples seem unlikely to have persuaded young readers to abstain from such literature. However, they acknowledged widespread public concerns about the issue and reinforced Dodge's larger goal of elevating her audience's appreciation of literature and art. She had once commiserated to Scudder about the "heavy responsibility as well as high privilege . . . [of having] the ear of Young America once a month." While that "responsibility" occasionally overlapped with Comstock's concerns about sensational stories "that make day-dreamers of our children and castle-builders of the student," in *St. Nicholas* it more often centered on her belief that children's books tended to be too prosaic rather than too imaginative.[41]

Here, too, she borrowed her views largely from the New England elites, particularly from the editors of the *Atlantic*. The Brahmin magazine had had a long, if contested, tradition of challenging readers to consumer more thoughtful literature, and its editors affirmed this approach in their position toward postwar sensational fiction. One *Atlantic* author compared the impact of those novels to that of classic works by Shakespeare and Sir Walter Scott:

> Tragedy lifts your whole nature—sentiment, conscience, reflection, imagination, whatever there is in you—altogether above actual life into the ideal world of art . . . With the melodrama, you are in the mind and dust of the earth all the time you listen; everything is intensely commonplace, not ex-

cepting the rant and the crimes; sensational authors transfer money from your pocket to theirs without going through the extremely tedious process of attempting to get a fine sentiment into your head or a new idea into your heart; the great defect of the romancers is that there's no romance in them . . . This power to interest you in society where you fear your pocket will be picked is not art.[42]

By the 1880s, the magazine was offering similar critiques of children's books, declaring that young readers "are drugged with a literature whose chief merit is its harmlessness . . . [It is] powerless to awaken a child's imagination or to stimulate his mental growth," and "children's reading is at present especially defective in stimulating the child's imagination."[43] In 1882, the *North American Review*'s editors begged authors to "refrain from moralizing and instruction" in children's literature.[44]

Dodge worked harder at achieving this goal than at eradicating sensational literature from children's reading diets. In addition to recommending classic literature in editorials and in "The *St. Nicholas* Treasure-Box of Literature," she created a feature called "Books for Boys and Girls," which listed modern books that might stimulate young readers' intellects and imaginations.[45] Neither of these features seems to have resonated with her young audience, however. She printed no readers' letters in praise of them (her standard technique for displaying her audience's enthusiasm for a *St. Nicholas* innovation), and she discontinued both departments after less than a year.[46] In 1881, she tried a different approach, polling her readers' opinions about *St. Nicholas*'s content in an attempt to raise their reading standards by offering more stories in the genres that pleased them most. She clearly did not like the responses, however, for in a subsequent editorial regarding their feedback she gently scolded them: "In this hurrying, busy, nineteenth-century life of ours, your present tastes will change or new tastes develop more rapidly than you can imagine, and *St. Nicholas*, if it is truly to be your magazine, must keep pace with, and even anticipate your growth."[47] Although Dodge continued such efforts throughout her tenure at the magazine, she consistently struggled to align her ambitions with children's interests.[48] As she had lamented to Scudder, "fair ideals . . . get so woefully squeezed under printing and binding presses!"[49]

With *St. Nicholas* authors, Dodge adopted an improvisational approach that affirmed the magazine's ambivalent attitude toward concerns about sensational literature.[50] Unlike the *Companion*, *St. Nicholas* did not institute specific guidelines for either the structure or the content of its fiction. Whereas Ford's contributors received a leaflet outlining the requirements for *Companion* fiction and discouraging creativity, Dodge's contributors received a generalized announcement: the one she sent out in 1873 indicated only that the magazine would be "entirely unsectarian in character" and reiterating many of the goals stated in her "Children's Magazine" article.[51]

St. Nicholas encouraged originality, but Dodge and her staff also maintained strict, though occasionally flexible, standards regarding the magazine's content. She refused to publish anything she found morally offensive, morbid, excessively sentimental, overly didactic or sectarian, or politically divisive. She altered illustrations she feared might offend pious sensibilities: skirts could not billow too widely, Tom Sawyer and Huck Finn could not appear in bare feet because they might be perceived as vulgar, and the cartoon characters known as the Goops could not stick out their tongues lest young readers do the same.[52] She had particularly difficult negotiations with Trowbridge, who favored a grittier style of realism than she would accept. Although she accepted "Fast Friends," she refused to illustrate scenes involving drinking or gambling.[53] After Trowbridge submitted another serial "His One Fault," Dodge's assistant William Fayal Clarke wrote to him, sharing "Mrs. Dodge's hearty appreciation & admiration of the story as a whole" but asking him to shorten an asthma attack, "tone down" a brutal beating, and de-emphasize a character's cruelty toward his wife. The letter emphasized that the editor's requests did not reflect her personal tastes: "Mrs. Dodge appreciates the truth to nature and dramatic value of these, as now described—if written for a book, for older readers—but for 'St. Nicholas' the changes suggested must be an improvement."[54] Regarding the dialect in the story, Clarke told Trowbridge, "St. Nicholas is seriously crippled in the use of dialect by the demands of parents & teachers for strictly grammatical language in the magazine." Ultimately, the parties compromised by having Trowbridge minimize but not completely eliminate the dialect.[55]

THE COMPANION's and St. Nicholas's contrasting approaches to both sensational literature and the regulation of their content established a pattern that continued as the two magazines addressed the broader issue of genteel children's roles in an industrializing and urbanizing nation. Dodge retained her improvised ambivalence on the subject, while Ford remained more doctrinal. As the rhetoric of Comstock and his associates continued to resonate across the nation during the 1870s and 1880s, Ford was adamant that young readers were safest when they stayed close to home.

The Companion had never favored allowing children, particularly younger ones, to wander far from home. The Civil War had reinvigorated this position; and even as commercial motivations after war had led him to portray young Americans who were venturing farther afield, he persisted in arguing that such endeavors harmed their moral development. The primary change he introduced into the *Companion*'s message during 1870s and 1880s was to associate these dangers more precisely with urban environments. While earlier stories had sometimes focused on the moral and physical corruption of cities, he now began presenting these strange and overwhelming environments as the root of the problem, particularly in the case of young men who were transitioning from small towns and rural communities.

Stories about "green" country boys (and occasionally girls) who struggled after moving to the city began appearing in the *Companion* early in the 1870s. The first wave of stories, such as Rufus Sargent's "Dandy Lyon's Visit to New York," suggested how poorly equipped country youths were for survival in the city: on his first day there, Dandy gets lost, is robbed, and is then accused of theft.[56] As the nation sank into an economic depression after the Panic of 1873, the consequences of their ill-preparation became more serious. In Trowbridge's 1877 serial "Awkward Andy: A Story of City Life," a young migrant spends money impetuously, escorts disreputable young women to saloons and theaters, and accrues so many debts that he steals money from his employer and becomes a wanted criminal.[57] The theme of profligacy recurred throughout the genre, allowing Ford to emphasize the dangers of excessive independence for young urban men and occasionally to highlight the value of reliable moral mentorship (most often by mother figures). In most of these stories, the young man ends up dead or disgraced, but protagonists who receive domesticated guidance are more likely to be redeemed.[58]

The *Companion*'s editorials and nonfiction articles presented similar problems but also tried to help young readers solve them. "A Green Boy in Boston" acknowledges that "many a boy who is bright and efficient at home, makes sorry blunders when thrown into new situations, and gets the reputation of being green." The article notes that experience might cure this problem but also attempts to comfort struggling young men by assuring them that poverty is a "great safeguard" against such difficulties because it protects them from attracting the attention of the devious and the dissolute.[59] To reach readers who did not view perpetual poverty as a reasonable solution, a series of editorials titled "Young Men in the City" warn against a focus on acquiring riches and caution youths to avoid entertainments such as the theater.[60] Another article counsels new arrivals to the city to maintain strong connections with their parents so as to increase the probability of honorable behavior, while several other pieces directly suggest that young people should return home.[61]

Gradually, as urbanization accelerated during the 1880s and early 1890s, the *Companion* shifted away from simply discouraging readers from moving to the city toward explaining how they could maintain their moral bearings in such an environment. Ford's fundamental answer was that young people should strive to retain the qualities that his magazine associated with small towns and rural communities. In "Awkward Andy," one of the earliest *Companion* stories to consider this issue, the title character fails to master the sophisticated posturing of his assimilated cousin (a failing that the narrator ascribes to his uncorrupted nature), but his determination and integrity enable him to surpass his peers in the business world.[62] This emphasis on avoiding artifice became the *Companion*'s consistent message. In contrast to 1870s editorials that describe young women who disappear after moving to the city and tell country girls to stay at home, Edgar Fawcett's 1885 serial "A Country Cousin" presents a young orphan who eventually prospers in urban society due to her courage and straightforward nature.[63] Similarly, Amanda M. Douglas's 1893 "Larry" is a coming-of-age tale about a young orphan raised by an adoptive country mother. After Larry learns that his birth family is among the wealthiest in New York, his newfound uncle moves him to the city so that he can assume his rightful place as heir. He encourages Larry to break ties with his modest country friends, but loyalty, intelligence, and determination compel the young man to maintain those bonds. As it happens, those same qualities also vault him into family leadership when his city cousins prove to be incapable of managing the family business.[64]

Even as these stories acknowledged that rural youths might prosper in the city if they could maintain their traditional values, they highlighted another concern: a belief that children reared in urban environments lacked physical, intellectual, and moral strength and thus threatened the nation's future. Whereas Larry and the "country cousin" possess the *Companion*'s traditionally esteemed qualities of honesty, directness, courage, and perseverance, their wealthy city peers are skilled primarily in artifices such as polite conversation, fashion, and dancing, talents that many nineteenth-century genteel Americans saw as dangerous to society as a whole.[65]

The city-born youths in *Companion* stories were often dissipated and disingenuous. One young male in "A Country Cousin" is a "little savage imp" who disparages any opinions that do not agree with his. His sister, who is the same age as her country cousin but appears to be older, is driven by "whims and caprices" and incapable of caring for herself. Much of the blame in this story falls on the parents, who are too busy with business and social obligations to properly raise their children, leaving that responsibility to a corrupt maid and a stoic butler. In "Larry," the young urban men lack both intelligence and ambition, while the young women are so obsessed with fashionable society that the country hero loses interest in their attractions. Other *Companion* stories about wealthy city children emphasize their nervousness, another sign of physical weakness that in some elite Protestant circles became emblematic of the dissipation that urban industrial life had inflicted on the nation's genteel classes.[66]

During this period the *Companion* also occasionally addressed the challenges of impoverished urban children. The story "Poor Little Bobby," for example, describes a newsgirl who dies of exposure while protecting an even smaller child on the streets of New York.[67] Nonfiction articles recommend removing such children to the country, which might cure many of their physical and emotional ailments. For instance, one article describes the Fresh Air Fund, which enabled poor city children to take summer vacations in the country; another lauds Charles Loring Brace's orphan trains, which delivered urban waifs into the homes of rural families.[68] Ford even asked subscriber families living outside the city to help by opening their homes to these children.[69]

These articles reinforced the magazine's broader promotion of the country as an environment that offered both the salutary benefits of traditional middle-class family life and frequent interactions with nature. One of its most frequent celebrators was Charles Asbury Stephens, an assistant editor and contributor to the *Companion* for more than half a century. The son of a Maine farmer, Stephens initially specialized in stories of boys who were hunting, fishing, and exploring the outdoors, which he described as "a wonderful respite from civilization."[70] Through their struggles with nature, these boys learned to overcome physical, mental, and emotional challenges, a concept that foreshadowed the muscular Christian ideals later promoted by Theodore Roosevelt and others.[71] Eventually Stephens expanded his repertoire to include pieces on domestic life in the country, beginning with nonfiction articles such as "Coasting! How to Slide with Girls" in the late 1870s and culminating at the turn of the century with a series called the Old Home Farm stories, which related the adventures of a family of orphans raised by their grandparents on a Maine farm.[72] These stories clearly resonated with the *Companion*'s readers, for they continued in various forms through the 1920s and inspired many readers to trek to the Stephens homestead and search for the individuals they portrayed.[73] The Old Home Farm stories exemplified values of rural living, personal sincerity, home production, and multigenerational family units; and these values continued to be the cornerstone of the *Companion*'s ideology, even as they became less prevalent as a lived experience among Americans of the early twentieth century.[74]

DURING THE 1870s and 1880s, *St. Nicholas* also consistently demonstrated a preference for stories that encouraged young people to live in the country, but its reasoning was different from the *Companion*'s. Ford's foremost concern was the moral corruption of city youth who had not been raised in traditional structures of authority. In contrast, Dodge and her contributors focused on the advantages of alternative environments, just as they had done when they were addressing the issue of sensational fiction. They particularly concentrated on the health benefits of rural living, not so much as a response to the immediate crises of urbanization and industrialization but as a continuation of the magazine's liberal Protestant heritage, which relied on eighteenth- and early nineteenth-century childrearing theories of thinkers such as Bronson Alcott, Johann Pestalozzi, and Jean-Jacques Rousseau.

Like the *Companion*, *St. Nicholas* was concerned about the growing effect of schools on children's lives. Dodge, however, believed that schools offered too much structure rather than too little supervision. Rather than supporting traditional teaching approaches such as rote memorization, she promoted Rousseau's ideal of greater exposure to nature, simple but hearty food, and the nurturing supervision of empathetic adults.[75] Among her writers, Louisa May Alcott was a particular advocate of this child- and nature-centered approach. In her serials "Eight Cousins" and "Jack and Jill," Alcott recommends an unpretentious and active outdoor lifestyle for both boys and girls and warns of the potential for illness if children overexert themselves at their studies. Both serials feature a boy whose excessive reading damages his eyes and his health, and at the end of "Jack and Jill" the children's guardian decides to take them out of school for a few years to "cultivate their bodies and let their minds rest."[76]

Other *St. Nicholas* stories addressed the contrast between urban and rural living, and they, too, extolled the physical benefits of country living rather than emphasized the dangers of city life. Edward Payson Roe's serial "Driven Back to Eden" follows a family of five to a farm in upstate New York, where they move after the father recognizes the health hazards they face in their Manhattan apartment. The stories follow the family's transition from city folk to farmers and is practically a manual for readers who might wish to make the same transition.[77]

Like the *Companion*, *St. Nicholas* supported the efforts of the Fresh Air Fund. Asking young readers for donations to help city children visit the country during the summer, Jack-in-the-Pulpit tells them, "Jack doesn't like to think of poor children in cities at times like this."[78] Nonfiction articles also promoted the moral benefits of country life and emphasized the salutary effects of productive rural trades such as farming. William M. Baker's "Sheep or Silver?" introduces yet another family who decides to move away from the city. Facing the dilemma of whether to focus on mining or herding, the parents choose the latter because it will teach their children to "develop rather than destroy nature." The narrator declares that "a miller or farmer is almost always a happier man than one who goes mining for silver or gold," thus reinforcing the anti-modern message of the genre.[79]

Another group of *St. Nicholas* stories highlighted what it saw as inappropriate aspects of urban industrial culture. They appeared frequently in the magazine during the 1870s, nearly as often as such stories appeared in the *Companion.* However, in keeping with Dodge's editorial approach, the *St. Nicholas* versions generally used humor to mitigate their severity. Celia Thaxter's "The Bear at Appledore," for example, denigrates the commercial impulses of a town's children through the voice of a bear who complains about the way they treat him when he wanders in from the country. One "awful girl" in particular humiliates him by selling tickets so others can watch him do tricks.[80] Even when other stories directly highlighted the differences between city and country youths, they borrowed Dodge's gently subversive strategies. Whereas George MacDonald's "Gone Astray," in the *Companion,* describes a young shepherd's son who goes off to college in Edinburgh and abandons his family, Trowbridge's "Bass Cove Sketches," in *St. Nicholas,* highlights the amusing incompetence of a wealthy city man whose inability to perform the basic outdoorsman tasks of shooting a rifle and rowing a boat confounds a much younger but more capable country boy.[81] *St. Nicholas* authors also handled the shortcomings of female city dwellers with humor. In E. Vinton Blake's "The Dalzells of Daisydown," the heroine returns to the city after a vacation in the country and rebels against her mother's emphasis on fashion and society.[82]

Like Ford, Dodge selected stories that criticized the artifice and physical weakness of male and female city dwellers, but her lighter touch reflected her ambivalence about the values that buttressed the anti-urban position. This ambivalence was evident in early *St. Nicholas* stories such as Trowbridge's serial "Fast Friends" and Elizabeth Stuart Phelps's "How Trotty Went to the Great Funeral," which displayed children successfully overcoming the obstacles of urban living.[83] Soon the magazine's fiction began to present cities as environments filled with advantages as well as challenges. Lucy S. Rider's "Dick Hardin Visits Philadelphia" highlights the novelties that excite a boy during his first visit to the city, where he attends the 1876 Centennial Exposition, the first World's Fair in the United States.[84] Richard Harding Davis's "Midsummer Pirates" praises the "excellent and

varied ... modern features" of city homes.[85] In 1890, William O. Stoddard's
"Crowded Out o' Crofield" became the first *St. Nicholas* serial story to acknowledge that certain young men might advance their careers more effectively in the city, and during the subsequent decade Dodge introduced
more examples of children who were thriving in both modern and ancient
cities.[86]

Nonfiction articles also promoted the opportunities of urban life. According to Charles Barnard's "Young Folks' Fun in Central Park," "country
kids think they have all the fun," but only Central Park has "sports without
end."[87] While recognizing that the city streets were not an appropriate
place for children, his piece, like others in that appeared in the magazine
by the 1890s, celebrated the new parks, gardens, libraries, museums, and
other institutions that were now making cities more enjoyable and healthy
for young urban dwellers. The cornerstone of this trend was the magazine's
1893–94 series on American cities, which was instigated by excitement over
the Columbian Exposition. To display the quality of cultural leadership
now available in the nation's urban environments, Dodge selected esteemed
residents to write eleven profiles of nine cities. They included Senator
Henry Cabot Lodge and author Frances Hodgson Burnett for Washington,
D.C., George Washington Cable for New Orleans, and Thomas Wentworth Higginson for Boston. All shared an interest in progressive reform;
and although none referred explicitly to the emerging City Beautiful movement, their focus on open spaces, natural beauty, and attractive architecture
revealed a common belief that such urban resources could inspire residents
to improve themselves.[88]

In "Boston," Higginson stresses the importance of schools, parks, and
playgrounds in the city's social fabric and focuses on the variety of public
and charitable institutions that oversee its physical, intellectual, and moral
development.[89] Burnett's "The City of Groves and Bowers" concentrates
almost exclusively on Washington, D.C.'s natural beauty, which inspires its
residents to be more "well dressed, well bred and respectable" than those of
other cities. James Ballantine's "Chicago" calls the city's parks its "crowning
glory" and highlights residents' access to game fish and birds within the city
limits.[90] Talcott Williams's "Philadelphia" promotes it as "A City of Homes"
and emphasizes the correlation between the physical layout of a city and the
character of its residents: "The only way to make families comfortable ...
is to put each in a separate house which it owns"; every homeowner is "a
capitalist ... [who] will never be a turbulent striker."[91] In his opinion, Philadelphia's unique capacity to offer homeownership to a broad swath of its
residents makes it a uniquely healthy and safe alternative to country living.

As these articles reveal, *St. Nicholas* was coming to accept that the American city was a respectable, safe environment in which to raise children. The *Companion,* however, was unpersuaded, and Ford continued to focus on the threats posed by social change. Despite their differences, both magazines survived the children's literature crisis of the 1870s and 1880s because their editors made decisions that sustained the long-standing ideals of their respective segments of the industry. During subsequent decades, however, this approach became insufficient. The cultural transformations that continued to sweep through American society introduced new challenges to genteel expectations of children's appropriate social roles, and both magazines struggled to adapt.

CHAPTER 8

Children's Magazines and Modern Childhood

"KEEP THE FAMILY together," repeats Grandma, a character in the opening chapter of the Marshall Saunders's 1903 *Youth's Companion* serial "Chronicles of the Graveleys." Her prodigal granddaughter Margaretta responds, "The old cry! I've heard that ever since I was born. What makes you say it so much?" Grandma explains that her father, while trapped in a burning building, had shouted this statement out the window to a friend, asking the man to carry the message to his wife. Decades later, Grandma is attempting to honor his wishes in the midst of her family's financial crisis. She says, "Keep the family together, . . . and you keep the nation together. Foster national love and national pride, and you increase the brotherhood of man." Her modern granddaughter, moved by this story, provides the lesson's conclusion: "Then the family is the rock on which the nation is built."[1]

"Chronicles of the Graveleys" exemplifies a wave of late nineteenth- and early twentieth-century *Companion* fiction celebrating the importance of family bonds in American society. In the 1890s, the magazine featured a group of stories about weddings and anniversaries, including Caroline Harwood Garland's "A Queer Golden Wedding" (1895) and Eva Wilder Broadhead's "The Wedding Gown of Felisita" (1899).[2] A trend toward family stories began with Charles Asbury Stephens's "Stories of the Old Home Farm" (1902) and by the end of 1903 included Walter Leon Sawyer's "Stories of the Merricks," Gwendolen Overton's "Tales of a Frontier Family," Mary Stewart Cutting's "The Doings of the Harlows," and Mary E. Mitchell's "The Broadening of the Hacketts."[3] In 1905, the magazine published Grace S. Richmond's serial "The Second Violin," which follows the Birch siblings' efforts to keep their home together in their parents' absence.

This story became so popular that it spawned four sequels during the next two years.[4]

Clearly, the *Companion*'s editors felt the need to remind their young audience of the importance of family and marriage, and they were not alone in their concern. By the late 1800s, many genteel Americans believed the nation's families were in a state of crisis. The birth rate was declining, particularly among white Protestants, a condition that inspired fears of "race suicide"; and at the same time, the country's divorce rate was the highest in the world.[5] Yet fears extended beyond these statistics. Industrialization and urbanization had transformed the purpose of genteel American families, eliminating their role as a unit of economic production. This change made it more difficult for parents to control their children's conduct. For a few decades after the Civil War, genteel Americans had managed to use fiction and other entertainments to, in the words of an *Atlantic Monthly* author, "keep our Young American under the thumb of his father and mother without breaking his spirit."[6] By the turn of the century, however, children's exposure to a growing number of outside influences hindered this agenda. Compared to previous generations, children from genteel northern families now attended school for more days per year, and their period of education extended down to kindergarten and up through high school and even college. They participated in extracurricular organizations such as athletic teams, social clubs, and scouting troops. A growing number of advertisers, publishers, retailers, and other consumer industries vied for children's attention; and scientific and social scientific experts offered advice about their psychological and physical development as well as their employment possibilities in the rapidly changing industrial economy.[7]

These changes did not eliminate parental authority over children, or even reduce it substantially, but they did force adults to change their approaches to maintaining control over children's socialization. Although the *Companion* and *St. Nicholas* had flourished for decades by helping parents with this process, they, too, had to reorient their formulas to compete with less didactic sources of entertainment: new toys such as Lincoln Logs and Raggedy Ann dolls, a burgeoning genre of cheap juvenile fiction, and entertainments for older youths ranging from nickelodeons to amusement parks to sporting events. Unlike the challenges of previous decades, these commercial competitors directly threatened the magazines' role as mediators between American families and consumer cultures. By questioning the genteel balance between didacticism and commerce at the heart of these publications, competitors suggested that not all forms of entertainment needed to be instructive, forcing the magazines to restructure their messages to remain relevant to a new generation of young readers.

In addition, the magazines faced a changing literary culture that, like consumer industries, was increasingly questioning the premises of gentility. *St. Nicholas* was particularly affected by this change because it relied more heavily than the *Companion* did on a prestigious roster of fiction writers. Between the end of the Civil War and the first years of the twentieth century, many respected and popular American writers—Harriet Beecher Stowe, Louisa May Alcott, Mark Twain, William Dean Howells, Edith Wharton, Jack London, Sarah Orne Jewett, Rudyard Kipling, and dozens more—had contributed to children's magazines. By 1910, these contributors had largely vanished, replaced by a growing class of workmanlike producers. This shift occurred for a number of reasons. Not only were many more magazines competing for the services of premier writers, but literary authors were growing disillusioned with the genteel conventions of children's fiction. New authors such as Theodore Dreiser and Kate Chopin, and later F. Scott Fitzgerald and William Faulkner (both of whom had read *St. Nicholas* as children), saw these conventions as prudish and socially damaging and sought to replace them with frank examinations of sex, violence, mental illness, and other topics inappropriate for young readers. In part because of their efforts to weaken genteel dominance over American literature, children's fiction became a specialized and less prestigious enclave of the publishing industry.[8]

A change in leadership at both magazines exacerbated these challenges. Following the death of Daniel Sharp Ford in 1899, his lieutenant Edward Stanwood assumed oversight of the *Companion*'s large staff of assistant and associate editors. After Mary Mapes Dodge died in 1905, her longtime assistant, William Fayal Clarke, took control at *St. Nicholas*. Although the new editors retained their predecessors' fundamental values, they struggled to integrate them with contemporary models of youth that reflected the increased social (if not physical or financial) freedoms of early twentieth-century American children.

As its family stories showed, the *Companion* continued its efforts to protect readers from the threats of contemporary society. Yet it also diversified its approach by further subdividing its audience on the basis of gender, class, age, and, for the first time, ethnicity and religion. For older Protestant boys on the cusp of manhood, particularly those from genteel families, the *Companion* still recommended an escape from urban industrial life, either through farming or professional work on the geographic margins of society. For everyone else, including poorer children from immigrant families (whom the *Companion* increasingly pursued as customers), wealthier children, and genteel girls, the magazine promoted incorporation into organizations—not only families but also unions, clubs, sports teams, and boarding schools—that might limit their exposure to society's harmful influences. This focus on the benefits of communal support networks brought the magazine closer to the formula of *St. Nicholas* that reinforced existing hierarchies of gender, class, and race.

St. Nicholas injected more competition and a more gendered approach into its formula. In 1899, the magazine introduced the St. Nicholas League, an organization dedicated to producing, discussing, and judging young readers' writings and artwork. Over the next thirty-seven years, this department became one of its most popular features as young people from all over the nation competed to receive prizes, including publication in the magazine. The next year, Dodge instituted an advertising competition, inviting children to produce copy and illustrations for selected products in a manner designed both to please sponsors and to make children more perceptive consumers.[9] Contests and challenges also began pervading the magazine's fiction, appearing in both professional and athletic settings, with the latter becoming particularly popular during the final decades of the nineteenth century.

Yet surprisingly, given *St. Nicholas*'s previous efforts to establish more gender equity in its fiction, these workplace and sports stories remained predominantly male. Equally remarkable was the traditionally patriarchal *Companion*'s willingness to revisit its gendered views. As it compartmentalized modern children's experiences, it also began offering stories of heroines who play sports and attend college, publishing such fiction far more often than *St. Nicholas* did. During the 1910s, Dodge's successor Clarke did introduce new methods of featuring female characters, employing them as protagonists in a wave of sensationalized historical serials that emerged in response to the growing popularity of series fiction and in domestic stories that portrayed parents as companionate "chums" rather than authority figures.[10]

Since the 1850s, children's magazines had been ardently pursuing male readers. This new focus on female readers was evidence that both the *Companion* and *St. Nicholas* had ceded the commercial vanguard of children's publishing to formats with fewer concerns about balancing entertainment with didacticism. The series fiction genre emerged to fill this vacuum, introducing contemporary, independent young characters who attracted large numbers of young readers. In the early twentieth century, the genre included the Stratemeyer syndicate's immensely popular Rover Boys,

Bobbsey Twins, and Tom Swift books. In contrast to *Companion* stories about quasi-independent boarding school students and young professional men and *St. Nicholas* stories about competent young women from history, series books introduced contemporary characters freely operating in both realistic and fantastic environments while retaining a genteel sensibility.[11] The success of these books reflected a subtle shift in American commercial culture, which was moving away from the view that children's entertainments had to please parents first. This change foreshadowed the decline of this generation of children's magazines, which had thrived on producing the genteel balance that adults wanted for American children and had provided an influential source of cultural authority for those children and their families.

GENTEEL AMERICAN children of the late nineteenth century collectively spent more time away from their families than had any previous generation of middle-class or wealthy children in the nation's history. By 1880, urban school systems were in session an average of nine months per year. Although only about 7 percent of American children between the ages of fourteen and seventeen attended high school by 1890, most who did came from white, urban, middle-class or wealthy households.[12] After-school and summer activities run by YMCAs, schools, or the children themselves kept this cohort occupied among peer groups for much of the day.[13] Homes increasingly featured separate bedrooms for each child as well as playrooms where youngsters could retreat from direct parental supervision.[14]

During the early 1880s, both the *Companion* and *St. Nicholas* began to explore the altered social dynamics that these changes had created. Rather than focusing on stories about individuals or small groups of young people who leave home, the magazines now introduced serial stories examining peer-centered youth cultures that existed beyond parental supervision. Not surprisingly, Ford and Dodge each approached this subject in an ideologically consistent manner.

Ford's *Companion* adopted a skeptical view of these developments. The magazine already had expressed its disapproval of peer groups because of the lack of responsible oversight in such environments.[15] Its new wave of stories concentrated on the moral dangers of competition, which these settings engendered. John Townsend Trowbridge's 1881 serial "The Pocket Rifle," for example, tells the tale of schoolchildren who are participating in an academic contest.[16] In the course of the contest, the students—particularly two boys who are best friends—become increasingly hostile toward and suspicious of each other. Attempts to undermine their competition damage both boys' reputations and eventually endanger their physical safety.[17] Ironically, the *Companion*'s opposition to such competitions peaked at the same time as its premiums program did, which offered prizes to young readers based on the number of new magazine subscribers they acquired. This inconsistency suggests that the magazine's stance on the issue derived from parental concerns rather than Ford's own ideals.

St. Nicholas displayed more confidence in young Americans' ability to self-regulate. Noah Brooks's 1880 serial "The Fairport Nine" introduces a boys' club whose members spend most of their time together, whether playing baseball or celebrating the Fourth of July. They perceive a boy as a "milk-sop" if he sleeps in a bed on the Fourth—a perspective that illustrates the magazine's inclination toward celebrating youthful independence.[18] William O. Stoddard's "Saltillo Boys," another serial about a peer group that freely roams through its local community, reinforced this message. As one of its characters exclaims, "Rules! What do we want with rules? The youngest boy in the lot is over thirteen. I'm sixteen now, and I think I knew enough to be decent, three years ago."[19]

Both magazines tentatively explored more contemporary coming-of-age experiences. Whereas "Fairport" and "Saltillo" depict traditional small-town childhoods, the *Companion*'s "Redmond of the Seventh" (which I discussed in the introduction to part III of this book) explores the peer-centered culture of a large New York City school. Set in the rambunctious, flirtatious environment of Manhattan adolescence, Mrs. Frank Lee's 1888 story focuses on the independent-minded protagonist's clashes with a patriarchal headmaster who prioritizes deference to authority and exercise of self-control.[20] Although Redmond never fully accepts these expectations, with the aid of an empathetic female teacher he learns to respect them. Moreover, his ultimate decision to become a missionary offers an idealistic but improbable conclusion to a late nineteenth-century American childhood.[21] The author's stand on the issue of independence is unclear, and Ford (or his audience) was probably dissatisfied with the story as he avoided tales of other institution-based versions of childhood for more than a decade.

St. Nicholas's early vision of modern childhood was similarly ambivalent, as "Mystery in a Mansion" (1880) makes clear. The only anonymous serial published during Dodge's tenure, the chapters of "Mystery" were all printed in the back half of the magazine at a time when most serials appeared, at least initially, near the beginning of issues.[22] The experimental story introduced many youthful behaviors that later became integral to *St. Nicholas*'s early twentieth-century fiction, such as allowing children to have significant input into family decisions. Like Ford, however, Dodge apparently decided that her late nineteenth-century audience was not ready to embrace such changed representations of American youth, for they did not appear again in the magazine until the 1910s.

"Mystery" focuses on a family's retreat into a pastoral environment. Yet even though the plot and setting are standard *St. Nicholas* fare, the story is among the earliest to focus on older children's familial relationships. The three teenaged Baird children interact collegially with each other and their parents and, in typical *St. Nicholas* fashion, puncture moralism with humor. The two older siblings tease the youngest brother about his carelessness, and the father gently mocks his daughter's vanity when she complains about the state of her hair. The children maintain substantial influence over family decisions. When they object to their father's choice of a seaside vacation, Mr. Baird explains his financial reasons but acquiesces when the siblings develop an alternative plan that satisfies everyone's interests.[23]

"Mystery" also uses the children's banter as a way to acknowledge the audience's cultural sophistication, an approach that was unprecedented in either magazine. In the opening scene, the oldest sibling recites a story that begins, "Once upon a time, there was a man who became rich and famous," a line that her brothers mocks for its predictability. This sequence parodies literary conventions by combining the opening line of most fairy tales with the widely criticized conclusion of many dime novels. The story the girl tells belongs to neither genre, but the joke is an authorial wink toward readers' capacity to recognize such clichés. Later in the scene, after a son describes how his teacher has blamed a student's poor grammar on his inadequate home life, the father quips, "It won't—will not, I mean—do to allow Fred to feel that his home interests are against his education." Again, the author presumes that the audience will understand a satirical remark about the convention of home as the primary site of children's instruction.[24]

Dodge's acknowledgment that some of her audience possessed such cultural understanding belied traditional liberal Protestant beliefs that adults could mold children as they deemed appropriate. Yet subsequent stories suggest that she believed her adult subscribers were still not prepared for the idea.[25] After "Mystery," such modern children disappeared from the magazine for nearly two decades; and when they returned, assessments of their propriety were more ambiguous.[26] By the time *St. Nicholas* began regularly reproducing such companionate parent-child relationships, consumer industries' inroads into American homes had converted such sophistication into a quality that many genteel circles admired.[27]

AFTER RETREATING from this experimental approach to modernity, Dodge and (slightly later) Ford took up a subject that enabled them to depict contemporary childhood in a manner more palatable to adult subscribers: the entry of young men into the workforce. Genteel Americans of all religious backgrounds expected older boys to enter public life as workers. Yet disagreement about appropriate employment options, and the magazines' suggestions about jobs illustrate their ambivalence about modern forms of youth, even in the context of this conventional topic.

For boys from late nineteenth-century genteel American families, preparing to move into the workplace meant considering a growing number of career choices, many of which required specialized training or extended schooling. Because such decisions often required more information than fathers could competently offer, both the *Companion* and *St. Nicholas* offered themselves as authorities on this subject—their first extended attempt to provide practical business advice.[28] During the 1880s, each magazine produced a series of articles aimed at young men, whose emerging need for career guidance revealed both the complexity of their choices and the diminution of parental control.[29] *St. Nicholas* made the latter point clear in the first article of George J. Manson's 1884 series "Ready for Business; or, Choosing an Occupation: A Series of Practical Papers for Boys." Explaining that "father . . . is no authority on this matter," the author presents himself as an expert who can provide "an inside view of various trades and businesses" to help young men select the most suitable profession.[30] He refrains from offering advice on how to succeed in those industries; instead, he supplies information about opportunities in contemporary professions such as electrical engineering and architecture as well as more traditional jobs such as boat building and captaining a ship.

The contrast between Manson's articles and the *Companion* series "Just the Boy That's Wanted" demonstrates how the magazines applied their distinct editorial formulas to the issue of employment. The *Companion's* series did not appear until 1889, five years after *St. Nicholas's*, a gap that indicates the magazine's lingering resistance to the integration of young men into the industrial economy. When articles did appear, most focused on traditional professions such as medicine, law, and the clergy, none of which appeared in Manson's series. While *St. Nicholas* focused on providing young readers with career information, the *Companion* emphasized the character traits they needed to succeed in the job. This approach enabled Ford to reinforce the magazine's traditional values rather than emphasize the need to adapt to cultural changes. Finally, while Manson, a journeyman writer, wrote all the articles in the *St. Nicholas* series, the *Companion* hired prominent specialists to discuss their own fields, including Massachusetts Supreme Court justice Oliver Wendell Holmes, Jr.; *Nation* and *New York Evening Post* editor E. L. Godkin; and prominent clergyman Lyman Abbott.[31] Thus, as Dodge adopted the corporate technique of branding the magazine itself as the trustworthy source, Ford continued to prefer placing authority in the hands of individuals rather than in institutions or communities.[32]

In addition to publishing nonfiction about career choices, both magazines began using fiction to address young men's employment options. (No stories about girls' career decisions appeared in either magazine until the 1890s.) Once again, *St. Nicholas* addressed the subject first. Its early stories generally guide boys away from business, using whimsical humor to emphasize how poorly prepared they are for entrepreneurship.[33] Later tales shift toward reluctant acceptance of this pursuit, either by showing boys who develop business skills only in emergency situations or by rewarding their entrepreneurial instincts even after they fail.[34]

The *Companion,* meanwhile, incorporated the subject into its genteel sensational template, highlighting the prevalence of unscrupulous business practices to discourage boys from becoming entrepreneurs. Ford often employed the trope of a son who is struggling to vindicate a father who has been vanquished physically or psychologically by a rival, most often a former assistant. This device emphasized parents' inability to protect children in hostile business environments as well as the danger of trusting individuals outside the family.[35]

Both magazines steered boys toward productive rather than entrepreneurial occupations, a decision that mirrored much of the advice literature of the period.[36] In the early 1880s, the *Companion* suggested that "the trades are nearer the professions than some would like to admit" and counseled boys to become mechanics or farmers because "the professions are overcrowded."[37] It also concentrated on the laboring classes. For example, George H. Bassett's "What One Man Can Do" profiles the work of the Grand Central Station dispatcher, and several serial stories from this period argued that blue-collar vocations were crucial to both the nation and young men's character development.[38] This focus enabled Ford to expand the *Companion*'s appeal to working-class audiences, affirm the moral benefits of physical labor, and create new settings for his successful story template. For instance, W. C. Grinnell's "Perils of a Linesman's Life" highlights the important work of laying the nation's new technological infrastructure, sharing tales of adventure and physical risk not associated with occupations such as banking and law.[39]

The *Companion* did not regularly produce fiction about young white-collar workers until 1897, when it ran a yearlong series written by members of these professions. Beginning with "Stories by Clergymen," the magazine offered three or four weeks' worth of tales by doctors, journalists, lawyers, and professors.[40] Yet these stories had little to do with the professions. Instead, the authors offered antimodern messages, emphasizing their encounters with marginalized individuals who displayed traditional values of selflessness, generosity, and loyalty. In "A Young Savage," for example, journalist P. Y. Black describes witnessing a young Indian boy's internal conflict between his desire for civilization and his tribal and racial loyalty. (The boy literally dies in the crossfire.) Homer Greene's "Starry Vint's Defence" celebrates the patriotism of a deaf-mute who defends the honor of the American flag.[41]

Even *Companion* stories that highlighted the work of modern young professionals generally did so in settings divorced from modern society. In Fanny M. Johnson's "Young Knight of Honor," a reporter stays in town to edit the local newspaper after every other healthy person flees an epidemic; and in Hayden Carruth's "Track's End," a young bank assistant protects a North Dakota community's assets from robbers and vandals during a snowbound winter when the rest of the respectable population has abandoned the town.[42] While celebrating the young men's efforts, these 1890s tales retained the *Companion*'s opposition to urbanization. In fact, the magazine's stories from this period show only immigrant and working-class youths achieving success in modern urban environments. The pattern demonstrates Ford's continuing emphasis on convincing youths with viable alternatives to avoid the dangers and temptations of urban industrial America.[43]

Dodge did not share his inherent suspicion of modernity but integrated elements of industrial society into *St. Nicholas*'s stories about young men's work. Her early attempts in the 1870s reinforced the magazine's interests in science and technology. In addition to publishing biographies of scientists (part of a popular movement of promoting such men as masculine ideals), she selected fiction that celebrated boys who had scientific and technological inclinations.[44] According to Major Traverse's nonfiction article "Something about Railroads," a civil engineer is "the genii of the age." Likewise, Trowbridge's serial "The Young Surveyor" features Jack Hazard, the prototypical *St. Nicholas* boy hero, as he teaches a frontier family to lay pipes for drinking and irrigation water using principles of engineering.[45]

These idealizations, however, did not lead *St. Nicholas* to embrace all aspects of the expanding industrial economy. Instead, Dodge, like Ford, distinguished between the value of productive work and the dangers of entrepreneurship. By the early 1890s, stories occasionally focused on boys who were using science in ways that were antithetical to the magazine's values. Whereas characters such as Jack Hazard had used technology to establish themselves as independent workingmen, newer protagonists employed it to gain quick wealth or personal advancement. Brander Matthews's "Tom Paulding (A Tale of Treasure Trove in the Streets of New York)," for example, satirizes the magazine's more sensational competitors, but its story still ends with a boy who uses engineering techniques to recover his great-grandfather's long-lost treasure from a vacant Harlem lot. Although the money saves the family home and sends Tom to engineering school, the story's presentation of science as an avenue to riches conveys a more consumer-driven perspective than Dodge previously had promoted.[46]

St. Nicholas did return to its original ideal of science as an instrument for bettering society rather than for gaining celebrity or wealth, even as its editors set its early twentieth-century stories within the context of an industrial economy in which youths more often worked for large corporations than for themselves. F. Lovell Coombs's 1909–10 "Young Railroaders" series, for example, focuses on a group of friends who are lower-tiered employees of a large railroad line. Like most adventure stories, these tales center on the boys' bravery and cool-headedness, but they also highlight the youths' technological abilities, which repeatedly save the conglomerate from disaster.[47] The heroes always place the company's welfare above their own safety, as in "A Race Through the Flames," in which a young engineer drives a train through a forest fire to deliver goods on time.[48]

Thus, when science reemerged as *St. Nicholas*'s preferred vehicle for integrating young men into industrial society, their ideal role shifted from independent worker to loyal company man. This reflected the workplace realities of most genteel young American men at the beginning of the twentieth century. Popular representations of scientists and engineers as individual achievers had always reflected aspiration rather than actual experience, and by the turn of the century, even the promotion of such ideals abated as these experts increasingly worked on large-scale projects funded by corporate wealth.[49] This emphasis on collective action not only meshed with *St. Nicholas*'s long-standing editorial philosophy but also paralleled an experience familiar to most of the magazine's readers by the 1910s: athletic competition.

DURING THE late nineteenth century, sports became an integral part of American childhood; and their appearance in the *Companion* and *St. Nicholas* was a crucial element of the magazines' attempt to reorient themselves toward more contemporary representations of American youth. Yet here, too, both magazines revealed continuing anxieties about the transition. In the 1870s and early 1880s, sports had been an occasional but not integral aspect of the world that *St. Nicholas* was presenting to readers.[50] Athletics promoted crucial elements of the magazine's approach to child-rearing, including communal effort and outdoor exercise, so their relatively infrequent appearance during these years may indicate a lack of audience demand. For Ford, however, the subject was problematic. Team sports promoted collective rather than individual responsibility, and many orthodox Protestants derided them as at best a distraction and at worst a source of moral corruption due to the close association between sports and gambling. The *Companion* expressed both of these opinions in editorials published during the late 1870s and early 1880s.[51] Nonetheless, by the end of the 1880s, both magazines dramatically expanded their presentations of sports, each in a manner that reinforced their own editorial philosophies.

St. Nicholas initially linked athletics with two of its favorite subjects: science and patriotism. In 1885, George B. M. Harvey's "How Science Won the Game" explained the physics of throwing a curve ball and, conversely, how sports could motivate boys to study.[52] A few years later Mrs. Burton Harrison's "Washington as an Athlete" described the president's passion for sports and argued that athletics helped mold him into the man who led both an army and a government.[53] "Washington" exemplified *St. Nicholas*'s most frequent justification for sports: the physical, moral, and intellectual benefits they offered to the nation's young men. For instance, Richard Harding Davis's "Richard Carr's Baby" focuses as much on the Princeton's football star's effort to use sports to strengthen a young fan as it does on his athletic accomplishments.[54] Beginning in 1889, Walter Camp, "the father of American football" and director of the Yale athletic program, wrote a series of articles describing the rules and physical benefits of various games, and Theodore Roosevelt promoted his vision of strenuous masculinity in his article "Buffalo Hunting" and a series of biographies of prominent American outdoorsmen.[55]

The *Companion* adopted similar arguments when it began to reverse its position on sports in the late 1880s. However, in a surprising decision that foreshadowed its early twentieth-century editorial policies, the magazine began this reversal by praising girls' athletic activities such as ice skating and swimming.[56] By the early 1890s, the genre expanded to include boys; and in an implicit acknowledgment of his changing policy, Ford published stories in which teachers and students combined to convince parents of the physical and moral benefits of sports.[57] His editorials took a similar approach, endorsing baseball as a game that calls into "vigorous action a larger number of muscles than almost any other" and even supporting the controversial game of football, arguing that "grownups should be glad boys favor it so strongly . . . [because it] promotes manliness of bearing, courage and 'push.'"[58]

His justification, like the association *St. Nicholas* was drawing between sports and Ivy League institutions, suggests that the magazines' growing interest in athletics derived at least partly from genteel concerns about white Protestants' capacity to maintain dominance over the transformed political and commercial environments of the late nineteenth century.[59] An 1889 *Harper's* article encapsulated concerns about this group's physical enervation:

> A hundred years ago there was more done to make our men and women hale and vigorous than there is to-day. Over eighty per cent of all our men then were farming, hunting, or fishing, rising early, out all day in the pure, bracing air, giving many muscles very active work, eating wholesome food, retiring early, and so laying in a good stock of vitality and health. But now hardly forty per cent are farmers, and nearly all the rest are at callings—mercantile, mechanical, or professional—which do almost nothing to make one sturdy or enduring.[60]

Perceptions of physical malaise instigated speculations about "race suicide" as birth rates fell among the prosperous classes but not the working-class or minority communities in the United States.[61] Sports offered a direct response to these problems, and their popularity also served the needs of evangelical Christian communities, which were concerned that religion had come to be seen as too "feminized."[62] This combination of factors persuaded Ford, like many Americans of the period, to shift toward advocating athletics.

Indeed, *Companion* stories of the late 1890s portrayed sports as a means of developing in boys the aggression and poise they needed to succeed in the industrial economy, a link that *St. Nicholas* generally did not make for another decade. In "Captain Benson's Last Rally," for example, author Frank H. Spearman suggests that students who participate in athletics are disciplined, self-motivated youths who will make superior citizens.[63] Other stories of the era focus less idealistically on how performances on the football gridiron or baseball diamond might lead to work opportunities.[64] One tale about a football star, Jesse Lynch Williams's "The Man in the Window," explicitly links these pursuits, arguing that "sports helped him to become a better worker."[65]

Ford occasionally made this connection in the other direction. In "Tales of the Toilers: At the Whitstone Mill," author Ray Stannard Baker suggests that the mill's labor leader "would have made a great stroke in a varsity crew."[66] However, most of the *Companion*'s sports stories focused on wealthy youths who were competing for elite preparatory schools. In fact, after the turn of the century, nearly all of them were written by Arthur Stanwood Pier, an assistant editor at the magazine and a teacher at St. Paul's School in Concord, New Hampshire. Pier set his tales at a fictional school called St. Timothy's; and while one story does describe his hero Clark Harding as "democratic," that assessment refers only to his tolerance for wealthy boys from less sophisticated backgrounds.[67]

Pier's St. Timothy's stories display boys who are learning how to succeed as part of a team both on and off the field.[68] Yet like *Companion* articles that supported women's participation in athletics and narratives about working-class Americans such as Baker's "At the Whitstone Mill," they also reflect a broader editorial policy restricting such collective activities, athletic or otherwise, to groups (such as women and elite men) who did not need to participate in the industrial workforce or to working-class Americans who needed organizational help to raise themselves to genteel levels of economic stability and social respectability. Stories about non-elite genteel young men continued to focus on their individual pursuit of careers, particularly on their ability to overcome obstacles on their own.[69]

This division of young men's experiences by class distinguished the *Companion*'s approach from *St. Nicholas*'s. Dodge and her successors generally targeted a wealthier, more educated audience and thus predominantly offered stories about students rather than young laboring men. Yet even when the magazine presented boys who were establishing themselves as newsboys or railroad workers, they succeeded partly through the support of some form of community.[70] Interestingly, *St. Nicholas* did not extend this pattern into girls' sports stories as the *Companion* did. Thus, both magazines diverged from their standard approaches when addressing appropriate roles for young women in modern American society.

BY THE late nineteenth century, genteel American girls were beginning to gain some of the freedom to roam beyond domestic environments that their male counterparts had achieved decades earlier. In about 1880, the novelist Henry James noted unhappily that Boston's schoolgirls were so pervasive as to be "in possession of the public scene."[71] A historian of girlhood during this period agrees with James's assessment that young women's growing public presence could be attributed to their extended time at school.[72] The

Companion drew similar conclusions, and in 1880s its editorials and articles began to address the topic of female education and its role in preparing girls for modern American life. Some of these pieces advocated distinct curricula for girls, claiming that young women did not need to learn classical languages as boys did but more "practical" skills such as sewing and cooking. Others openly discussed "The Girl's Problem," counseling parents to either "resolv[e] her back into a state of unquestioning and uncomplained of dependence, or [help] her to independence on the same broad and general lines by which boys reach that desired and desirable goal."[73] During this decade, the *Companion* did not declare which course it preferred.

St. *Nicholas* more actively supported the expansion of girls' prospects during this period, although it focused more on economic opportunities than on education. An 1883 biography of artist Elizabeth Butler noted that marriage did not interfere with her work, implying that author was encouraging young women to continue their artistic endeavors after marriage.[74] Elizabeth Stuart Phelps's article "Supporting Herself" went farther, telling girls they should prioritize family and marriage but also develop skills to support themselves in case they ever needed to do so.[75] Such practical advice reflected Dodge's own experiences as an impoverished widow, but St. *Nicholas* did not return to this topic very often in subsequent years.

Both publications initially addressed the subject primarily through nonfiction, but during the 1880s St. *Nicholas* began to present stories about young women who were building communities that encouraged them to expand their ambitions beyond home duties and social gatherings. In "Nan's Revolt," for example, author Rose Lattimore Alling introduces girls who declare "treason on polite society" and determine to become useful by securing jobs.[76] By the 1890s, these communities became more institutionalized; and in 1895, female college students made their first appearance in St. *Nicholas.* The heroines of Jessie M. Anderson's serial "The Three Freshman: Ruth, Fran and Nathalie" display traditionally feminine instincts for homemaking, but they also read ancient languages, take rhetoric classes, and produce plays that lampoon Socrates. The author balances these impulses throughout the narrative, culminating with Ruth's announcement that she wants to become a doctor, though she immediately explains that "she doesn't want to do anything in the women's rights line."[77]

The *Companion* largely avoided specific examples of modern girlhood until the 1890s. When Ford did venture into this field, he focused predominantly on stories about the lives of working girls, a decision that both distinguished such activities from the realm of genteel femininity and continued his efforts to expand his audience into the laboring classes. These young urban women helped to support their families and developed a small degree of economic independence by working in factories, department stores, and other venues that needed cheap labor.[78] In 1898, the *Companion* ran a series of laudatory stories about such girls that reinforced its growing interest in collective activities (except for middle-class males) by highlighting the clubs they created for both social and educational purposes.[79]

Yet the *Companion* offered more for female readers than a working-class equivalent of the stories in *St. Nicholas*. In fact, it surpassed its elite contemporary in the variety of representations it offered to turn-of-the-century young women. It occasionally presented independent girls who achieved commercial success, although usually, as in *St. Nicholas*, such stories involved emergent circumstances that required them to save the family business.[80] More often, young women thrived as nurses, teachers, reporters, and artists thanks to the support of various peer communities.[81]

The 1897 Alice Balch Abbot story "How Cousin Marian Helped" had established Dodge's template for *St. Nicholas*'s discussion of girls' participation in sports.[82] While it supported the idea, it kept such endeavors out of both the main storyline and the accompanying illustrations. In contrast, by the early twentieth century, the *Companion* began to consistently promote girls' athletic and educational endeavors, perhaps because Ford's death in 1899 had shifted control of the magazine to a new generation of editors. After 1902, *Companion* stories and pictures regularly promoted sports as a means of strengthening girls' bodies and characters.[83] The magazine applied a similar logic to a new argument that college education could benefit girls whose families could afford it.[84] While earlier *Companion* stories had presented college girls primarily as members of the social elite, this new genre described mentally and morally self-disciplined young women who became doctors and lawyers.

The caveat to such portrayals was the *Companion*'s insistence that these pioneers should reinvest their skills in domestic activities, a demand it never made of male professionals. Women who became doctors, nurses, or librarians in *Companion* stories inevitably returned to their small towns so that their entire community could benefit from their knowledge.[85] These women were similarly expected to use their learning to support the family. As one editorial opined, "whatever criticisms may be made on women as scholars, none can be made on those women who dedicate their scholarship to the service of the home."[86] Yet even with these restrictions, the *Companion*'s presentation of such female models legitimized girls' ambitions to pursue educational and work opportunities in the world beyond their homes.

Furthermore, as young women in *Companion* and *St. Nicholas* stories returned home with new skills, experiences, and interests, they altered the culture of their traditional familial environments. One example of this shift occurred in the *Companion* family stories that I introduced at the beginning of this chapter. These serials focused primarily on the families' girls, who assumed substantial responsibilities within and outside the household. In "Chronicles of the Graveleys," for example, the sister becomes a political activist and reformer, lobbying the mayor and the police chief for a new park in the poorest section of the city.[87] Young women characters were also displaying more interest in the pursuit of leisure. Early twentieth-century stories were filled with dances, sporting events, and other peer activities, and the *Companion* even eased its edict against romance as long as the affair resulted in marriage.[88] In *St. Nicholas* during the 1910s, young women also became the heroines of adventure and mystery serials, although the magazine either kept these stories situated in the past or restricted the heroines' movements to home, school, or summer camp environments. (A heroine of Augusta Huiell Seaman's "The Sapphire Signet" is literally confined to a wheelchair.)[89]

As young magazine characters assumed more active roles within their families and communities, representations of traditionally authoritarian parent-child relationships became untenable. This issue was a particular concern in stories about girls; the magazines were already featuring boys' actions outside the home. *St. Nicholas* girls often described their parents as "real chums" or "best friends," and the *Companion* also shifted toward a more companionate dynamic in its family stories, particularly those about leisure activities.[90] In an episode of Mary Stewart Cutting's "The Doings of the Harlows" (1903), the father finds his daughter an escort for the school dance, an impulse that is reversed in an installment of Margaret Ashmun's "Stories of the Carleton Family" (1916), when a daughter gives up her own consumer desires to buy concert tickets for her parents.[91] This story's inversion of parent and child roles exemplifies how far the *Companion* had diverged from its traditional formula by the 1910s.

In the decades before World War I, both *St. Nicholas* and the *Companion* had shifted their approaches to match the pace of change in American children's lives. Magazine stories now incorporated companionate familial relationships; described educational, athletic, and workplace opportunities for boys and girls; and introduced an expanding array of leisure activities. These changes, however, were still contained within the magazines' traditional genteel framework, which required their editors to balance commercial appeal with lingering Protestant anxiety about market influences on children. As twentieth-century commercial products for children began to move away from such moral concerns, both magazines became increasingly anachronistic and struggled to maintain cultural relevance and financial stability.

Epilogue

WHEN THE United States entered World War I in April 1917, *St. Nicholas* launched a new department, "For Country and for Liberty: Patriotic Service for American Boys and Girls," which announced, "The boys and girls of America are as eager as their elders to do their share in this great conflict, and it is the earnest wish of *St. Nicholas* to aid them in every way in this endeavor." The editors suggested that children could volunteer for the Red Cross or serve in the U.S. Boys' Working Reserve, which the U.S. Department of Labor had formed to help solve the wartime farm-labor shortage. They showed photographs of "The Girls in Khaki" as they trained at the National Service School.[1] They presented stories of young people's military heroism in France and at home, describing a submarine spotter in the North Atlantic, a female ambulance driver, girls who helped harvest wheat, and a thirteen-year-old boy who supplied bread for two villages.[2] British lieutenant general Tom Bridges summarized *St. Nicholas*'s perspective: "The huge organization which the nation must erect, if it is to carry on war with success, involves a great increase in the number of those who are now serving the state. There is much work to be done in which quite young persons are as efficient as their elders."[3]

Although the *Youth's Companion* produced eye-catching patriotic covers during the war, it was less aggressive in its call to action and made fewer efforts to use the war for dramatic purposes. Until March 1918, the editors offered no suggestions for how young Americans could assist the war effort—almost a year after *St. Nicholas* had first begun focusing on the subject.[4] The *Companion* presented few fictional stories about the conflict and none that focused on American youth's efforts overseas.[5] In general,

194 Epilogue

the war and children's involvement in it played a much smaller role in the content of the *Companion* than it did in *St. Nicholas*.

The two magazines' contrasting approaches to the national war effort were consistent with their long-standing editorial formulas. *St. Nicholas*, with its optimistic and confident liberal Protestant perspective on childhood, had from its inception worked to integrate young Americans into the nation's public cultures and had embraced community and collective action as the best instruments for successfully adapting genteel childrearing practices to the changing conditions of an urbanizing, industrializing society. In contrast, the *Companion* had begun with an orthodox Protestant belief in innate depravity; and though its emphasis on the sinfulness of youth had faded over the course of the nineteenth century, its anxiety about nondomestic influences and its emphasis on personal responsibility continued to lead the editors to marginalize public collective action, which they saw as appropriate only for wealthy and feminine segments of American society. Young men were supposed to rely on their individual skills and character to improve their station and their society, for the *Companion*'s cautionary perspective toward the integration of youth into public life had developed into a perception that boys who were attempting to establish themselves could not trust the motives of individuals from outside their families.[6]

Yet even as the two publications continued to adhere to the opposing ideological perspectives that the children's magazine industry had used to instruct and entertain young Americans for nearly a century, their approaches to World War I revealed the extent to which genteel standards for addressing young readers had changed over that period. The Civil War began in 1861, but children's magazines barely mentioned the conflict during that first year, preferring to adopt a strategy that, by 1917, *St. Nicholas* believed was appropriate for only the very youngest children: "to protect them as far as possible from any intimate knowledge of the horrors which war always carries in its train."[7] The Civil War–era strategy had been the product of a prevailing belief in the power of gentility among liberal and orthodox white Protestants. By the turn of the century, though, this genteel perspective was an impediment: with continued economic expansion, Americans were increasingly less threatened by the role of consumer culture in their lives.

In terms of children, this shift was evident in a number of new commercial practices, including the introduction of children's sections into department stores and the emergence of advertisements aimed directly at young consumers.[8] In the children's publishing industry, one of the clearest signals was the growth of series books. This genre of fiction, which generally follows the adventures of the same characters through a number of volumes, dates back in the United States to Jacob Abbott's 1830s Rollo books. In the early 1900s, however, a new generation of publishers, led by the New Jersey entrepreneur and author Edward Stratemeyer, used the concept to seize the attention of young American readers and take control of the industry away from children's magazines.

Stratemeyer, like children's magazine editors from previous generations, had struggled to find an appropriate avenue for his talents and ambitions. Beginning his career as a store clerk, he got his start in publishing by ghostwriting juvenile novels for famous authors such as Horatio Alger and Oliver Optic. Eventually he produced some fairly successful series under his own name, and he edited a boys' story paper. In 1905, he began to create what one scholar has described as a "production factory for series books," contracting with writers to produce books based on outlines he had created under pseudonyms he had selected.[9] Such a process was not new: before the Civil War, Samuel Goodrich had employed Nathaniel Hawthorne and other writers to do similar work on his Peter Parley books. But as Ford had done in the children's magazine industry from the 1860s through the 1890s, Stratemeyer changed the scale of this process. Between 1910 and 1930, his syndicate averaged thirty-one titles per year, and his most popular series eventually included as many as a hundred volumes each.[10]

Those series, which featured the Bobbsey Twins and Tom Swift and later the Hardy Boys and Nancy Drew, were not quality literature. Many educators hated them. Franklin K. Mathiews, chief librarian for the Boy Scouts of America, exclaimed, with a hyperbolic ire that recalled Anthony Comstock's, that such literature was "Blowing Out the Boy's Brains."[11] Yet these intentionally formulaic books sold millions of copies because they offered American children representations of youthful independence at a level that children's magazines, constrained by traditional genteel values, refused to match.

One of Stratemeyer's earliest endeavors, the Old Glory series, signaled his intentions. First published in 1898, the books follow the exploits of three brothers during the Spanish-American War. The first volume, *Under Dewey at Manila; or, The War Fortunes of a Castaway,* describes a boy's transformation from a castaway into a soldier; and the next five show young Americans fighting for their nation in a dramatic yet unrealistic manner— one that both the *Companion* and *St. Nicholas* were still refusing to imitate two decades later.[12] Stratemeyer's first huge success, the Rover Boys series, advanced his formula by making his young protagonists' adventures increasingly improbable. The first volume, *The Rover Boys at School; or, the Cadets of*

Putnam Hall, keeps its heroes relatively contained, but subsequent volumes send them (among other adventures) alone down the Hudson River to rescue a girl and to Africa to rescue their father.[13]

To an extent, Stratemeyer's series combined Ford's and Dodge's philosophies about the best way to reach young readers. Like the *Companion,* they favored the sensational, unrealistic plotlines featured in working-class publications such as story papers and the penny press; like *St. Nicholas,* they displayed an unwavering confidence in the capacity of young people to overcome these fantastic circumstances. They departed from these formulas by continuing to loosen the constraints that genteel society had imposed on respectable youth. Whereas the magazines allowed only marginalized children from poor or nonwhite families to act independently in stories set in contemporary American society, Stratemeyer featured boys, and eventually girls, from genteel homes who traveled the world—in Tom Swift's case, even flew above it—without adult oversight.

It is difficult to determine why series books moved away from gentility earlier than children's magazines did. Ford's death in 1899 and Dodge's in 1905 meant that both the *Companion* and *St. Nicholas* had a new generation of editors in the years when Stratemeyer was launching his career. Yet like the writers who predominantly contributed to the magazines after 1910, these new editors were professional but not visionary. Unlike Stratemeyer, both Edward Stanwood at the *Companion* and William Fayal Clarke at *St. Nicholas* were longtime assistants who had trained within the corporate bureaucracy that was standardizing the publishing industry. In their new positions, they emphasized continuity rather than the constant adaptation that had marked the successful tenures of their mentors.

After World War I, as the nature of childhood continued to change, this choice became increasingly problematic. Young Americans were spending more time in school and in extracurricular programs such as scouting. They had more access to entertainments such as movies and radio, and the spread of automobiles gave older youths more physical independence. These activities, along with a growing divide in subject matter between adult and children's fiction, meant that families spent less time reading together, a trend that further weakened children's magazines, which had traditionally been a conduit between family and commercial interests.[14] Publishers responded by creating specialized magazines for young readers—for instance, *American Boy* and the *American Girl,* which chronicled the nation's booming scouting movements—a shift that inflicted more damage on the *Companion* and *St. Nicholas.*[15]

As (in one historian's words) "the Victorian taint of sin associated with consumer desire" faded, the industry's two behemoths gradually became anachronisms.[16] Both survived temporarily on their reputations, but their slow declines became precipitous during the 1920s. The *Companion,* ironically, was purchased in 1925 by Ellery Sedgwick, the publisher responsible for revitalizing the *Atlantic Monthly,* the liberal Protestant institution that had launched *Our Young Folks* in 1865 as a potential competitor for Ford's ascendant magazine. Sedgwick's purchase may have been a sentimental attempt to rescue a dying industry giant, but the *Companion* lasted for only four more years under his management, discontinuing in 1929 after 102 years of publication. *St. Nicholas*'s final stage began in 1927, when Clarke retired after twenty-two years as editor and more than half a century at the magazine. Six editors followed him during the next thirteen years, but the magazine ceased publication in 1940; and a seventh editor failed to resurrect it in 1943.

No subsequent periodicals achieved a level of authority comparable to these fallen institutions. Successful twentieth-century publications such as *Highlights* and *Cricket* carried on elements of their agendas (*Cricket* explicitly presented itself as a successor to *St. Nicholas*), but the production of children's reading had become an enclave for academic and literary specialists; thus, the magazines garnered much smaller market shares and less public interest that their nineteenth-century predecessors had.[17] Like the genteel cultures that had spawned them, those predecessors, with their combined service to adult and young readers, were part of the nation's transition from a set of predominantly rural, localized producer societies into a compilation of more urban, industrial, and centralized consumer cultures. Although its peak influence was past, the children's magazine industry had helped white Protestant families adapt their standards of children's behavior to the conditions of those cultures. In doing so, it had established a basis from which twentieth- and twenty-first-century adults would continue to contest the commercial roles of young people in American society.

NOTES

ABBREVIATIONS

JM	*Juvenile Miscellany*
OYF	*Our Young Folks*
SN	*St. Nicholas*
YC	*Youth's Companion*
YF	*Youth's Friend*

Introduction

1. "George Cook," *Teacher's Offering, or Sabbath Scholar's Magazine* (November 1823): 5–6.

2. Frank Luther Mott, *A History of American Magazines*, vol. 1, *1741–1850* (1930; Cambridge: Belknap Press of Harvard University Press, 1957), 144.

3. Katherine Carleton, "Dorothy the Motor Girl," *SN* 38 (May 1911): 627.

4. Frank Luther Mott, *A History of American Magazines*, vol. 3, *1865–1885* (Cambridge: Harvard University Press, 1938), 501.

5. Bernard Wishy has argued that "nationally read writers" for children (for instance, Lydia Sigourney and Jacob Abbott) "gradually abandoned much of the orthodoxy of their forefathers," while Anne Scott Macleod has claimed that "the children of children's fiction, rational, sober, and imperfect at the beginning of the nineteenth century, had become innocent, charming and perfect" by the onset of the twentieth. Neither author, however, considers the continued orthodoxy of the *Youth's Companion*, which persisted into the twentieth century. See Bernard Wishy, *The Child and the Republic: The Dawn of American Child Nurture* (Philadelphia: University of Pennsylvania Press, 1968), 21; and Anne Scott MacLeod "From Rational to Romantic: The Children of Children's Literature in the Nineteenth Century," *Poetics Today* 13 (spring 1992): 141.

6. "Address to the Young," *JM* 1 (September 1826), iii; Gillian Avery, *Behold*

the Child: American Children and Their Books, 1621–1922 (Baltimore: Johns Hopkins University Press, 1994), 96–114.

7. Mott, *A History of American Magazines*, 1:144.

8. My focus on the cultural conditions in which these magazines' formulas were produced was inspired by Richard Brodhead's call for attention to "literature's working conditions—the history of the diverse and changing worlds that have been constructed around writing in American social life" and indeed by much of the scholarship in the field known as the history of the book. See Richard H. Brodhead, *Culture of Letters: Scenes of Reading and Writing in Nineteenth-Century America* (Chicago: University of Chicago Press, 1995), 8; and Cathy N. Davidson, "Toward a History of Books and Readers," and Robert Darnton, "What Is the History of Books?," both in *Reading in America: Literature and Social History*, ed. Cathy N. Davidson (Baltimore: Johns Hopkins University Press, 1989), intro. and chap. 1. On the importance of editorial formula as historical evidence, see John G. Cawelti, *Adventure, Mystery, and Romance: Formula Stories As Art and Popular Culture* (Chicago: University of Chicago Press, 1977).

9. See, for example, Lisa Jacobson, *Raising Consumers: Children and the American Mass Market in the Early Twentieth Century* (New York: Columbia University Press, 2004); Daniel Thomas Cook, *The Commodification of Childhood: The Children's Clothing Industry and the Rise of the Child Consumer* (Durham, N.C.: Duke University Press, 2004); William Leach, *Land of Desire: Merchants, Power, and the Rise of a New American Culture* (New York: Vintage, 1993), 85–90, 248–60; Leonard Marcus, *Minders of Make-Believe: Idealists, Entrepreneurs, and the Shaping of American Children's Literature* (New York: Houghton Mifflin, 2008); and R. Gordon Kelly, *Mother Was a Lady: Self and Society in Selected Children's Periodicals, 1865–1890* (Westport, Conn.: Greenwood, 1974),

10. Avery, *Behold the Child*, especially part 2; Anne Scott MacLeod, "Children's Literature for a New Nation," in *American Childhood: Essays on Children's Literature of the Nineteenth and Twentieth Centuries* (Athens: University of Georgia Press, 1994), 87–98; Richard O'Brien, *The Story of American Toys: From the Puritans to the Present* (New York: Abbeville, 1990).

11. Testimonial, *YF* 1 (1823–24): 2.

12. The literature on this subject is voluminous. See, for example, Steven Mintz, *Huck's Raft: A History of American Childhood* (Cambridge: Belknap Press of Harvard University Press, 2004), especially chaps. 1, 3, and 4; Karin Calvert, *Children in the House: The Material Culture of Early Childhood, 1600–1900* (Boston: Northeastern University Press, 1992); and Wishy, *The Child and the Republic*.

13. My definition of sentimentality is derived from June Howard, "What Is Sentimentality?," *American Literary History* 11 (spring 1999): 63–81; and Gillian Silverman, "Sympathy and Its Vicissitudes," *American Studies* 43 (fall 2002): 5–28.

14. Influential editors such as Lydia Maria Child and Horace Scudder, despite their shorter tenures at children's magazines, went on to success in other publishing venues.

15. Many scholars have identified these ideals as middle class or bourgeois, which they were. However, the children's magazines I examine in this book rarely used those terms, particularly before the Civil War. Instead, they described such practices almost exclusively as genteel or respectable. I prefer the term *genteel* for this reason and because it emphasizes performance over financial or professional status. For descriptions of these ideals as middle class or bourgeois, see, for example, Karen Halttunen, *Confidence Men and Painted Women: A Study of Middle-Class Culture in America, 1830–1870* (New Haven: Yale University Press, 1982); Mintz, *Huck's Raft,* especially chap. 4; and Sven Beckert, *The Monied Metropolis: New York City and the Consolidation of the New York Bourgeoisie, 1850–1896* (Cambridge: Cambridge University Press, 2001).

16. Richard Bushman, *The Refinement of America: Persons, Houses, Cities* (New York: Vintage, 1992), especially part 2; John Kasson, *Rudeness and Civility: Manners in Nineteenth-Century America* (New York: Hill and Wang, 1990), especially chap. 2; C. Dallett Hemphill, *Bowing to Necessities: A History of Manners in America, 1620–1860* (New York: Oxford University Press, 1999), especially part 3.

17. Mintz, *Huck's Raft,* 76; Joseph E. Illick, *American Childhoods* (Philadelphia: University of Pennsylvania Press, 2002), part 2.

18. Viviana Zelizer, *Pricing the Priceless Child: The Changing Social Value of Children* (Princeton: Princeton University Press, 1985), 11–12.

19. On children's roles as historical actors in the nineteenth-century United States, see Karen Sánchez-Eppler, *Dependent States: The Child's Part in Nineteenth-Century American Culture* (Chicago: University of Chicago Press, 2005).

20. R. Gordon Kelly, *Children's Periodicals of the United States* (Westport, Conn.: Greenwood, 1984), xix–xx.

21. Ronald J. Zboray, *A Fictive People: Antebellum Economic Development and the American Reading Public* (New York: Oxford University Press, 1993), especially chap. 1.

22. I borrow the term *primitive orthodoxy* from H. Crosby Englizian, *Brimstone Corner: Park Street Church, Boston* (Chicago: Moody, 1968), 18.

23. Kelly, *Children's Periodicals,* xxii–xxiii.

24. Howard Chudacoff, *How Old Are You? Age Consciousness in American Culture* (Princeton: Princeton University Press, 1989), 9; Joseph F. Kett, *Rites of Passage: Adolescence in America, 1790 to the Present* (New York: Basic Books, 1977), 11–37.

25. Chudacoff (*How Old Are You?,* 29) argues that the process of age grading began with the education and medical care of children. I agree with that assessment but would add commerce as an accelerant in this process.

26. One of the twentieth-century inheritors of this paternalistic perspective was E. B. White, who in 1934 smugly and erroneously dismissed *Youth's Companion* readers as "people whose childhood was spent on the other side of the railroad tracks." Ironically, he made this comment in an article celebrating *St. Nicholas,* which distinguished itself from New England publications such as *Our Young Folks* and the *Riverside* by puncturing the attitude that White was displaying. See E. B.

White, "Onward and Upward with the Arts: The *St. Nicholas* League," *New Yorker,* December 8, 1934, 42.

27. Jacobson, *Raising Consumers,* 1–15.

28. Anne Scott MacLeod, "Children, Adults, and Reading at the Turn of the Century," in *American Childhood,* 123.

Part I: Establishing Children's Magazines, 1823–1856

1. "The Busy Bee," *YC* 5 (August 10, 1831): 47; "Sabbath Scholar Drowned," *YC* 13 (September 13, 1849): 79.

2. *JM,* 2 and 3 (1828–29).

3. Neil Brody Miller, "'Proper Subjects for Public Inquiry': The First Unitarian Controversy and the Transformation of Federalist Print Culture," *Early American Literature,* 43, no.1 (2008): 103.

4. Thomas O'Connor, *The Athens of America: Boston, 1825–1845* (Amherst: University of Massachusetts Press, 2006), 1–4.

5. The historian John L. Brooke addresses this struggle in a broader context, arguing that what resulted was a "variable and uneven fabric of consent, legitimacy, and institutions woven in thousands of localities across the new Republic." See John L. Brooke, *Columbia Rising: Civil Life on the Upper Hudson from the Revolution to the Age of Jackson* (Chapel Hill: University of North Carolina Press, 2010), 3.

6. David Paul Nord, *Faith in Reading: Religious Publishing and the Birth of Mass Media in America* (New York: Oxford University Press, 2004).

7. Anne D. Jordan, "Youth's Friend and Scholar's Magazine," in *Children's Periodicals of the United States,* ed. R. Gordon Kelly (Westport, Conn.: Greenwood, 1984), 523–26. The range of circulation numbers comes from Frank Luther Mott, *A History of American Magazines,* vol. 1, *1741–1850* (1930; Cambridge: Belknap Press of Harvard University Press, 1957), 144.

8. Nathaniel Willis, letter to Lydia Sigourney, May 28, 1844, Connecticut Historical Society. The italics are mine.

1. Deacon Willis's *Companion*

1. "The Twins," *YC,* June 6, 1827, 5.

2. James Janeway, "A Preface: Containing Directions to Children," in *A Token for Children* (1676; New York: Garland, 1977), n.p. This edition reprints the 1676 version, but earlier versions appeared in 1671 and 1672.

3. Gillian Avery, *Behold the Child: American Children and Their Books, 1621–1922* (Baltimore: Johns Hopkins University Press, 1994), 31–34; Gail Schmunk Murray, *American Children's Literature and the Construction of Childhood* (New York: Twayne, 1998), 6.

4. James Janeway, "To all Parents, School-Masters and School Mistresses, or any that have any hand in the Education of Children," in *Token,* n.p.

5. Peter Gregg Slater, *Children in the New England Mind: In Death and in Life* (Hamden, Conn.: Archon, 1977), 134; Murray, *American Children's Literature*, 7.

6. Charles R. King, *Children's Health in America* (New York: Twayne, 1993), 43.

7. Janeway, "Example I. Of one eminently converted between Eight and Nine years old, with an account of her Life and Death," and "Example II. Of a Child that was admirably affected with the things of God, when he was between two and three years Old, with a brief account of his Life and Death" in *Token*, 5, 22.

8. The church building also had been a repository for gunpowder during the War of 1812. See Joyce W. Warren, *Fanny Fern: An Independent Woman* (New Brunswick, N.J.: Rutgers University Press, 1992), 6.

9. Ibid., 10, 14; Nancy A. Walker, *Fanny Fern* (New York: Twayne, 1993), 7.

10. "Accounts of the Happy Deaths of Two Young Christians," (Boston: Nathaniel Willis, 1819). Archived at the Baldwin Library, University of Florida.

11. "To a Child Who 'Forgot to Pray,'" *YC*, April 16, 1827, 4; "The Dying Child," *YC*, November 8, 1856, 116.

12. David Paul Nord, *Faith in Reading: Religious Publishing and the Birth of Mass Media in America* (New York: Oxford University Press, 2004); Neil Brody Miller, "'Proper Subjects for Public Inquiry': The First Unitarian Controversy and the Transformation of Federalist Print Culture," *Early American Literature* 43 (2008): 101–35.

13. "Reminiscences from Mrs. H. B. Stowe," in *Autobiography, Correspondence, Etc. of Lyman Beecher*, ed. Barbara M. Cross (Cambridge: Belknap Press of Harvard University Press, 1961), 2:81–82.

14. Thus, as Neil Brody Miller suggests about the broader Federalist turn toward print as a vehicle for communicating with audiences, Willis's shift should not be seen as "disingenuous" or "crassly manipulative" but as an accommodation made to broaden his audience (Miller, "Proper Subjects for Public Inquiry," 104).

15. Editorial, *YC*, April 16, 1827, 1.

16. Exodus 19:5; 1 Peter 2:9. In both cases, the word *peculiar* appears in the King James version but not in subsequent translations.

17. The phrase "peculiar institution" as a popular means of referring to slavery appears to derive from a September 11, 1830, letter from John C. Calhoun to Vernon Maxcy. It later appears in the South Carolina Protest to the Tariff of 1828. See *The Papers of John C. Calhoun, 1824–1832* (Columbia: University of South Carolina Press, 1978), 229.

18. According to one source, the first Willis in New England was George Willis, who settled in the Massachusetts Bay Colony in 1630; another source describes a great-great grandfather born in Duxbury (part of the Plymouth colony) in 1637. See Warren, *Fanny Fern*, 6.

19. On the seventeenth-century use of the word *peculiar*, see Sacvan Bercovitch, *The American Jeremiad* (Madison: University of Wisconsin Press, 1978), 7, 15.

20. John Cotton, *Milk for Babes. Drawn Out of the Breasts of Both Testaments. Chiefly, for the Spirituall Nourishment of Boston Babes in Either England: But May*

Be of Like Use for Any Children (1646), http://digitalcommons.unl.edu, 1–2. See also Michael Wigglesworth, *The Day of Doom; or, A Poetical Description of the Great and last Judgment: With Other Poems* (New York: American News Company, 1867). For more on seventeenth-century New England writings for children, see Avery, *Behold the Child,* 13–35.

21. Avery, *Behold the Child,* 31, 33.

22. Janeway, "To All Parents, School-Masters and School-Mistresses."

23. Jonathan Edwards, *Edwards on Revivals: Containing a Faithful narrative of the Surprising Work of God in the Conversion of Many Hundred Souls in Northampton, Massachusetts, A.D. 1735* (New York: Dunning and Spalding, 1832), 46.

24. Jonathan Edwards, *The Works of Jonathan Edwards* (London: William Ball, 1809), 2:937.

25. Watts's poems went through more than three hundred editions in America during the next two hundred years, including at least one printed by Nathaniel Willis. (His son Nathaniel Parker later recalled preparing the type for that edition.) They appeared in the *New England Primer* and, during the nineteenth century, in *McGuffey's Readers.* See Avery, *Behold the Child,* 44–45; and Thomas Baker Nelson, *Sentiment and Celebrity: Nathaniel Parker Willis and the Trials of Literary Fame* (New York: Oxford University Press, 1999), 3.

26. Isaac Watts, *Divine and Moral Songs for Children* (New York: Hurd and Houghton, 1866), 74.

27. "The Busy Bee," *YC,* August 10, 1831, 47.

28. Mark A. Noll, *America's God: From Jonathan Edwards to Abraham Lincoln* (New York: Oxford University Press, 2002), 13, 43–44.

29. Mary Kupiec Cayton, "Who Were the Evangelicals? Conservative and Liberal Identity in the Unitarian Controversy in Boston, 1804–1833," *Journal of Social History* 31 (fall 1997): 101; Marc M. Arkin, "The Force of Ancient Manners: Federalist Politics and the Unitarian Controversy Revisited," *Journal of the Early Republic* 22 (winter 2002): 575–610.

30. Biographical information comes from Nathaniel Willis, "Autobiography of a Journalist," in Frederic Hudson, *Journalism in the United States, from 1690–1872* (New York: Harper and Brothers, 1873); Warren, *Fanny Fern,* 5–10; Walker, *Fanny Fern,* 5–25; Nelson, *Sentiment and Celebrity,* 13–20; and "Nathaniel Willis," *Dictionary of American Biography* (New York: Scribner, 1936), 20:305–6.

31. J. M. Opal, *Beyond the Farm: National Ambitions in Rural New England* (Philadelphia: University of Pennsylvania Press, 2008); Joyce Appleby, *Inheriting the Revolution: The First Generation of Americans* (Cambridge: Belknap Press of Harvard University Press, 2000).

32. Frederick Garner Fassett, *A History of the Newspapers in the District of Maine, 1785–1820* (Orono: University of Maine Press, 1932), 107–40; Willis, "Autobiography," 290.

33. Fassett, *A History of the Newspapers,* 137; Willis, "Autobiography," 290; Nelson, *Sentiment and Celebrity,* 16; Warren, *Fanny Fern,* 8.

34. Fassett, *A History of the Newspapers*, 136–40; Willis, "Autobiography," 291.

35. H. Crosby Englizian, *Brimstone Corner: Park Street Church, Boston* (Chicago: Moody Press, 1968), 18.

36. Willis printed several editions of Reverend Jedidiah Morse's 1815 pamphlet "American Unitarianism," which, as historian Conrad Wright argues, may have cemented the breach between the city's Calvinist and Unitarian clergies. He also printed the lectures of Reverend Edward Griffin, the first minister of Park Street Church. See Willis, "Autobiography," 291; and Conrad Wright, "Ministers, Churches, and the Boston Elite, 1791–1815," in *The Unitarian Controversy: Essays on American Unitarian History* (Boston: Skinner House, 1994), 57.

37. Warren, *Fanny Fern*, 10, 11, 14; Nelson, *Sentiment and Celebrity*, 13–14.

38. Warren, *Fanny Fern*, 6–9.

39. "Prospectus of the Youth's Companion: Conditions," *YC*, April 16, 1827, 1; "Unitarian Universalism," *Boston Recorder*, April 20,, 62. See also "Effects of Unitarian Theology," *Boston Recorder*, November 3, 1821, 180.

40. Lyman Beecher, letter to Dr. [Edward] Griffin, March 1, 1828, in *The Autobiography of Lyman Beecher*, 1:96.

41. M. A. DeWolfe Howe, "The Hundredth Anniversary of the *Youth's Companion*: One Century of Joyful Service to Youth," *YC*, November 4, 1926, 822.

42. "Prospectus of the Youth's Companion," 1. Lorinda Cohoon rightly notes that Willis's stance on advertisements was more complicated than he claimed; he did occasionally incorporate indirect advertisements into the paper as instructional pieces designed to teach children about commerce. Nonetheless, advertisements did not become a regular feature until he sold the magazine. See Lorinda Cohoon, *Serializing Boyhoods: Periodicals, Books, and American Boys, 1840–1911* (Lanham, Md.: Scarecrow, 2006), 3–4.

43. See, for example, "A Good Use of a Shilling," *YC*, April 16, 1827, 3; and "Another Year Gone," *YC*, May 17, 1839, 4.

44. On the American Sunday School Union's role in spreading Sunday schools, see Anne Boylan, *Sunday School: The Formation of an Institution, 1790–1880* (New Haven: Yale University Press, 1990), especially 60–100.

45. Edwin Wilbur Rice, *The Sunday School Movement, 1780–1917, and the American Sunday School Union, 1817–1917* (Philadelphia: American Sunday School Union, 1917), 143.

46. Packard expressed these views in his correspondence with educator Horace Mann, who rejected the organization's texts as too "sectarian" for Massachusetts schools. See Boylan, *Sunday School*, 55–57.

47. Title page, *Teacher's Offering* 1 (1823–24): 1. The bound volume also included a review of the magazine (which I quoted in this book's introduction) that suggested the power a commodity created expressly for children might have over young minds. See testimonial, *Teacher's Offering* 1 (1823–24): 2.

48. Because the only available copies of the *Teacher's Offering / Youth's Friend* are bound volumes, I cannot tell exactly when the epigram was removed. However,

volume 1, page 4, includes an advertisement for six complete volumes of the *Youth's Friend,* making it likely that these volumes were published no earlier than 1829 or 1830. I doubt that the American Sunday School Union would have later added that epigram only to the first volume, so I am guessing that it appeared in the original issues of 1823–24.

49. Preface, *Teacher's Offering* 1 (1823–24): 1.

50. Boylan, *Sunday School,* 44, 156.

51. Kristen Drotner, *English Children and Their Magazines, 1751–1945* (New Haven: Yale University Press, 1988), 24–26.

52. "The Teacher's Offering," *YF* 3 (February 1826): 23–25.

53. Announcement, *Boston Recorder,* April 20, 1827, 62.

54. "Good Use of a Shilling," 3.

55. Avery, *Behold the Child,* 93–114.

56. "The Beginning," *YF* 15 (January 1838): 1.

57. Nathaniel Willis, letter to Lydia Sigourney, May 28, 1844, Connecticut Historical Society. The italics are mine.

58. "From One of Our Auxiliaries," *YF* 1 (1823–24): 2; "Preface to the Original Edition," *YF* 1 (1823–24): 3.

59. "Death of Francis A. Brown," *YF* 1 (January 1824): 152–53.

60. "The Sabbath; or, The Three Cousins," *YF* 1 (January 1824): 39–40. Other *Youth's Friend* stories that mitigate the traditionally frightening language of evangelical orthodoxy include "An Extraordinary Dream," *YF* 1 (December 1823): 23–27; and "The Fruitless Fig Tree," *YF* 8 (January 1831): 11–12.

61. "The Orphan Boys," *YF* 1 (1823–24): 9–11.

62. "The Knowledge of a Little Boy Astonishing a Priest," *YF* 1 (November 1823): 8–9. Such denigration of non-Protestant faiths occurred periodically in the magazine. See also "Visit to the Synagogue" *YF* 12 (February 1835): 19–22.

63. "Hannah More; or, The Advantages of Sunday Schools," *YF* 3 (January 1826): 3–9. See also "A Child's Reproof" *YF* 1 (December 1823): 29–30; "A Good Boy." *YF* 1 (December 1823): 30–31.

64. "She Sobbed Herself to Death," *YF* 15 (January 1838): 15–16.

65. "Frances Stone," *YC,* June 6, 1827, 5. See also "Editorial: Little Edward," *YC,* February 8, 1832, 152.

66. "A Death Bed Scene of a Child Six Years Old," *YC,* April 16, 1827, 2. See also "Lines,: On the Death of W. who died at Bloomingburg, Ohio, July 14, 1845," *YC,* January 14, 1846, 144.

67. "To Children and Youth," *YC,* June 6, 1827, 7.

68. "To the Youthful Reader," *YC,* June 20, 1827, 15.

69. "Prospectus," 1.

70. "A Father's Dying Advice," *YC,* June 20, 1827, 14.

71. See, for example, "The Man Who Suddenly Became Rich," *YC,* November 30, 1827, 103.

72. Caroline Gilman, "Mother, What is Death?" *YC,* January 11, 1828, 132.

73. "Woman," *YC,* June 6, 1827, 7. See also "The Contented Mother," *YC,* May 17, 1839, 3; and Mrs. L. H. Sigourney, "Narrative: The Farmer and the Soldier. A Tale," *YC,* November 13, 1835, 101.

74. A Lady, "Self-Denial, or, The Two Cousins," *YC,* January 7, 1847, 141–42.

75. "The Choice of Companions," *YC,* October 12, 1831, 83.

76. Mrs. Hofland, "The Captive Boy," *YC,* July 27, 1831, 37; Washington Irving, "The Mother and Her Son," *YC,* June 5, 1840, 13; The Little Drunkard, *YC,* July 31, 1835, 42.

2. Aunt Maria's *Miscellany* and the Limits of Gentility

1. "Adventure in the Wood," *JM* 1 (September 1826): 5–13.

2. For purposes of clarity, I refer to the editor as Lydia Maria Child (the name by which she is generally known) throughout the book.

3. Carolyn Karcher, *The First Woman in the Republic: A Cultural Biography of Lydia Maria Child* (Durham, N.C.: Duke University Press, 1994), 56; review, *Ladies' Magazine* 1 (January and July 1828): 47–48, 336; "Works of Mrs. Child," *North American Review* 37 (July 1833): 138–64.

4. The only other contemporary female authors in Boston during this time were novelist Catharine Sedgwick and the elderly historian Hannah Adams. See Deborah Clifford, *Crusader for Freedom: A Life of Lydia Maria Child* (Boston: Beacon, 1992), 49.

5. See, for example, "Ruined Cities," *JM* 1 (September 1826): 30.

6. Patricia Okker, *Our Sister Editors: Sarah J. Hale and the Tradition of Nineteenth-Century American Women Editors* (Athens: University of Georgia Press, 1995); Sharon M. Harris, ed., *Blue Pencils and Hidden Hands: Women Editing Periodicals, 1830–1910* (Boston: Northeastern University Press, 2004); Mary Kelley, *Private Woman, Public Stage: Literary Domesticity in Nineteenth-Century America* (New York: Oxford University Press, 1984).

7. Lydia Maria Child, "The First and Last Book," in *The Coronal: A Collection of Various Pieces, Written at Various Times* (Boston: Carter and Hendee, 1832), 282.

8. Okker, *Our Sister Editors,* 16.

9. Karcher, *The First Woman in the Republic,* 6; Melissa J. Homestead, "Behind the Veil: Catharine Sedgwick and Anonymous Publication," in *Catharine Maria Sedgwick: Critical Perspectives,* ed. L. L. Damon-Bach and V. Clements (Boston: Northeastern University Press, 2002), 30.

10. Thomas O'Connor, *The Athens of America: Boston, 1825–1845* (Amherst: University of Massachusetts Press, 2006), 165.

11. "Address to the Young," *JM* 1 (September 1826): iii–iv.

12. Milton Rugoff, *The Beechers: An American Family in the Nineteenth Century* (New York: Harper and Row, 1981), 71.

13. Conrad Wright, "Institutional Reconstruction in the Unitarian Controversy," in *American Unitarianism, 1805–1865,* ed. Conrad Wright (Boston: Massachusetts

Historical Society and Northeastern University Press, 1989), 5; Irving Bartlett, "Introduction," in *Unitarian Christianity and Other Essays*, by William Ellery Channing (Indianapolis: Bobbs-Merrill, 1957), xviii.

14. Daniel Walker Howe, *The Unitarian Conscience: Harvard Moral Philosophy, 1805–1861* (Cambridge: Harvard University Press, 1970), 5; John Locke, *An Essay Concerning Human Understanding* (1689; London: John Beecroft, 1775), 13, 67; *Rousseau's Émile or Treatise on Education* (1762; New York: Appleton, 1909), 1.

15. Gillian Avery, *Behold the Child: American Children and Their Books, 1621–1922* (Baltimore: Johns Hopkins University Press, 1994), 65–67.

16. Lydia Maria Child, letter to Lucy Osgood [?], December 17, 1870, in Karcher, *The First Woman in the Republic*, 8. Subsequent biographical information is from pp. 1–15.

17. Victoria Clements, "Introduction," in *A New-England Tale; or, Sketches of New England Character and Manners*, by Catharine Maria Sedgwick (1822; New York: Oxford University Press, 1995), xii–xiv.

18. Joyce W. Warren, *Fanny Fern: An Independent Woman* (New Brunswick, N.J.: Rutgers University Press, 1992), 13–14.

19. Karcher, *The First Woman in the Republic*, 3–4, 8; Clifford, *Crusader for Freedom*, 12–13.

20. On Elizabeth Peabody's experience as a teacher, see Megan Marshall, *The Peabody Sisters: Three Women Who Ignited American Romanticism* (Boston: Houghton Mifflin, 2005), part 3.

21. Karcher, *The First Woman in the Republic*, 17.

22. Cathy Davidson, "Preface," in Sedgwick, *A New-England Tale*, vii; Kelley, *Private Woman, Public Stage*, 180–83.

23. Clifford, *Crusader for Freedom*, 44; "Recent American Novels," *North American Review* 21 (July 1825): 87.

24. An American Lady [Lydia Maria Child], *Evenings in New England. Intended for Juvenile Amusement and Instruction* (Boston: Cummings, Hilliard, 1824), iii.

25. Ibid., 56.

26. See, for example, "Personification" and "The Little Master and His Little Slave," in [Child], *Evenings in New England*, 1, 138.

27. Lydia Maria Child, letter to Mary Francis Preston, undated, in *The Collected Correspondence of Lydia Maria Child, 1817–1880*, ed. Patricia G. Holland, Milton Meltzer, and Francine Krasno (Millwood, N.Y.: Kraus Microform, 1980), microfiche 1, letter 19; Karcher, *The First Woman in the Republic*, 60; Review, *North American Review* 20 (January 1825): 230–31.

28. Karcher, *The First Woman in the Republic*, 39–40.

29. Child was a lifetime spiritual seeker who never settled long on a religious faith. During this period, she appears to have been attracted to the spiritual ideas of the Swedish thinker Emanuel Swedenborg. See ibid., 13–14.

30. Lydia Maria Child, letter to Mary Francis Preston, 1826, in *Collected Correspondence*, microfiche 1, letter 22; Clifford, *Crusader for Freedom*, 43; Karcher, *The First Woman in the Republic*, 66.

31. Karcher, *The First Woman in the Republic*, 79. Also see William Charvat, "The Conditions of Authorship in 1820," in *The Profession of Authorship in America, 1800–1870: The Papers of William Charvat*, ed. Matthew J. Bruccoli (Columbus: Ohio State University Press, 1968), 29–48., Nearly all of the writers of the period had to supplement their income by doing work other than the writing they viewed as their primary vocation. (James Fenimore Cooper was a notable exception.) See Karcher, *The First Woman in the Republic*, 632.

32. Lydia Maria Child, letter to Mary Francis Preston, January 6, 1827, in *Lydia Maria Child: Selected Letters, 1817–1880*, ed. Milton Meltzer, Patricia G. Holland, and Francine Krasno (Amherst: University of Massachusetts Press, 1982), 8.

33. Clifford, *Crusader for Freedom*, 53–54.

34. Cornelia Meigs, Elizabeth Nesbit, Anne Eaton, and Ruth Hill Vigeurs, *A Critical History of Children's Literature* (New York: Macmillan, 1953), 275.

35. "Address to the Young," iii–iv.

36. The following all appear in *JM* 1 (September 1826): "The American Traveller," 14; "Letter from Summer to Winter," 21; "Ruined Cities," 30; "The Dwarf," 54; "The Little Rebels," 48, 53.

37. "The Tulip and the Tri-Colored Violet," *JM* 1 (September 1826): 37.

38. "The American Traveller," 19–20.

39. Caroline Healey Dall, recollection, *Unitarian Review* 11 (June 1883): 525–26. Perhaps this remembrance is overly nostalgic, but no similar recollections of either the *Companion* or the *Youth's Friend* have surfaced.

40. Child, letter to Preston, January 6, 1827.

41. See, for example, "The Brothers, or . . . the Influence of Example," *JM* 3 (November 1827): 209–26; and "Mary French and Susan Easton," *JM* 6 (May–June 1834): 186–202.

42. "Attention," *JM* 1 (September 1826): 72, 82.

43. Karcher, *The First Woman in the Republic*, 66–67.

44. "Maria and Frances, or, The Birthday Present," *JM* 1 (November 1826): 1. See also "The French Orpha, or, New Year's Reward," 1 (January 1827): 1.

45. See, for example, "Maria and Frances," 1; and "Adventure in the Wood," 5.

46. "An American Traveller," 14; "Remarkable Boys," *JM* 6 (March–April 1831): 331–32; "Benjamin Franklin," *JM* 2 (March 1827): 22–23.

47. "Adventure in the Wood," 5; "The Little Rebels," 48; "The Industrious Family," *JM* 6 (July–August 1831): 217.

48. Karcher, *The First Woman in the Republic*, 72, 78.

49. "Life in the Desert," *JM* 6 (May–June 1831): 161–62.

50. "Brenda, A Lapland Story," *JM* 6 (July–August 1831): 298.

51. "The Indian Boy," *JM* 2 (May 1827): 31; "Pol Sosef. The Indian Artist," *JM* 5 (January–February 1831): 278.

52. "Extracts from a Journal," *JM* 3 (November 1827): 227–36.

53. "Some Talk about Cuba," *JM* 2 (May–June 1832): 198; "All about Brazil," *JM* 3 (September–October 1832): 31.

54. "New Books," *JM* 2 (July–August 1832): 320.

55. "William Peterson, the Brave and Good Boy," *JM* 6 (March–April 1834): 66–67.

56. "Jumbo and Zairee," *JM* 5 (January–February 1831): 285–99.

57. "Mary French and Susan Easton," 186–202.

58. Editorial, *JM* 6 (July–August 1834): 323.

59. John Crandall, "Patriotism and Humanitarian Reform in Children's Literature, 1825–1860," *American Quarterly* 21 (spring 1969): 6, 10.

60. Samuel Goodrich, *Tales of Peter Parley about Africa* (Boston: Gray and Bowen, Carter and Hendee, 1830), n.p.

61. "Carrier's Address," *Merry's Museum and Parley's Magazine* 33 (January 1857): 1–2.

62. "Slavery," *YC*, July 18, 1828, 32; "Slavery," July 25, 1828, 36.

63. *YC*, February 8, 1844, 160.

64. B. Green, letter to William Lloyd Garrison, March 8, 1833, Boston Public Library, Special Collections; John Farmer, letter to F. Jackson, January 8, 1835, Boston Public Library, Special Collections.

65. Letter to the editor, *YC*, November 14, 1850, 116.

Part II: Commercializing Children's Magazines, 1857–1873

1. "A True Story," *YC*, October 26, 1871, 337–38.

2. Frank R. Stockton, "What Might Have Been Expected," *SN* 1 (November 1873): 24, (February 1874): 225, (April 1874): 363.

3. Daniel Straubel, "National Police Gazette," in *American Mass-Market Magazines,* ed. Alan Nourie and Barbara Nourie (New York: Greenwood, 1990), 285; Lewis Lapham and Ellen Rosenbush, eds., *An American Album: One Hundred and Fifty Years of Harper's Magazine* (New York: Franklin Square, 2000), xvi; Ruth K. MacDonald, "Merry's Museum," in *Children's Periodicals of the United States,* ed. R. Gordon Kelly (Westport, Conn.: Greenwood, 1984), 296.

3. Perry Mason and Sensational Gentility

1. "Fejee Islanders," *YC*, January 1, 1857, 1.

2. "Pearl Divers," *YC*, January 8, 1857, 5; "The Thugs of India," *YC*, January 15, 1857, 9; "The Bastinado," *YC*, February 26, 1857, 33.

3. "Red Snow" and "Volcanoes," *Parley's Magazine,* March 16, 1863, 10, 17; "The Adventures of Gilbert Go-Ahead," *Merry's Museum* 16 (January 1851): 1; "The Dwarf" *JM* 1 (September 1826): 54; "Crocodiles," *JM* 6 (March–April 1831): 69.

4. David Greene, "*Youth's Companion,*" in *Children's Periodicals of the United States,* ed. R. Gordon Kelly (Westport, Conn.: Greenwood, 1984), 509.

5. Ford assumed the pseudonym "Perry Mason" in 1867 when he became the magazine's sole proprietor, and his real name never again appeared in the *Companion* until his obituary was published ("Daniel Sharp Ford," *YC*, February 1, 1900, 53).

His concerns about privacy are discussed in the obituary and in George W. Coleman, *Democracy in the Making: Ford Hall and the Open Forum Movement* (Boston: Little, Brown, 1915), 9–10. Erle Stanley Gardner, the author of the Perry Mason novels, read the *Companion* as a boy and borrowed Ford's pseudonym in the 1930s, when he began producing his legal thrillers. See Dennis J. Bounds, *Perry Mason: The Authorship and Reproduction of a Popular Hero* (Westport, Conn.: Greenwood, 1996), 5.

6. Shelly Streeby, *American Sensations: Class, Empire, and the Production of Popular Culture* (Berkeley: University of California Press, 2002), especially 3–37.

7. For examples of this culture, see David B. Sachsman and David W. Bulla, eds., *Sensationalism: Murder, Mayhem, Mudslinging, Scandals and Disasters in 19th-Century Reporting* (New Brunswick, N.J.: Transaction, 2013); and Patricia Cline Cohen, Timothy J. Gilfoyle, and Helen Lefkowitz Horowitz, *The Flash Press: Sporting Male Weeklies in 1840s New York* (Chicago: University of Chicago Press, 2008).

8. Gillian Avery, *Behold the Child: American Children and Their Books, 1621–1922* (Baltimore: Johns Hopkins University Press, 1994), 184–90; E. Anthony Rotundo, *American Manhood: Transformations in Masculinity from the Revolution to the Modern Era* (New York: Basic Books, 1993), 31–55.

9. Frank Luther Mott suggests that Ford's generally silent partner, Reverend John W. Olmstead, incited these changes. The argument makes sense because the two men also disagreed about the use of advertising and a premiums program designed to spur circulation. See Frank Luther Mott, *A History of American Magazines*, vol. 2, *1850–1865* (1938; Cambridge: Belknap Press of Harvard University Press, 1938), 266.

10. Lorman A. Ratner, Paula T. Kaufman, and Dwight L. Teeter, Jr., *Paradoxes of Prosperity: Wealth-Seeking versus Christian Values in Pre–Civil War America.* (Urbana: University of Illinois Press, 2009).

11. Ronald Story, *The Forging of an Aristocracy: Harvard and the Boston Upper Class, 1800–1870* (Middletown, Conn.: Wesleyan University Press, 1980), 135–71.

12. Thomas H. O'Connor, *Civil War Boston: Home Front and Battlefield* (Boston: Northeastern University Press), 4; William G. McLoughlin, *Revivals, Awakenings, and Reform* (Chicago: University of Chicago Press, 1978), 141–42.

13. Mott, *A History of American Magazines*, 2:266.

14. "Young Samuel, A Servant of God," *YC*, December 18, 1856, 137; "Emma Winifred; or, The Little Girl Who Was Punished for Sabbath Breaking," *YC*, November 27, 1856, 125.

15. Evidence of the *Companion*'s precarious financial situation in 1856 appears in Nathaniel Willis, business ledger for the *Boston Recorder* and the *Youth's Companion*, Unitarian Archives, Harvard Divinity School.

16. Mott, *A History of American Magazines*, 2:266. Mott offers no evidence to support his claim that Ford assumed control of the magazine, but its editorial patterns validate his thesis. The initial push to commercialize the magazine, which

diminished after the first few months, resurged after Ford and Olmstead dissolved their partnership in 1866.

17. "New Arrangement," *YC,* December 25, 1856, 144.

18. Masthead, *YC,* January 1, 1857, 1.

19. Willis's explanation appeared in the April 16, 1827, prospectus for the *Companion* and was reprinted periodically in the magazine throughout his tenure. See, for example, his editorial *YC,* December 6, 1839, 120.

20. David Reed, "Growing Up: The Evolution of Advertising in *Youth's Companion* during the Second Half of the Nineteenth Century," *Journal of Advertising History* 10, no. 1 (1987): 21.

21. "To Our Friends," *YC,* January 1, 1857, 3.

22. Reed, "Growing Up," 21.

23. Masthead, *YC,* January 1, 1857, 4; Greene, *"Youth's Companion,"* 509, 511.

24. "To Our Friends," *YC,* January 1, 1857, 3.

25. Louise Harris, *None but the Best; or, The Story of Three Pioneers: The Youth's Companion, Daniel Sharp Ford, [and] C. A. Stephens* (Providence: Brown University, Stephens Collection, 1966), 20.

26. Ratner et al., *Paradoxes of Prosperity,* 19.

27. Biographical information is from "Daniel Sharp Ford," 53; Mott, *A History of American Magazines,* 2:266–74; Lesley Ginsberg, "Daniel Sharp Ford," in *American National Biography,* ed. John A. Garraty and Mark C. Carnes (Oxford: Oxford University Press, 1999), 8:221; Richard Cutts, *Index to the "Youth's Companion," 1871– 1929* (Metuchen, N.J.: Scarecrow, 1972), v–xvi; Harris, *None but the Best,* 19–23; and "Daniel Sharp Ford Dead," *New York Times,* December 25, 1899, 1.

28. One historian of the city's religious cultures describes Boston's Baptists during this period as "upstart evangelicals." See Benjamin L. Hartley, *Evangelicals at a Crossroads: Revivalism and Social Reform in Boston, 1860–1910* (Durham: University of New Hampshire Press, 2011), 1.

29. Story, *Forging of an Aristocracy,* 135–71.

30. Peter Benson, "Gleason's Publishing Hall," in *Publishers for Mass Entertainment in Nineteenth-Century America,* ed. M. B. Stern (Boston: Hall, 1980), 141; Streeby, *American Sensations,* 89, 85.

31. For an analysis of the relationship between technological development and the growth of the U.S. publishing industry, see Ronald J. Zboray, *A Fictive People: Antebellum Economic Development and the American Reading Public* (New York: Oxford University Press, 1993), 3–16. Circulation numbers are from William Huntzicker, *The Popular Press, 1833–1865* (Westport, Conn.: Greenwood, 1999), 169; Gerald Baldasty, *The Commercialization of News in the Nineteenth Century* (Madison: University of Wisconsin Press, 1992), 49; and Henkin, *City Reading: Written Words and Public Space in Antebellum New York* (New York: Columbia University Press, 1998), 105.

32. Michael Denning, *Mechanic Accents: Dime Novels and Working-Class Culture in America* (New York: Verso, 1987) 10; Lori Merish, "Story Papers," in *The Oxford*

History of Popular Print Culture, vol. 6, *U.S. Popular Print Culture, 1860–1920*, ed. Christine Bold (New York: Oxford University Press, 2012), 46–47.

33. On this backlash, see Huntzicker, *The Popular Press;* Baldasty, *The Commercialization of News;* Henkin, *City Reading*, especially chap. 5; and Michael Schudson, *Discovering the News: A Social History of American News* (New York: Basic Books, 1978).

34. A Physician, *Confessions and Experience of a Novel Reader: Respectfully Dedicated to Every Young Man and Woman, and Especially to Every Parent* (Chicago: William Stacy, 1855), 27, 62; Edwin Whipple, *Essays and Reviews* (Boston: Ticknor and Fields, 1851), 74–75.

35. Lambert A. Wilmer, *Our Press Gang; or, A Complete Exposition of the Corruptions and Crimes of American Newspapers* (Philadelphia: Lloyd, 1859), 173, 340, 375; George Thompson, *Venus in Boston: and Other Tales of Nineteenth-Century Life*, ed. David S. Reynolds and Kimberly R. Gladman (Amherst: University of Massachusetts, Press, 2002), xxvii–xxviii.

36. Avery, *Behold the Child*, 87–91, 114–18; Ann Douglas, *The Feminization of American Culture* (New York: Knopf, 1977), 1–2.

37. Physician, *Confessions*, 48.

38. On Ford's philanthropic efforts to foster religious education for workers, see Coleman, *Democracy in the Making*, 11–12.

39. Mary Noel, *Villains Galore: The Heyday of the Popular Story Weekly* (New York: Macmillan, 1954), 15–16.

40. Supplement, *YC*, October 28, 1868, n.p.

41. "Fejee Islanders," 1; "The Bastinado," 33; "Grape Harvest in Syria," *YC*, February 5, 1857, 21.

42. "Moral Tale: Setting Up for a Gentleman," *YC*, April 16, 1857, 61. On sporting papers, see Cohen et al., *The Flash Press*.

43. "Wanted—A Boy from the Country," *YC*, June 25, 1857, 101.

44. A Lady, "Self-Denial, or, The Two Cousins," *YC*, January 7, 1847, 141–42.

45. Lydia Sigourney, "The Farmer and the Soldier," *YC*, February 12, 1846, 161–62. See also "Andrew Jackson—His Mother," a tepid memorial of the recently deceased president that revealed Willis's disdain for Jackson's model of masculinity (*YC*, September 25, 1845, 83).

46. Oliver Optic [William Taylor Adams], *The Boat Club; or, The Bunkers of Rippleton: A Tale for Boys* (Boston: Brown, Bazin, 1855); Thomas Hughes, *Tom Brown's Schooldays* (Cambridge, U.K.: Macmillan, 1857). Historians disagree about whether the gender divide that the publishing industry perceived actually existed among readers. Some scholars claim that girls read boys' books and men and boys read sentimental literature with equal alacrity, but they do not dispute the industry's perception of a gendered difference in antebellum reading habits and its particular pursuit of male readers. See Anne Scott MacLeod, "American Girlhood in the Nineteenth Century: Caddie Woodlawn's Sisters," in *American Childhood: Essays on Children's Literature of the Nineteenth and Twentieth Centuries* (Athens: University

of Georgia Press, 1994), 3–29; and Emily Hamilton-Honey, *Turning the Pages of American Girlhood: The Evolution of Girls' Series Fiction, 1865–1930* (Jefferson, N.C.: McFarland, 2013).

47. Adams wrote five more books in this series before 1860 and edited the *Student and Schoolmate* from 1855 through 1872, serializing Alger's novel *Ragged Dick* in 1868. On Adams's *Boat Club* series, see Lorinda Cohoon, *Serialized Citizenships: Periodicals, Books, and American Boys, 1840–1911* (Lanham, Md.: Scarecrow, 2006), 57–87.

48. "Frank Norton, or, The Unheeded Admonition," *YC,* April 2, 1857, 52.

49. "Deception," *YC,* January 1, 1857, 2.

50. Thomas Augst, *The Clerk's Tale: Young Men and Moral Life in Nineteenth-Century America* (Chicago: University of Chicago Press, 2003); Brian P. Luskey, *On the Make: Clerks and the Quest for Capital in Nineteenth-Century America* (New York: New York University Press, 2010); Priscilla Ferguson Clement, *Growing Pains: Children in the Industrial Age, 1850–1890* (New York: Twayne, 1997), 92.

51. Clement, *Growing Pains,* 6, 92; Viviana Zelizer, *Pricing the Priceless Child: The Changing Social Value of Children* (New York: Basic Books, 1985), 77.

52. An example of Ford's attempt to balance both adult and juvenile interests appears in his appeal for subscription renewals at the end of his first year as editor. Despite its title, "To Our Young Readers" addresses both audiences. In the first paragraph, he tells children, "We have made arrangements to give you a real good paper next year . . . We shall have tales, and adventures, and stories too." In the second paragraph, he shifts his attention to parents, promising that the *Companion* will continue its efforts to improve young readers, whom he calls "the flowers of our land," by showing them "what is good, and true, and pure, and noble, and beautiful—in religion, morality and nature" (*YC,* December 31, 1857, 212).

53. "The Swiss Basket Maker," *YC,* January 1, 1857, 1.

54. "The Good Deed in Season," *YC,* January 22, 1857, 13.

55. "Mother's Apron Strings," *YC,* January 1, 1857, 3.

56. A Republican, "The Motherless," *YC,* January 1, 1857, 4; "James Miller," *YC,* January 8, 1857, 5.

57. "A Mother's Love," *YC,* April 2, 1857, 54.

58. "Women of the Revolution: Flora McDonald," *YC,* January 29, 1857, 18; "Women of the Revolution: Frances Allen," *YC,* January 8, 1857, 6; "Women of the Revolution: Susannah Livingston," *YC,* January 22, 1857, 14.

59. "Biography: Original: Grace Darling," *YC,* December 20, 1855, 138; "Moral Tale: The Story of Grace Darling," *YC,* June 18, 1857, 97.

4. The *Youth's Companion* and the Civil War

1. "William Walker, A Story of the War," *YC,* December 19, 1861, 199.

2. Harry S. Stout, *Upon the Altar of the Nation: A Moral History of the Civil War* (New York: Viking, 2006), 101–2.

3. "The Patriot Boy," *YC*, December 31, 1863, 209.

4. James McPherson, *For Cause and Comrades* (New York: Oxford University Press, 1998); Melinda Lawson, *Patriot Fires: Forging a New American Nationalism in the Civil War North* (Lawrence: University Press of Kansas, 2002), 2, 14–49, 98–128.

5. On broader trends of children's politicization during the war, see James Marten, *The Children's Civil War* (Chapel Hill: University of North Carolina Press, 2000).

6. "Beadle's Dime Novels," *North American Review* 49 (July 1864): 303–9.

7. David L. Greene, *"Youth's Companion,"* in *Children's Periodicals of the United States*, ed. R. Gordon Kelly (Westport, Conn.: Greenwood, 1984), 511; Frank Luther Mott, *A History of American Magazines*, vol. 2, *1850–1865* (1938; Cambridge: Belknap Press of Harvard University Press, 1957), 268.

8. *YC*, April 18, 1861, 61, 64.

9. *YC*, July 25, 1861, 117, 120.

10. Stout, *Upon the Altar of the Nation*, 36–37, 101; Marten, *The Children's Civil War*, especially chap. 5.

11. "Russell's Paint-Box," *YC*, May 2, 1861, 69; "Susie's Mistake," *YC*, October 3, 1861, 155.

12. Steven Mintz, *Huck's Raft: A History of American Childhood* (Cambridge: Belknap Press of Harvard University Press, 2004), 126–27.

13. "William Walker's War," 199.

14. Stout, *Upon the Altar of the Nation*, 101–2.

15. "The Great National Tragedy," *YC*, April 27, 1865, 66.

16. "Give to the Soldiers," *YC*, February 5, 1863, 22; "Do Our Part for the Country," *YC*, March 26, 1863, 50.

17. "The Patriot Boy," 209.

18. "Myself or My Country?" *YC*, June 9, 1864, 88.

19. Stout, *Upon the Altar of the Nation*, 36; Marten, *The Children's Civil War*, 32.

20. "The Michigan Drummer Boy," *YC*, February 26, 1863, 34; "The Boy Soldier," *YC*, July 9, 1863, 111; Alice Fahs, *The Imagined Civil War: Popular Literature of the North and South, 1861–1865* (Chapel Hill: University of North Carolina Press, 2001), 263.

21. "Gen. Mitchel and the News-boys," *YC*, February 26, 1863, 34; "General Grant's Boyhood," *YC*, January 28, 1864, 14.

22. "The Brother's Letter," *YC*, May 14, 1863, 78; "Army Life," *YC*, April 2, 1863, 55.

23. Marten, *The Children's Civil War*, 167–69.

24. Fahs, *The Imagined Civil War*, 258–59; "A Little Drummer Boy," 130.

25. Anne Scott MacLeod, *A Moral Tale: Children's Fiction and American Culture, 1820–1860* (Hamden, Conn.: Archon, 1975), 60–65.

26. "The Drummer-Boy of Marblehead," *Merry's Museum* 44 (July 1862): 8–9.

27. Edmund Kirke, "The Little Prisoner" [part 1], *OYF* 1 (January 1865): 32–37.

28. John Townsend Trowbridge, *The Drummer Boy: A Story of Burnside's Expedition* (Boston: Tilton, 1863); Horatio Alger, *Frank's Campaign; or, What Boys*

Can Do on the Farm for the Camp (Boston: Loring, 1864); Oliver Optic [William Taylor Adams], *The Soldier Boy; or, Tom Somers in the Army,* Army and Navy Series, vol. 1 (Boston: Lee and Shepard, 1863); Jane Goodwin Austin, *Dora Darling: The Daughter of the Regiment* (Boston: Tilton, 1864). Optic's Army and Navy Series began with *The Soldier Boy* and ran through six volumes over the next three years. *Dora Darling* sold well enough for Austin to produce a sequel but remained anomalous in a genre primarily written by and for males. Also see Fahs, *The Imagined Civil War,* 263–79.

29. For examples of these departments, see "The Teacher's Desk," *Student and Schoolmate* (May 1865): 158–59; "Chats with Readers and Correspondence," *Forrester's Playmate* (February 1864): 160; John Townsend Trowbridge, "Half-Hours with Father Brighthopes" *OYF* 1 (August 1865): 534; and "Round the Evening Lamp," *OYF* 1 (January 1865): 80.

30. Optic, *The Soldier Boy,* 5.

31. Lawson, *Patriot Fires,* 160–62.

32. J. Randolph Cox, "Dime Novels," in *The Oxford History of Popular Print Culture,* vol. 6, *U.S. Popular Print Culture, 1860–1920,* ed. Christine Bold (New York: Oxford University Press, 2012), 63.

33. Edward S. Ellis, preface, *Seth Jones* (1860; New York: Dillingham, 1907), 14–15.

34. Albert Johannsen, *The House of Beadle and Adams and Its Dime and Nickel Novels: The Story of a Vanished Literature,* 3 vols. (Norman: University of Oklahoma Press, 1950–1962), 1:62.

35. Fahs, *The Imagined Civil War,* 19–20; Johannsen, *House of Beadle and Adams,* 1:9–11.

36. Information on antebellum and dime-novel marketing practices is from Cox, "Dime Novels," 64; Johannsen, *House of Beadle and Adams,* 1:31, 33, 40; Edmund Pearson, *Dime Novels; or, Following an Old Trail in Popular Literature* (Boston: Little, Brown, 1929), 7–8, 46; Charles M. Harvey, "The Dime Novel in American Life," *Atlantic Monthly* 100 (July 1907): 37; and David Henkin, *City Reading: Written Words and Public Space in Antebellum New York* (New York: Columbia University Press, 1998), 39–100.

37. "Publishers Notice from the First Edition," in *Malaeska: The Indian Wife of the White Hunter,* by Mrs. Ann S. Stephens (1860; New York: Blom, 1971).

38. Stephens was a contemporary writer of some renown. See Jennifer Blanchard, " 'Her Object is Good': Ann S. Stephens and *Portland Magazine,*" in *Blue Pencils and Hidden Hands: Women Editing Periodicals, 1830–1910,* ed. Sharon M. Harris (Boston: Northeastern University Press, 2004), 41–59. Other frequent early contributors had similarly respectable reputations: for instance, Metta J. Victor edited several women's magazines during the 1850s, and Mary A. Denison published widely, including in the *Companion.*

39. The psychic appeared in Mary A. Denison, *Florida; or, The Iron Will. A Story of To-Day,* Beadle's Dime Novels, vol. 20 (New York: Beadle and Adams, April 1, 1861).

40. John R. Edson, "*Youth's Casket,*" in Kelly, *Children's Periodicals,* 496–501.

41. Johannsen, *House of Beadle and Adams,* 1:49.

42. "Erastus Beadle," *Banner Weekly,* November 30, 1889, quoted ibid., 39; Pearson, *Dime Novels,* 49.

43. Cox, "Dime Novels," 64.

44. William A. Settle, Jr., "The Dime Novel As an Historian's Tool," *Dime Novel Roundup* 40 (September 1970): 93; M. Bertrand Couch, "Blood and Thunder Novels for Boys," *Reckless Ralph's Dime Novel Roundup* 6 (November 1937): 5–6.

45. Michael Denning uses this terminology in *Mechanic Accents: Dime Novels and Working-Class Culture in America* (London: Verso, 1987), 202. Also see Harvey, "The Dime Novel in American Life," 37; Johannsen, *House of Beadle and Adams,* 1:9–11; and Pearson, *Dime Novels,* 7–8.

46. Twain's examples were not Beadle books, but Johannsen suggests that he adapted the duke and dauphin's theatricals in *The Adventures of Huckleberry Finn* from a Beadle volume titled *Richard Talbot of Cinnabar; or, The Brothers of the Red Hand.* See Johannsen, *House of Beadle and Adams,* 1:9–11.

47. "Beadle's Dime Novels," 303–9.

48. Ibid., 306–8.

49. "A Story of the Backwoods," *YC,* April 9, 1863, 57. See also "Indian Attack on a Settler," *YC,* May 7, 1863, 73.

50. "A Dead Man's Revenge," *YC,* October 29, 1863, 173, 178.

51. For a chronological listing of the publication dates of American children's magazines, see Kelly, *Children's Periodicals,* 552–61.

52. No war-related pictures appeared on the *Companion*'s cover until "Our Exchanged Prisoners," *YC,* January 5, 1865, 2.

53. My Revenge," *YC,* September 24, 1863, 153. See also "After the Battle," *YC,* January 8, 1863, 5.

54. "The Rebel Officer," *YC,* January 21, 1864, 9. See also "The Soldier Boy and His Sock," *YC,* March 12, 1863, 42; and "A Soldier's Regard for His Mother," *YC,* February 5, 1863, 24.

55. "Vermont Strategy," *YC,* February 19, 1863, 30; "The Way a Rebel Officer Was Trapped," *YC,* January 21, 1864, 10. See also "Capturing a Rebel by Strategy," *YC,* June 18, 1863, 100.

56. "A Brave Woman," *YC,* March 12, 1863, 44. See also "The Boys vs. the Rebels," *YC,* July 23, 1863, 117; and "The Trooper Captain," *YC,* February 12, 1863, 25.

57. "A Southern Boy's Idea of the Yankees," *YC,* October 15, 1863, 164. The *Companion* claimed that planters also bred such ignorance in blacks. See "Granny and the Yankees," *YC,* March 3, 1864, 34.

58. "The Iron Yoke," *YC,* January 7, 1864, 4; "Celia the Contraband," *YC,* January 28, 1864, 14; "General Butler and the Slave Whipper," *YC,* December 3, 1863, 196; "Granny and the Yankees," 34.

59. "The Faithful Negro," *YC,* September 24, 1863, 156. See also "Little Starlight," *YC,* December 1, 1864, 189; and "Among the Contrabands," *YC,* January 14, 1864, 8.

60. "The Great National Tragedy," 66.

61. See, for example, "Joe Sears," *YC*, March 26, 1863, 48; "Courage," *YC*, July 30, 1863, 120; and "The Pirate and the Savages," *YC*, February 25, 1864, 30.

62. "The Wronged Shepherd," *YC*, May 4, 1865, 69; "Agnes Briarly," *YC*, May 18, 1865, 77; "At the Gate," *YC*, November 30, 1865, 189. Not all cover illustrations of this period presented imperiled children and women, but these images distinguished the postwar genre from its prewar antecedents.

63. "The Lighthouse on the Skeve Mhoil," *YC*, July 20, 1865, 112.

64. "Reclaimed," *YC*, August 17, 1871, 257.

65. "The Slave's Crime," *YC*, November 14, 1867, 180.

66. "Under the Snow," *YC*, June 16, 1870, 186; "Over the Falls," *YC*, March 3, 1870, 65; "Nobody's Child," *YC*, September 28, 1871, 303.

67. Rose Terry Cook, "A Midsummer Madness," *YC*, September 27, 1877, 307; Ruth Chesterfield, "The Eagle's Nest," *YC*, January 16, 1873, 17; Mrs. E. D. Kendall, "Nannie Hapgood," *YC*, February 10, 1876, 43; "Aunty Di," *YC*, August 16, 1877, 261.

68. Edward Eggleston, "Kitty's Forty," *YC*, January 1, 1874, 1; " 'Piggy,' " *YC*, May 8, 1873, 143; Julia A. Eastman, "The Boys at Beechwood," *YC*, August 27, 1874, 277; Marion Harland, "Haunted," *YC*, May 29, 1879, 176.

69. "Hints to Teachers," *YC*, June 22, 1882, 258.

70. E. E. Hale, "Life at School," *YC*, January 20, 1870, 20; "White Slaves," *YC*, March, 9, 1865, 38; "The Tumbling Lassie," *YC*, May 23, 1867, 81; "Robby and His Brothers," *YC*, Jan. 1, 1869, 1.

71. Edward S. Ellis, "In the Chippewa Country: A Story of the Border," *YC*, March 18, 1869, 82.

5. The Cultural Custodians

1. John Townsend Trowbridge, "Jack Hazard and His Fortunes," *OYF* 7 (January 1871): 2.

2. Michael Winship, *American Literary Publishing in the Mid-Nineteenth Century: The Business of Ticknor and Fields* (Cambridge: Cambridge University Press, 1995), 17; Shirley Marchalonis, *The Worlds of Lucy Larcom, 1824–1893* (Athens: University of Georgia Press, 1989), 155; W. S. Tryon, *Parnassus Corner: A Life of James T. Fields, Publisher to the Victorians* (Boston: Houghton Mifflin, 1963), 289.

3. R. Gordon Kelly, ed., *Children's Periodicals of the United States* (Westport, Conn.: Greenwood, 1984), xxii.

4. In 1882, the *Youth's Companion*'s claimed a circulation of 263,000. By that date, *Our Young Folks*, which had peaked at a circulation of approximately 75,000, was out of business, and *St. Nicholas*, which became the most successful liberal Protestant children's magazine after its demise, had a circulation of approximately 70,000. See David L. Greene, *"Youth's Companion,"* Joan Brest Friedberg, *"Our Young Folks,"* and Fred Erisman, *"St. Nicholas,"* ibid., 511, 330, 378.

5. Marchalonis, *The Worlds of Lucy Larcom*, 153–56, 283; Tryon, *Parnassus Corner*, 290.

6. Thomas Wentworth Higginson, *Cheerful Yesterdays* (Boston: Houghton Mifflin, 1898), 167; Susan Goodman, *Republic of Words: The Atlantic Monthly and Its Writers, 1857–1925* (Hanover, N.H.: University Press of New England, 2011), x; Ellery Sedgwick, *The Atlantic Monthly, 1857–1909: Yankee Humanism at High Tide and Ebb* (Amherst: University of Massachusetts Press, 1994), 4; Paul DiMaggio, "Cultural Entrepreneurship in Nineteenth-Century Boston: The Creation of an Organizational Base for High Culture in America," *Media, Culture and Society* 4 (1982): 33–50.

7. Sedgwick, *Atlantic Monthly*, 2–4.

8. David L. Greene, "*The Riverside Magazine for Young People*," in Kelly, *Children's Periodicals*, 367; Leonard Marcus, *Minders of Make-Believe: Idealists, Entrepreneurs, and the Shaping of American Children's Literature* (New York: Houghton Mifflin, 2008), 32–70.

9. Biographical information in this chapter about Fields's childhood and youth is from Tryon, *Parnassus Corner*, 1–92; James C. Austin, *Fields of the Atlantic Monthly: Letters to an Editor, 1861–1870* (San Marino, Calif.: Huntington Library, 1953), 7–10; Sedgwick, *Atlantic Monthly*, 70–71; Rita K. Gollin, *Annie Adams Fields: Woman of Letters* (Amherst: University of Massachusetts Press, 2002), 18–20; Winship, *American Literary Publishing*, 17–18; and Annie Fields, *James T. Fields, Biographical Notes and Personal Sketches, with unpublished fragments and tributes from men and women of letters* (Boston: Houghton Mifflin, 1881), 1–19.

10. Sedgwick, *Atlantic Monthly*, 70; Winship, *American Literary Publishing*, 17–18. The firm name changed to Ticknor and Fields in 1854.

11. Tryon, *Parnassus Corner*, 329; Marchalonis, *The Worlds of Lucy Larcom*, 154.

12. Larcom worked in the Lowell mills and then as a teacher in the western states, publishing her first poems in the *Atlantic* only in 1861. As magazine editor, she was paid fifty dollars a month, although Fields doubled that salary when he made her editor-in-chief. In contrast, Howells, as assistant editor of the *Atlantic*, received one hundred dollars a week. See Marchalonis, *The Worlds of Lucy Larcom*, especially 166, 285.

13. Tryon, *Parnassus Corner*, 329–32.

14. According to Larcom's biographer, Fields's wife and Larcom's friend, Annie Adams Fields, who hosted a kind of literary salon, was the "guiding spirit of the magazine," although her husband retained control over its content. See Marchalonis, *The Worlds of Lucy Larcom*, 283, n. 1; and Rita Gollin, "Subordinated Power: Mr. and Mrs. James T. Fields," in *Patrons and Protegees: Gender, Friendship, and Writing in Nineteenth-Century America*, ed. Shirley Marchalonis (New Brunswick, N.J.: Rutgers University Press, 1988), 141–60.

15. Tryon, *Parnassus Corner*, 279–99.

16. Sedgwick, *Atlantic Monthly*, 70.

17. Edward Waldo Emerson, *The Early Years of the Saturday Club* (Boston: Houghton Mifflin, 1918), 380–81; Caroline Ticknor, *Hawthorne and His Publisher* (Boston: Houghton Mifflin, 1913), 254. The Emerson quotation is from Annie

Adams Fields, notebooks, May 4, 1868, Massachusetts Historical Society. Also see Tryon, *Parnassus Corner*, 322–23.

18. Frank Luther Mott, *A History of American Magazines*, vol. 3, *1865–1885* (1938; Cambridge: Belknap Press of Harvard University Press, 1957), 338.

19. James Russell Lowell, letter to Charles Eliot Norton, October 1859, in Horace Elisha Scudder, *James Russell Lowell: A Biography* (Boston: Houghton, Mifflin, 1901), 450–51. Norton, another Harvard alumnus, was the editor of the *North American Review*.

20. Sedgwick, *Atlantic Monthly*, 5. See also Daniel Walker Howe, *The Unitarian Conscience: Harvard Moral Philosophy, 1805–1861* (Cambridge: Harvard University Press, 1970), 8.

21. The phrase "defy the public" is from Emerson's comments during an 1857 meeting about the founding of the *Atlantic Monthly*. See *The Journals of Ralph Waldo Emerson*, ed. Susan Smith and Harrison Hayford (Cambridge: Harvard University Press, 1978–1982), 14:167.

22. Gillian Avery, *Behold the Child: American Children and Their Books, 1621–1922* (Baltimore: Johns Hopkins University Press, 1994), 123.

23. Samuel Griswold Goodrich, *Recollections of a Lifetime; or, Men and Things I have seen: in a series of familiar letters to a friend, historical, biographical, anecdotical, and descriptive* (New York: Miller, Orton, and Mulligan, 1857), 1:166, 169–71.

24. Samuel Griswold Goodrich, *Fairy Land, and Other Sketches for Youth* (Boston: Munroe, 1844), 34.

25. James T. Fields, letter to Thomas Delf, December 19, 1849, in Sarah Wadsworth, *In the Company of Books: Literature and its "Classes" in Nineteenth-Century America* (Amherst: University of Massachusetts Press, 2006), 41–42.

26. Nathaniel Hawthorne, letter to James T. Fields, April 7, 1851, in *The Letters, 1843–1853: Centenary Edition of the Works of Nathaniel Hawthorne*, ed. Thomas Woodson, L. Neal Smith, and Norman Holmes Pearson (Columbus: Ohio State University Press, 1987), 16:417.

27. Wadsworth, *In the Company of Books*, 39.

28. Guilian Verplanck, ed., *The Fairy Book* (New York: Harper and Brothers, 1836).

29. Review, *Graham's Magazine* 43 (September 1853): 333–35. On Hawthorne's transition from a hack writer to a literary writer for children, see Wadsworth, *In the Company of Books*, 25–43.

30. Wadsworth, *In the Company of Books*, 35.

31. Avery, *Behold the Child*, 61, 65–66, 68–69.

32. Lydia Maria Child, letter to Lucy Larcom, March 12, 1873, in *Lydia Maria Child: Selected Letters, 1817–1880*, ed. Milton Meltzer, Patricia G. Holland, and Francine Krasno (Amherst: University of Massachusetts Press, 1982), 511.

33. "Thumbling," *OYF* 1 (January 1865): 9.

34. Horace Elisha Scudder, diary, October 24, 1866, Houghton Library, Harvard University; Hjalmar Hjorth Boyesen, "Hans Christian Andersen," *SN* 3 (December 1875): 65.

35. John Townsend Trowbridge, "Andy's Adventures; or, The World Bewitched," *OYF* 1 (January 1865): 44.

36. William Dean Howells, "Criticism and Fiction," in *Criticism and Fiction* (New York: Harper, 1892), iii, 1.

37. Harriet Beecher Stowe, "Hum, the Son of Buz," *OYF* 1 (January 1865): 1, 7; Lucy Larcom, "The Volunteer's Thanksgiving," *OYF* 1 (January 1865): 7–8.

38. Larcom had read Child's *Miscellany* as a young mill girl, and she credited it with having given her older sister the idea to found the *Lowell Offering*, a monthly periodical produced by female textile workers, where Larcom had first published her writing. In addition to turning to Child for advice, she corresponded with Sara Jane Lippincott, who under the pseudonym "Grace Greenwood" had been editing another children's magazine, the *Little Pilgrim*, for more than a decade. See Larcom, *New England Girlhood: Outlined from Memory* (1899; Boston: Northeastern University Press, 1986), 170; and Marchulonis, *The Worlds of Lucy Larcom*, 174.

39. "Literary Notices," *Ladies' Magazine* 1 (November 1828): 522.

40. "Editor's Table," *Godey's Lady's Book* (February 1857): 29.

41. Patricia Okker, *Our Sister Editors: Sarah J. Hale and the Tradition of Nineteenth-Century American Women Editors* (Athens: University of Georgia Press, 1995), especially 38–58. Also see Nina Baym, *Women's Fiction: A Guide to Novels by and about Women in America, 1820–1870*, 2nd ed. (Urbana: University of Illinois Press, 1995).

42. Stowe was the nominal editor of *Hearth and Home*, where future *St. Nicholas* editor Mary Mapes Dodge worked as associate editor and oversaw daily operations. I discuss this professional relationship further in chapter 6.

43. Nearly every major children's magazine produced between 1840 and 1865 had a woman on its editorial staff: Lippincott at the *Little Pilgrim*, Louisa May Alcott at *Merry's Museum*, and Mary Mapes Dodge at *Hearth and Home*. A prominent exception was the *Companion*, a difference we might attribute to its patriarchal orthodox ideals.

44. John Townsend Trowbridge, "Jack Hazard and His Fortunes," *OYF* 7 (March 1871): 135; *OYF* (April 1871): 194.

45. Thomas Wentworth Higginson, "The Baby of the Regiment," *OYF* 1 (February 1865): 102–8. See also Ruth Chesterfield, "The Disobedient Crow," *OYF* 2 (March 1866): 129; and Nora Perry, "The Little Dunbars," *OYF* 8 (January 1872): 11.

46. See, for example, "Winning His Way," *OYF* 1 (January 1865): 48.

47. Scudder, diary, August 4, 1866.

48. Vieux Moustache [Clarence Gordon], "The Midnight Coast," *Riverside* 1 (January 1867): 14. See also Vieux Moustache [Clarence Gordon], "How the Captain Came by a Legacy," *Riverside* 4 (March 1870): 101.

49. Harriet Prescott, "The Portrait," *OYF* 1 (February 1865): 85, Charles J. Foster, "Sports, Games and Pastimes," *OYF* 3 (February 1867): 110; Trowbridge, "Andy's Adventures; or, The World Bewitched," 44.

50. Thomas Bailey Aldrich, "Story of a Bad Boy," *OYF* 5 (January 1869): 1.

51. Ibid., *OYF* 5 (June 1869): 345; *OYF* 5 (July 1869): 425.

52. Lorinda Cohoon, *Serialized Citizenships: Periodicals, Books, and American Boys, 1840–1911* (Lanham, Md.: Scarecrow, 2006), 93, 90.

53. Aldrich, "Story of a Bad Boy" (January 1869), 3; (June 1869), 352. Cohoon presents compelling evidence to support this interpretation of the story, but her assessment of Ticknor and Fields as a "consensus-seeking Congregationalist publishing house" is inaccurate. Neither Ticknor nor Fields was a Congregationalist; and as I discuss later in this chapter, *Our Young Folks* was the most aggressively and persistently anti-Confederate of all reputable children's magazines of this era. See Cohoon, *Serialized Citizenships*, 91.

54. Aldrich, "Story of a Bad Boy," *OYF* 5 (April 1869): 208.

55. Ibid., *OYF* 5 (December 1869): 790.

56. Anne Scott MacLeod, "Caddie Woodlawn's Sisters," in *American Childhood: Essays on Children's Literature of the Nineteenth and Twentieth Centuries* (Athens: University of Georgia Press, 1994), 5–7. MacLeod's evidence is limited to women who wrote autobiographies, which suggests that her insights apply to a literate and prosperous genteel minority of the population.

57. Twain's failure to follow this template is one reason why *Huckleberry Finn* was not (and is not) considered a children's novel.

58. Scudder, diary August 4, 1866.

59. "About Some Picture Books," *OYF* 3 (December 1867): 752.

60. Amy Kaplan, *The Social Construction of American Realism* (Chicago: University of Chicago Press, 1988), ix.

61. Stowe's "Hum, Son of Buz," for example, naturalizes the lives of these magazines' genteel audiences by mentioning that the family encounters the hummingbird on a beach vacation, at a time when most U.S. families did not have the opportunity to enjoy such vacations (1).

62. Sedgwick, *Atlantic Monthly*, 69–111; Oliver Optic [William Taylor Adams], "Cruise of the Leopold," *OYF* 1 (October 1865): 631; Mayne Reid, "Afloat in the Forest, or, A Voyage Among the Tree-Tops," *OYF* 1 (January 1865): 67.

63. Charles Dickens, "Holiday Romance," *OYF* 4 (January 1868): 1; Henry Wadsworth Longfellow, "Christmas Bells," *OYF* 1 (February 1865): 123; Henry Wadsworth Longfellow, "The Castle Builder," *OYF* 3 (January 1867): 57. Fields also paid for regular contributions from leading nonfiction writers such as the reforming minister Edward Everett Hale and the physical education expert Dio Lewis.

64. Tryon, *Parnassus Corner*, 323–24, 377.

65. Lydia Maria Child, "Grandfather's Chestnut Tree," *OYF* 1 (October 1865): 613; Gaston Fay, "Master Horsey's Excursion," *OYF* 1 (August 1865): 500.

66. Trowbridge, "Jack Hazard and His Fortunes" (January 1871), 1; Aldrich, "Story of a Bad Boy" (December 1869), 790. See also Caroline Augusta Howard, "A Clean Sweep," *OYF* 6 (February 1870): 105; and Aldrich, "Story of a Bad Boy," (December 1869): 785.

67. Shaun O'Connell, *Remarkable, Unspeakable, New York: A Literary History* (Boston: Beacon Press, 1995), 43. See also Sedgwick, *Atlantic Monthly*, 76.

68. In a letter Scudder wrote, "I am unwilling to introduce in the education of the coming generation any element which will serve to keep alive sectional hostility . . . The old questions then fought over on the field will doubtless in one form or another be fought over again . . . but I do not think it necessary to make them play a part in our magazine." See Scudder, diary transcription of letter to F. R. Goulding, June 16, 1866. In contrast, as late as September 1873 *Our Young Folks* was still publishing stories that emphasized the evils of slavery—e.g., Jane G. Andrews, "Patty's Responsibility," *OYF* 9 (September 1873): 554.

69. Edmund Kirke, "The Boy of Chancellorsville," *OYF* 1 (September 1865): 603.

70. See, for example, Edmund Kirke, "The Little Prisoner," *OYF* 1 (April 1865): 242; and Elizabeth Kilham, "Tobe's Monument," *OYF* 8 (February 1872): 80.

71. Scudder, diary transcriptions: letter to D. Hayes, Aug. 22, 1866; letter to Mary Mapes Dodge, July 30, 1866; letter 1 to Mrs. Prentiss, July 6, 1866; letter 2 to Mrs. Prentiss, July 6, 1866.

72. Domestic fiction in the *Riverside* was exemplified by Gordon's Vieux Moustache series and Helen C. Weeks's vignettes about a little white boy named Ainslee and his black friend Sinny. See, for example, Weeks, "Winter Time," *Riverside* 2 (January 1868): 1; and Weeks, "Amanda's Party," *Riverside* 2 (April 1868): 153.

73. The *Riverside's* nonfiction stories had a similar lack of historical context. While *Our Young Folks* addressed subjects such as military camp life and the Paris Exposition of 1868, the *Riverside* described topics such as "Life in a German Village" and offered letters describing the culture of Egypt. This approach had the added benefit of keeping stories suitable for any segment of his potential audience, another point Scudder stressed in his private writings. See Edmund Kirke, "Three Days at Camp Douglas," *OYF* 1 (April 1865): 252; Charles Shanly, "The French Exposition for Twenty-Four Cents," *OYF* 4 (March 1868): 170; B. G., "Life in a German Village," *Riverside* 2 (February 1868): 61; and T. D. B., "A Letter from Egypt," *Riverside* 4 (February 1870): 70.

6. The Jack-in-the-Pulpit

1. John Townsend Trowbridge, "Doing His Best," *OYF* 8 (December 1873): 710.

2. John Townsend Trowbridge, "Fast Friends," *SN* 1 (January 1874): 157, 159; (February 1874): 184.

3. Ibid., *SN* 1 (March 1874): 293.

4. Daniel H. Borus, *Writing Realism: Howells, James, and Norris in the Mass Market* (Chapel Hill: University of North Carolina Press, 1989), 27–64.

5. Stephen Nissenbaum, *The Battle for Christmas* (New York: Knopf, 1996).

6. "Children's Magazines," *Scribner's* 6 (July 1873): 352–54.

7. Mrs. Hance, "Den Falidjen Weg Fehend," *SN* 1 (November 1873): 41; M.M.D., "Mieux Vaut Avoir La Moitie D'Un Pain Que ne Pas Avoir De Pain," *SN* 1 (December 1873): 86; J. H. Morse, "Sancti Petri Aedes Sacra," *SN* 1 (June 1874): 493.

8. "The *St. Nicholas* Treasure-Box of Literature," *SN* 8 (December 1880): 139.

9. Mary Mapes Dodge, letter to Horace Elisha Scudder, September 24, 1868, Mary Mapes Dodge Collection, Huntington Library. See also their correspondence of March 31, 1868, Dec. 13, 1866, May 9, 1867, Dodge Collection, Huntington Library.

10. Mary Mapes Dodge, "The Artist and the Newsboy," in *The Irvington Stories* (New York: O'Kane, 1865), 247.

11. On the connection between literary realism and elite New England culture, see Nancy Glazener, *Reading for Realism: The History of a Literary Institution, 1850–1910* (Durham, N.C.: Duke University Press, 1997).

12. Mary Mapes Dodge, "My Mysterious Foe," *Harper's* 26 (April 1863): 659–64.

13. Dodge, "Cushamee," in *Irvington Stories*, 54.

14. "Po-No-Kah: An Indian Tale," in *Irvington Stories*, 161.

15. Information about Dodge's childhood is from Catharine Morris Wright, *Lady of the Silver Skates: The Life and Correspondence of Mary Mapes Dodge* (Jamestown, R.I.: Clingstone Press, 1979), 1–7; and Susan R. Gannon and Ruth Anne Thompson, *Mary Mapes Dodge* (New York: Twayne, 1992). I also consulted archival materials in the Dodge and Scribner collections at Princeton University, the letters of Mary Mapes Dodge at the Huntington Library, the DeGrummond Collection at the McCain Library of the University of Southern Mississippi, and the papers of Mary Mapes Dodge at the Alderman Library of the University of Virginia.

16. The four Dodge girls learned English, French, Latin, drawing, and music from a tutor. The parallels between James Mapes and Bronson Alcott are significant; both were brilliant but impractical educators and ineffective financial providers. Yet the Mapes family, though not wealthy, does not seem to have suffered the extreme poverty of the Alcotts. See Wright, *Lady of the Silver Skates*, 1–7; Gannon and Thompson, *Mary Mapes Dodge*, 1–5; and Eve LaPlante, *Marmee and Louisa: The Untold Story of Louisa May Alcott and Her Mother* (New York: Free Press, 2012), especially chap. 6.

17. Wright, *Lady of the Silver Skates*, 2.

18. *Hans Brinker* also demonstrated Dodge's urge to give children more entertainment in their books. Published in 1865, the novel was an intermediate step between the antebellum stories about Rollo and Peter Parley, which offered more information than plot, and the narrative-driven novels that followed, such as *Little Women* (1868) and *Story of a Bad Boy* (1870).

19. On New York's role in the popularization of Christmas in the United States, see Penne L. Restad, *Christmas in America* (New York: Oxford University Press, 1995), especially chaps. 3 and 4; and Nissenbaum, *The Battle for Christmas*, especially chap. 2.

20. Mary Mapes Dodge, "Santa Claus," *Hearth and Home*, December 26, 1868, 1.

21. "Holiday Whispers Concerning Toys and Games," *Riverside* 2 (January 1868): 41.

22. "A Real Christmas," *Hours at Home* 10 (January 1870): 209.

23. Wright, *Lady of the Silver* Skates, 74.

24. On publishing's postwar shift from Boston to New York, see David R. Shumway, *Creating American Civilization: A Genealogy of American Literature As an Academic Discipline* (Minneapolis: University of Minnesota Press, 1994), 43–46.

25. William Dodge's death has never been adequately explained, but most scholars have labeled his death a suicide. See Wright, *Lady of the Silver Skates*, 14–17; and Gannon and Thompson, *Mary Mapes Dodge*, 6–7.

26. Stowe gave the prestige of her name to the periodical but did not actively participate in its business. A letter to Dodge indicates the nature of their relationship. Writing about an article submitted by Thomas Wentworth Higginson, Stowe said, "I could wish Colonel Higginson's letter had been on some other subject. Still, I am quite willing to leave the matter to your judgment ... [for] you can judge better in this case what is expedient ... I give out to my numerous correspondents & applicants that I am not the person to decide upon manuscripts ... I sympathize with you in that sort of labor." Yet in the same letter Stowe recommended including an innocuous article by a Hartford colleague of "social influence and position ... whose interest in our magazine it is in every way worth while to cultivate." See Harriet Beecher Stowe, letter to Mary Mapes Dodge, January 8, 1869, Mary Mapes Dodge Collection, Princeton University.

27. John N. Dickie, "Bobby and the Demon," *Hearth and Home*, May 25, 1872, 11. See also Eleanor Burr, "Jimmy Drake, The Apple Peddler," *Hearth and Home*, April 12, 1873, 12.

28. Mary Mapes Dodge, *Hans Brinker; or, The Silver Skates, A Story of Life in Holland* (New York: O'Kane: 1865); Gannon and Thompson, *Mary Mapes Dodge*, 135.

29. One scholar has estimated that the number of magazines in the nation increased from approximately 700 in 1865 to 3,300 in 1885. See Frank Luther Mott, *A History of American Magazines*, vol. 3, *1865–1885* (1938; Cambridge: Belknap Press of Harvard University Press, 1957), 5.

30. Michael Winship, *American Literary Publishing in the Mid-Nineteenth Century: The Business of Ticknor and Fields* (Cambridge: Cambridge University Press, 1995), 15–18; W. S. Tryon, *Parnassus Corner: A Life of James T. Fields, Publisher to the Victorians* (Boston: Houghton Mifflin, 1963), 277–79, 285. The quotation is from Maury Klein, *The Flowering of the Third America: The Making of an Organizational Society, 1850–1920* (Chicago: Dee, 1993), 43.

31. Mark J. Noonan, *Reading the "Century Illustrated Monthly Magazine": American Literature and Culture, 1870–1893* (Kent, Ohio: Kent State University Press, 2010), xii, 1–3, 6.

32. Ibid., xi–xiv.

33. Arthur John, *The Best Years of the Century: Richard Watson Gilder, "Scribner's Monthly," and the "Century Magazine," 1870–1909.* (Urbana: University of Illinois Press, 1981), ix.

34. Noonan, *Reading the "Century,"* especially 11–31. The concluding assessment of the magazine is from Robert J. Scholnick, "*Scribner's Monthly* and the Pictorial

Representation of Life and Truth in Post–Civil War America," *American Periodicals* 1 (1991): 49–50.

35. "Topics of the Time," *Scribner's* 1 (November 1870): 106; "Preface," *Century* 23 (January 1881): 1.

36. David Shi, *Facing Facts: Realism in American Thought and Culture, 1850–1920* (New York: Oxford University Press, 1995), 3.

37. "Topics of the Time," *Scribner's* 1 (November 1870): 106; Scholnick, "*Scribner's Monthly*," 49.

38. Scholnick, "*Scribner's Monthly*," 49–50.

39. Noonan, *Reading the "Century*," 20–21.

40. The Scribner group purchased the *Riverside* in 1870 and *Our Young Folks* in 1872. In the years between those purchases they bought the *Children's Hour, Schoolday Magazine,* and the *Little Colonel.* See Susan R. Gannon, " 'Here's to Our Magazine'": Promoting *St. Nicholas, 1873–1905,*" in *"St. Nicholas" and Mary Mapes Dodge: The Legacy of a Children's Magazine Editor, 1873–1905,* ed. Susan R. Gannon, Suzanne Rahn, and Ruth Anne Thompson (Jefferson, N.C.: McFarland, 2004), 77–82.

41. Noonan, *Reading the "Century*," 37.

42. "Children's Magazines," 352–54. Dodge expressed this opinion even more emphatically in a letter to Scudder: "The poor children! *We* have the privilege of hiring our preachers and selecting our own wise counsel but they, poor things, are beridden with our preaching and counseling and teaching and often, most dismal of all, amusing, from the hour of their toddlehood . . . We often pour the lees of our experience upon them in a stream of twaddle, expecting them to be edified and delighted, while we smack our own lips over the wine." See Mary Mapes Dodge, letter to Horace Elisha Scudder, July 23, 1866, Dodge Collection, Huntington Library.

43. Gannon and Thompson, *Mary Mapes Dodge,* 13; Wright, *Lady of the Silver Skates,* 68.

44. Daniel H. Borus, *Writing Realism,* 34, 35, 39; Wright, *Lady of the Silver Skates,* 25, 35.

45. Mary Mapes Dodge, letters to Charles Scribner, June 19, 1876, June 22, 1876, Dodge Collection, Princeton University. (The emphasis is in the original.) See also their correspondence of September 12, 1878, November 20, 1878, October 27, 1879, May 15, 1883, Dodge Collection, Princeton University.

46. Louisa May Alcott, letter to Mary Mapes Dodge, September 17, 1882, Dodge Collection, Princeton University.

47. Trowbridge's notes about his income appear regularly in his unpublished journals. For example, see the entries for July 22, 1867, December 12, 1869, April 7, 1872, Houghton Library, Harvard University. Also see John Townsend Trowbridge, letter to Mary Mapes Dodge, November 29, 1873, Dodge Collection, Princeton University.

48. Richard H. Brodhead, *Culture of Letters: Scenes of Reading and Writing in Nineteenth-Century America* (Chicago: University of Chicago Press, 1993), 80–81.

49. John Townsend Trowbridge, *My Own Story: With Recollections of Noted Persons* (Boston: Houghton Mifflin, 1903), chap. 10; Susan Cheever, *Louisa May Alcott* (New York: Simon and Schuster, 2010). Trowbridge was able to emphasize youthful depravity in *Companion* stories while simultaneously focusing on boys' redemption and achievement in serials for *Our Young Folks* and *St. Nicholas*. Compare "Awkward Andy: A Story of City Life," *YC*, August 30, 1877, 277; and "The Boy Schoolmaster" *YC*, February 7, 1878, 41; with "The Tinkham Brothers' Tide Mill," *SN* 10 (November 1882): 17. Alcott generally submitted her less accomplished stories to the *Companion*, reserving her best material for *St. Nicholas*. Compare "Uncle Smiley's Boys," *YC*, February 3, 1870, 33; and "Mother's Trial," *YC*, May 26, 1870, 161; with "Eight Cousins," *SN* 2 (January 1875): 132; "Under the Lilacs," *SN* 5 (December 1877): 94; "Jack and Jill," *SN* 7 (December 1879): 89; and "The Spinning Wheel Stories," *SN* 11 (January 1884): 209.

50. Wright, *Lady of the Silver Skates*, 69–71; Fred Erisman, "*St. Nicholas*," in *Children's Periodicals of the United States*, ed. R. Gordon Kelly (Westport, Conn.: Greenwood, 1984), 378. Larcom's salary information comes from Joan Brest Friedberg, "*Our Young Folks*," in *Children's Periodicals*, 330. The quotation appears in Julia Tutwiler, "Mary Mapes Dodge in New York," in *Women Authors of Our Day in Their Homes: Personal Descriptions and Interviews*, ed. Francis Whiting Halsey (New York: Pott, 1903), 264.

51. John Townsend Trowbridge, letter to Roswell Smith, March 3, 1874, quoted in "What Some Eminent Men Think of *St. Nicholas*," advertising supplement, *SN* 2 (January 1875): 1.

52. The cover of the earliest issues of *St. Nicholas* noted that "*Our Young Folks* has been merged into *St. Nicholas*," and the January 1874 supplement noted that James Osgood, the publisher of *Our Young Folks*, "commends" *St. Nicholas* to *Our Young Folks* readers as "a worthy successor . . . and even more deserving of public acceptance." The July 1874 prospectus contained a quotation from a review: "The king is dead, long live the king! *Our Young Folks* gracefully drops its mantle upon the shoulders of her younger rival and hereafter all the little boys and girls will be obliged to take *St. Nicholas*." This material, available only in unbound copies of the magazine, is archived in the Children's Magazine Collection, George A. Smathers Library, University of Florida.

53. Lucia Runkle, "Mary Mapes Dodge," in *Our Famous Women* (Hartford, Conn.: Worthington, 1884), 280.

54. Premiums offer, *SN* 1 (January 1874), table of contents page.

55. [Josiah G. Holland], "Topics of the Time," *Scribner's* 1 (November 1870): 106.

56. "Willy by the Brook," *SN* 1 (November 1873): 31. See also L.G.M., "Pete," *SN* 1 (January 1874): 117; and Charles Barnard, "Tommy, the Soprano," *SN* 2 (January 1875): 148.

57. Alcott, "Eight Cousins," *SN* 2 (January 1875): 132. For another example of such mentoring, see Rebecca Harding Davis, "Naylor O' the Bowl," *SN* 1 (December 1873): 65.

58. Frances Hodgson Burnett, "Little Lord Fauntleroy," *SN* 13 (November 1885): 3.

59. See, for example, the biographies published in the magazine's first year: Clarence Cook, "Edward Jenner," *SN* 1 (March 1874): 241; Donald Mitchell, "Who Printed the First Bible? [Johannes Gutenberg]," *SN* 1 (April 1874): 313; D.G.M., "A Nice Old Gentleman [Isaac Newton]," *SN* 1 (June 1874): 478.

60. Frank R. Stockton, "What Might Have Been Expected," *SN* 1 (November 1873): 24, 225, 363; John Townsend Trowbridge, "The Young Surveyor" *SN* 2 (January 1875): 169; Trowbridge, "The Tinkham Brothers' Tide Mill," 17.

61. See, for example, "Letter Box," *SN* 1 (March 1874): 308.

62. Noah Brooks, "The Boy Emigrants," *SN* 3 (November 1874): 3. For a similar family structure, see Trowbridge, "The Tinkham Brothers' Tide Mill."

63. John Townsend Trowbridge, "His Own Master," *SN* 4 (December 1876): 81. See also Trowbridge, "The Young Surveyor."

64. Charles Dudley Warner, "Being a Boy," *SN* 1 (January 1874): 165–66.

65. See, for example, Rossiter Johnson, "How the Heavens Fell," *SN* 1 (February 1874): 193; Sarah Winter Kellog, "Story of a 'Toler'bul' Bad Boy," *SN* 4 (November 1876): 25; and Stockton's fairy tales, including "The Floating Prince," *SN* 8 (December 1880): 94; and "The Queen's Museum" *SN* 11 (September 1884): 837.

66. Stockton, "What Might Have Been Expected," 24.

67. Trowbridge, "The Young Surveyor," 169.

68. Alcott, "Eight Cousins," *SN* 2 (June 1875): 464. For similar examples, see Sarah Orne Jewett, "The Water Dolly," *SN* 1 (December 1873): 52; Alice Chadbourne, "The Last Pie," *SN* 1 (March 1874): 301; and Mary L. Bolles Branch "Jenny Paine's Hat," *SN* 2 (October 1875): 767.

69. Charles Barnard, "Rebecca the Drummer," *SN* 1 (July 1874): 503.

70. Mary E. Bradley, "Mrs. Pomeroy's Page," *SN* 1 (April 1874): 341.

Part III: Sustaining Children's Magazines, 1873–1918

1. Mrs. Frank Lee, "Redmond, of the 'Seventh,'" *YC*, January 5, 1888, 1–2.

2. Lee, "Redmond," *YC*, February 2, 1888, 49; February 10, 1888, 74.

3. Kate Douglas Wiggin, "Polly Oliver's Problem," *SN* 20 (November 1892): 3, 5, 8.

4. A July 1874 circular for *St. Nicholas* offered the following evaluation from the *Youth's Companion:* "The first number of *St. Nicholas* was good, the second better, and the last, in our judgment, surpasses even the *RM* [*Riverside*] in its palmist [*sic*] days; which leaves nothing to be said except to wish the enterprise success." The circular is archived in the Children's Magazine Collection, George A. Smathers Library, University of Florida.

5. Steven Mintz, *Huck's Raft: A History of American Childhood* (Cambridge: Belknap Press of Harvard University Press, 2004), 154–84; Priscilla Ferguson Clement, *Growing Pains: Children in the Industrial Age, 1850–1890* (New York: Twayne, 1997), 188–218; David I. MacLeod, *The Age of the Child: Children in America, 1890–1920* (New York: Twayne, 1998), especially 75–152.

6. Mintz, *Huck's Raft*, 135, 174; MacLeod, *The Age of the Child*, 2, 76.

7. Mintz, *Huck's Raft*, 174–75.

8. Lisa Jacobson, *Raising Consumers: Children and the American Mass Market in the Early Twentieth Century* (New York: Columbia University Press, 2004); Jane H. Hunter, *How Young Ladies Became Girls: The Victorian Origins of American Girlhood* (New Haven: Yale University Press, 2002); William Leach, *Land of Desire: Merchants, Power, and the Rise of a New American Culture* (New York: Vintage, 1993), 85–90, 248–60.

9. David L. Greene, "*Youth's Companion,*" in *Children's Periodicals of the United States*, ed. R. Gordon Kelly (Westport, Conn.: Greenwood, 1984), 512.

7. Tales and the City

1. Louisa May Alcott, "Eight Cousins," *SN* 2 (August 1875): 616–18.

2. Madeleine Stern, *Louisa May Alcott: From Blood & Thunder to Hearth & Home* (Boston: Northeastern University Press, 1998).

3. Gene Gleason, "Whatever Happened to Oliver Optic? Looking Back at a Literary Quarrel," *Wilson Literary Bulletin* 49 (May 1975): 647–50.

4. "Books for Boys and Girls," *SN* 1 (November 1873): 44; "Books for Boys and Girls: Books Received," *SN* 1 (December 1873): 102; "Jack-in-the-Pulpit: Bad Reading," *SN* 1 (January 1874): 173.

5. "Bad Books and What They Make," *YC*, February 27, 1873, 68; "Bad Books," *YC*, April 22, 1875, 126; "A Boy's Career," *YC*, January 4, 1877, 6; "Obscene Literature," *YC*, May 3, 1877, 142; "Poisoned Minds and Souls," *YC*, April 3, 1884, 132.

6. Mrs. Kate Gannett Wells, "The Responsibility of Parents in the Selection of Reading for the Young," *Library Journal* 4 (September–October 1879): 325.

7. "Literature for Boys," *Scribner's* 7 (January 1890): 370.

8. Papers from the "Fiction in Libraries and the Reading of Children" conference, *Library Journal* 4 (September–October 1879).

9. "Bad Books and What They Make," 68; "Obscene Literature," 142; Anthony Comstock, *Traps for the Young* (1883; Cambridge: Belknap Press of Harvard University Press, 1967), ix, 50.

10. "The *St. Nicholas* Treasure-Box of Literature," *SN* 8 (December 1880): 139.

11. Steven Mintz, *Huck's Raft: A History of American Childhood* (Cambridge: Belknap Press of Harvard University Press, 2004), 154–84; Michael Grossberg, "Changing Conceptions of Child Welfare in the United States, 1820–1935," in *A Century of Juvenile Justice*, ed. Margaret K. Rosenheim, Franklin E. Zimring, David S. Tanenhaus, and Bernardine Dohrn (Chicago: University of Chicago

Press, 2002), 22–27; Anthony M. Platt, *The Child Savers: The Invention of Delinquency* (Chicago: University of Chicago Press, 1977); Priscilla Ferguson Clement, *Growing Pains: Children in the Industrial Age, 1850–1890* (New York: Twayne, 1997), 188–218.

12. New York Society for the Suppression of Vice, "Seventh Annual Report," 1881, 9.

13. Peter Hall, *Cities of Tomorrow* (Oxford: Blackwell, 1988), 44; Greta Little, "*St. Nicholas* and the City Beautiful, 1893–1894," in *"St. Nicholas" and Mary Mapes Dodge: The Legacy of a Children's Magazine Editor, 1873–1905,* ed. Susan R. Gannon, Suzanne Rahn, and Ruth Anne Thompson (Jefferson, N.C.: McFarland, 2004), 241.

14. Comstock, *Traps for the Young,* 5, 9, 21, 41. (The emphasis appears in the original.)

15. Anthony Comstock, *Frauds Exposed; or, How the People Are Deceived and Robbed, and Youth Corrupted* (New York: Brown, 1880), 5, 389.

16. Wells, "The Responsibility of Parents," 325.

17. Comstock regularly boasted about his efforts, displaying scars from assailants and bragging that he had arrested enough men, women, and children to fill sixty-one coaches of a passenger train. See Comstock, *Traps for the Young,* xvii, xi, xviii.

18. Nicola Beisel, *Imperiled Innocents: Anthony Comstock and Family Reproduction in Victorian America* (Princeton: Princeton University Press, 1997), 36–103; Anna Louise Bates, *Weeder in the Garden of the Lord: Anthony Comstock's Life and Career* (Lanham, Md.: University Press of America, 1995), 69–95.

19. Mintz, *Huck's Raft,* 164–68, 177–78; Clement, *Growing Pains,* 197–202; Grossberg, "Changing Conceptions of Child Welfare," 19–29; Douglas E. Abrams, *A Very Special Place in Life: The History of Juvenile Justice in Missouri* (Jefferson City: Missouri Juvenile Justice Association, 2005).

20. "Beadle's Dime Novels," *North American Review* 49 (1864): 303–9.

21. Mark I. West, *Children, Culture, and Controversy* (Hamden, Conn.: Archon, 1988), 8.

22. Miss A. A. Bean, "The Evil of Unlimited Freedom in the Use of Juvenile Fiction," *Library Journal* 4 (September–October 1879): 341.

23. Wells, "The Responsibility of Parents," 326.

24. Charles Francis Adams, "The Public Libraries and the Public Schools," *Library Journal* 2 (August 1877): 437; Charles Francis Adams, "Fiction in Public Libraries and Educational Catalogues," *Library Journal* 4 (September–October 1879): 330.

25. "Address of T. W. Higginson," *Library Journal* 4 (September–October 1879): 357.

26. Beisel, *Imperiled Innocents,* 9, 49–75.

27. "Bad Books," *YC,* April 22, 1875, 126; "A Boy's Career," *YC,* January 4, 1877, 6; "A Boy Suicide," *YC,* April 24, 1879, 140; "Boy Burglars," *YC* 59 (Sept. 2, 1886): 332. Antebellum examples include "Lotteries—An Extract," *YC,* April 16, 1827, 3; C.,

"I Think I Will Not Change," *YC,* April 13, 1848, 199; and "The Boy That Learned to Drink," *YC,* October 25, 1839, 95.

28. "Deception," *YC,* January 1, 1857, 2; "Modest Apparel," *YC,* September 24, 1857, 154.

29. J.D.C., "The Best of a Bad Bargain," *YC,* January 2, 1873, 2. During the 1870s and 1880s, the *Companion* ran such stories nearly every month. See also "Betty Fanning," *YC,* September 24, 1874, 309; M.A.D., "A Dangerous Lover," *YC,* January 25, 1883, 26; and "Mary Ames' Novel," *YC,* August 12, 1886, 302.

30. Ruth Chesterfield, "A Boarding-School Romance," *YC,* August 5, 1875, 245.

31. John Townsend Trowbridge, "The Jolly Rover," *YC,* January 5, 1882, 1.

32. Ray Stannard Baker, *American Chronicle: The Autobiography of Ray Stannard Baker* (New York: Scribner's, 1945), 69–70.

33. Although I was not able to find a copy of Ford's leaflet, I gleaned much of its content from correspondence between *Companion* staff members and various writers (Daniel Sharp Ford Collection, Houghton Library, Harvard University). The correspondence between Ford and Louisa May Alcott during the 1870s was particularly helpful.

34. Daniel Sharp Ford, letter to Louisa May Alcott, February 17, 1875, Ford Collection. (The emphasis appears in the original.) In a letter to Dodge, Rebecca Harding Davis recounted a similar interaction. "Mr. Ford at the *Youth's Companion*" asked her to write a boys' story for his publication, telling her he would pay a "huge price" if "it united their ideas." He ultimately rejected it because it was "too dramatic" and "had a faint hint of love in it, too." She subsequently submitted the story to *St. Nicholas,* but because the title is not included in this undated letter, I have no way of telling whether it appeared there. See Rebecca Harding Davis, letter to Mary Mapes Dodge, undated, Mary Mapes Dodge Collection, Princeton University.

35. Baker, *American Chronicle,* 69.

36. Mayne Reid, *The Boy Hunters; or Adventures in Search of the White Buffalo* (Boston: Ticknor and Fields, 1868); Mary Mapes Dodge, letter to Horace Elisha Scudder, January 23, 1867, Mary Mapes Dodge Collection, Huntington Library.

37. Mary Mapes Dodge, letter to Horace Elisha Scudder, January 31, 1868, Dodge Collection, Huntington Library.

38. "Jack-in-the-Pulpit: Bad Reading," 173.

39. John Townsend Trowbridge, "Fast Friends," *SN* 1 (May 1874): 399.

40. Susan Coolidge, "The Fox and the Turkeys, or Charley and the Old Folks," *SN* 5 (September 1878): 756.

41. Mary Mapes Dodge, letter to Horace Elisha Scudder, July 23, 1866, Dodge Collection, Huntington Library; Anthony Comstock, *Traps for the Young* (New York: Funk and Wagnalls, 1883), 10.

42. "Mr. Hardhack on the Sensational in Literature and Life," *Atlantic* 13 (August 1870): 195.

43. Agnes Repplier, "What Children Read," *Atlantic* 30 (January 1887): 23; *Atlantic* 35 (May 1882): 569.

44. "Literature for Children," *North American Review* 138 (April 1884): 383.

45. "Books for Boys and Girls," *SN* 1 (November 1873): 44.

46. For more on Dodge's difficulties in getting children to read what she wanted, see Susan R. Gannon and Ruth Anne Thompson, *Mary Mapes Dodge* (New York: Twayne: 1992), 118–19.

47. "Letter Box," *SN* 10 (January 1882): 260.

48. The most successful of these efforts was the "Books and Reading" department, reinstated in November 1899 under the editorship of Hildegard Hawthorne, Nathaniel Hawthorne's granddaughter. This section commented on classic and contemporary literature as well as articles on various reading topics, and it ran until 1907, two years after Dodge's death. See, for example, "Books and Reading: Are Fairy Tales Babyish?" *SN* 33 (October 1906): 1148.

49. Mary Mapes Dodge, letter to Frank R. Stockton, December 4, 1866, Dodge Collection, Huntington Library.

50. Stockton was Dodge's assistant editor during the first decade of *St. Nicholas's* existence and a frequent contributor thereafter. He had a more cynical view than Dodge did and frequently made jokes in the office about incurring the wrath of the censors. Nonetheless, he recognized the necessity of avoiding any appearance of impropriety. In an 1897 letter to Dodge about a nonfiction series on pirates he was preparing for the magazine, he offered to call his protagonists "buccaneers" if this would avoid any potential difficulties. Dodge accepted his proposal and titled the series "The Buccaneers of Our Coasts," *SN* 25 (November 1897): 4. See Frank Stockton, letter to Mary Mapes Dodge, June 5, 1897, Dodge Collection, Princeton University.

51. In its emphasis on the importance of providing pleasure for young readers, the announcement was very similar to Dodge's *Scribner's* article, "Children's Magazines," which had earned her the editorship of *St. Nicholas:* "The spirit of mirthfulness shall be invoked from the first, and all things fresh, true and child-like, heartily commended, while every way to juvenile priggishness shall be bolted and barred as far as the management can affect." See "Announcement to Prospective Contributors," undated, Dodge Collection, Huntington Library. This document remains available only because it has a note to Scudder on the back and thus was preserved among his personal papers.

52. Susan R. Gannon, "Fair Ideals and Heavy Responsibilities: The Editing of *St. Nicholas* Magazine," in *"St. Nicholas" and Mary Mapes Dodge,* 38–39.

53. John Townsend Trowbridge, *My Own Story: With Recollection of Noted Persons* (Boston: Houghton Mifflin, 1903), 325.

54. William Fayal Clarke, "Memoranda Concerning *His One Fault,*" Rare Books Collection, New York Public Library. Clarke's assessment that Dodge distinguished between her individual tastes and her editorial standards is supported by an earlier letter from Dodge to Scudder, in which she comments on her submission to the *Riverside:* "Perhaps you may think my children [in the article "Kaleidoscopes and

Burglars"] talk and act rather roughly—they certainly would shock *some* persons— but then I draw from life, and do we not owe some allegiance to naturalness and simple fact?" Of course, this contrast may simply reflect her shift in perspective as she switched from writer to editor. Other authors recognized the pressures Dodge faced and tried to censor themselves when writing for her audience. Twain, who was her close personal friend, told his publisher that when writing "Tom Sawyer Abroad" for the magazine, he "tried to leave the improprieties all out" and was confident that, if he had failed to do so, "Mrs. Dodge can scissor them out." She did that and more, cutting more than 2,000 words from his 40,000-word narrative to improve the structure of the story (which Twain had written in a month because he needed the money) and tone down the dialect and racist references. See Mary Mapes Dodge, letter to Horace Elisha Scudder, November 16, 1867, Dodge Collection, Huntington Library; and Mark Twain, letter to Fred J. Hall, August 10, 1892, in *Mark Twain's Letters to His Publishers, 1867–1894,* ed. Hamlin Hill (Berkeley: University of California Press, 1967), 324.

55. In another story, Dodge also accepted the inclusion of some dialect, this time because the narrative opened with the caveat that the tale "won't hurt you even with its language if you remember that under the street children are tender warm feelings and true hearts." See Lucy G. Morse, "The Ash-Girl," *SN* 3 (April 1876): 386.

56. Rufus Sargent, "Dandy Lyon's Visit to New York," *YC* 46, June 5, 1873, 177. See also J.D.C., "'Prince Albert' and the City Girls," *YC*, June 12, 1873, 186; and M. A. Denison, "Sally's Trip to the City," *YC*, January 14, 1875, 10.

57. John Townsend Trowbridge, "Awkward Andy: A Story of City Life," *YC*, August 30, 1877, 277. See also John Townsend Trowbridge, "Lottery Ticket," *YC*, May 2, 1895, 213.

58. See, for example, Ruth Chesterfield, "Aunt Tennant's Wedding Present," *YC*, September 25, 1873, 305; Rebecca Harding Davis, "At the Races," November 26, 1874, 393; "The C.C.C.C.s," *YC*, August 3, 1876, 249; John Townsend Trowbridge, "The Missing Letters: Richard Borden's Story," *YC*, June 16, 1879, 17; and John Townsend Trowbridge, "How Rueben William was Saved," *YC*, April 12, 1877, 116.

59. "A Green Boy in Boston," *YC*, February 25, 1875, 58.

60. "Young Men in the City," *YC*, December 9, 1875; 407; December 16, 1875, 415.

61. "Write to Your Parents," *YC*, Sept. 20, 1877, 314; "American Cities: New York," *YC*, October 2, 1873, 316; "Go Back to the Farm," *YC*, January 31, 1878, 36.

62. Trowbridge, "Awkward Andy," *YC*, September 13, 1877, 293.

63. "The Dangers of the City," *YC*, April 30, 1879, 124; "Country Girls in the City," *YC*, November 25, 1875, 391; Edgar Fawcett, "A Country Cousin," *YC*, May 7, 1885, 189.

64. Amanda M. Douglas, "Larry," *YC*, January 5, 1893, 1.

65. For a discussion of this nineteenth-century fear of artifice and hypocrisy, see Karen Halttunen, *Confidence Men and Painted Women: A Study of Middle-Class*

Culture in America, 1830–1870 (New Haven: Yale University Press, 1986), especially 33–56; and John F. Kasson, *Rudeness and Civility: Manners in 19th Century Urban American* (New York: Hill and Wang, 1990).

66. Ruth Chesterfield, "Phoebe's Fright," *YC*, August 21, 1873, 265; M. R. Housekeeper, "Our New York Cousin," *YC*, February 7, 1884, 49. On cultural concerns about the " 'lowering of the mental nerve' among the [American] urban bourgeoisie" at the end of the nineteenth century, see T. J. Jackson Lears, *No Place of Grace: Antimodernism and the Transformation of American Culture, 1880–1920* (New York: Pantheon, 1981), 47–58.

67. "Poor Little Robby," *YC*, May 30, 1878, 171. See also "Life in New York: Driven to Desperation," *YC*, February 7, 1878, 43; and "The Story of One Dark Corner in a City," *YC*, October 9, 1879, 334.

68. "Children's Week," *YC*, July 27, 1882, 308; "Done for the Children," *YC*, September 21, 1882, 376; Charles Loring Brace, "The Street Children of New York," *YC*, November 15, 1883, 473.

69. "Practical Schools," *YC*, May 3, 1888, 220.

70. Charles Asbury Stephens, "In the Woods," *YC*, January 9, 1873, 8.

71. Stephens produced hundreds of such stories for the *Companion* between the 1870s and 1920s, including "Skip's Narrative: A Story of the Labrador," *YC*, April 3, 1873, 107; "Breaking Steers," *YC*, February 17, 1876, 53; "My Fast Horse: A Question of Moral Character," *YC*, April 11, 1878, 117; and "A Forest Incident," *YC*, April 20, 1882, 153.

72. Charles Asbury Stephens, "Coasting! How to Slide with Girls," *YC*, February 6, 1879, 43.

73. The Old Home Farm stories began on December 5, 1901, with "Medicine Bottle" and continued through January 1929 (the last year of the *Companion*'s publication), with "Julia." According to one reporter, Stephens had received 2,000 letters a year from readers and hosted countless visitors who wanted to meet the models for Addison, the Old Squire, Grandmother Ruth, and the other characters in his stories. See Katherine Crosby, "More Than Half a Century with Charles Asbury Stephens," *Boston Evening Transcript*, January 9, 1926, book sec., 1, Charles Asbury Stephens Collection, Bowdoin College.

74. According to Mark Anthony DeWolfe Howe, assistant editor of the *Companion* from 1888 to 1893 and editor from 1899 to 1913, Stephens "thought the thoughts and spoke the language of a vast body of Americans throughout the country." Reporter Katherine Crosby said that he "noted the homely features of life on the farm and in the village . . . [and] a vast audience responded to the absolute authenticity of his perceptions . . . His stories are never "jazzed up," and modern mechanics play small part in them. They are not keyed up to movie speed. But their readers, being boys, know them what they are, the Real Thing. They ring true, in their simplicity, their unpretentious directness." Interestingly, her antimodern realist language is almost identical to that used by New England cultural elites in their post–Civil War prescriptions for children's literature. See Mark Anthony

DeWolfe Howe, *A Venture in Remembrance* (Boston: Little, Brown, 1941), 111; and Crosby, "More Than Half a Century."

75. On prevailing pedagogical methods in nineteenth-century American schools, see Barbara Finkelstein, *Governing the Young: Teacher Behaviour in Popular Primary Schools in Nineteenth-Century United States* (New York: Falmer, 1989).

76. Alcott, "Eight Cousins," *SN* 2 (January 1875): 132; Louisa May Alcott, "Jack and Jill," *SN* 7 (October 1880): 932.

77. Edward Payson Roe, "Driven Back to Eden," *SN* 12 (February 1885): 241.

78. "Jack-in-the-Pulpit: Tom Hughes on Fighting," *SN* 2 (July 1875): 586; I. N. Ford, "The Fresh Air Fund," *SN* 10 (June 1883): 616.

79. William M. Baker, "Sheep or Silver?" *SN* 12 (June 1885): 575. Other stories that emphasized the benefits of country living for city children included Amalie LaForge, "Little Christie," *SN* 2 (March 1875): 280; The Author of "Rutledge," "Pleasant-Spoken," *SN* 2 (May 1875): 411; Emily Huntington Miller, "Partners," *SN* 4 (November 1876): 45; and E. Vinton Blake, "The Dalzells of Daisydown," *SN* 11 (September 1884): 828.

80. Celia Thaxter, "The Bear at Appledore," *SN* 3 (August 1876): 602.

81. George MacDonald, "Gone Astray," *SN* 4 (September 1877): 713; John Townsend Trowbridge, "Bass Cove Sketches: Young Joe and the Ducks," *SN* 3 (November 1875): 35; John Townsend Trowbridge, "Off to the Island," *SN* 3 (December 1875): 117. "Bass Cove" was not only a typical example of *St. Nicholas*'s pedagogical tactics but also a contrast to the more melodramatic style of Trowbridge's *Companion* stories—for instance, "Awkward Andy."

82. Blake, "Dalzells of Daisydown," *SN* (September 1884): 828. Like the magazine's assessments of masculine behavior, its considerations of the distinctions between city and country females did occasionally become earnest. In Louisa May Alcott's "The Cooking Class," for example, a country girl makes "simple but good" foods while a city cousin attempts a fancy dish and burns it. Yet even here the consequences of misbehavior are small; and unlike city children in most *Companion* stories, the miscreant successfully works to reform her shortcomings (*SN* 12 [November 1884]: 11).

83. Trowbridge, "Fast Friends"; Elizabeth Stuart Phelps, "How Trotty Went to the Great Funeral," *SN* 2 (November 1874): 11.

84. Lucy S. Rider, "Dick Hardin in Philadelphia," *SN* 4 (October 1876): 756.

85. Richard Harding Davis, "Midsummer Pirates," *SN* 16 (August 1889): 745.

86. William O. Stoddard, "Crowded Out o' Crofield," *SN* 17 (January 1890): 246. See also Kate Douglas Wiggin, "Polly Oliver's Problem," *SN* 20 (November 1892): 6; Elbridge S. Brooks, "A Boy of the First Empire," *SN* 22 (November 1894): 3; and James Otis, "Teddy and Carrots: Two Merchants of Newspaper Row," *SN* 22 (May 1895): 539.

87. Charles Barnard, "Young Folks' Fun in Central Park," *SN* 4 (September 1877): 705. The article's reference to playing sports in Central Park highlights the movement toward organized urban athletics as a replacement for the routine daily

exercise of country children. I discuss the growing role of sports in the lives of modern children in chapter 8.

88. Little, "*St. Nicholas* and the City Beautiful," 230–42.

89. Thomas Wentworth Higginson, "Boston," *SN* 20 (January 1893): 170. D. C. Gilman's "Baltimore" also focuses on the good works of the city's elite, with a particular emphasis on the charitable contributions of Johns Hopkins (*SN* 20 [August 1893]: 723).

90. Frances Hodgson Burnett, "A City of Groves and Bowers," *SN* 20 (June 1893): 563; James Ballantine, "Chicago," *SN* 20 (July 1893): 658. Similarly, Charles H. Shinn's "San Francisco" notes that its parks "are a surprise to every visitor" and describes its people as "an outdoor race . . . overflowing with health and vitality (*SN* 21 [April 1894]: 519).

91. Talcott Williams, "Philadelphia: A City of Homes," *SN* 20 (March 1893): 324.

8. Children's Magazines and Modern Childhood

1. Marshall Saunders, "Chronicles of the Graveleys," *YC*, February 5, 1903, 61.

2. Caroline Harwood Garland, "A Queer Golden Wedding, *YC*, December 5, 1895, 621; Eva Wilder Broadhead, "The Wedding Gown of Felisita," *YC* 73, March 9, 1899, 110. See also Annie Hamilton Donnell, "Cousin Agatha's Wedding Present," *YC*, August 19, 1897, 382; Alice Morgan, "On Their Wedding Journey," *YC*, May 18, 1899, 249; May Kelsey Champion, "A Colonial Bride," *YC*, September 7, 1899, 436; and Margaret Dodge, "Aunt Tabitha's Wedding Gown," *YC*, December 14, 1899, 658.

3. Charles Asbury Stephens, "Stories of the Old Home Farm," *YC*, December 5, 1901, 638; Walter Leon Sawyer, "Stories of the Merricks," *YC*, April 16, 1903, 188; Gwendolen Overton, "Tales of a Frontier Family," *YC*, August 6, 1903, 365; Mary Stewart Cutting, "The Doings of the Harlows," *YC*, September 24, 1903, 441; Mary E. Mitchell, "Broadening of the Hacketts," *YC*, December 29, 1904, 658.

4. Grace S. Richmond: "The Second Violin," *YC*, February 23, 1905, 85; "The Churchill Latch String," *YC*, December 14, 1905, 629; "The Readiness of the Regises," *YC*, September 13, 1906, 436; "Round the Corner in Gay Street," *YC*, August 1, 1907, 358; "Worthington Square," *YC*, December 12, 1907, 625.

5. Steven Mintz and Susan Kellogg, *Domestic Revolutions: A Social History of American Family Life* (New York: Free Press, 1968), 107–9.

6. "Books for Our Children," *Atlantic* 16 (December 1865): 724.

7. Steven Mintz, *Huck's Raft: A History of American Childhood* (Cambridge: Belknap Press of Harvard University Press, 2004), 185–99, 213–32; Lisa Jacobson, *Raising Consumers: Children and the American Mass Market in the Early Twentieth Century* (New York: Columbia University Press, 2004); David I. MacLeod, *The Age of the Child: Children in America, 1890–1920* (New York: Twayne, 1998), especially 75–152; Jane H. Hunter, *How Young Ladies Became Girls: The Victorian Origins of*

American Girlhood (New Haven: Yale University Press, 2002); William Leach, *Land of Desire: Merchants, Power, and the Rise of a New American Culture* (New York: Vintage, 1993), 85–90, 248–60.

8. Anne Scott MacLeod, "Children, Adults, and Reading at the Turn of the Century," in *American Childhood: Essays on Children's Literature of the Nineteenth and Twentieth Centuries* (Athens: University of Georgia Press, 1994), 114–26.

9. Ellen Gruber Garvey, "The *St. Nicholas* Advertising Competition: Training the Magazine Reader," in *"St. Nicholas" and Mary Mapes Dodge: The Legacy of a Children's Magazine Editor, 1873–1905,* ed. Susan R. Gannon, Suzanne Rahn, and Ruth Anne Thompson (Jefferson, N.C.: McFarland, 2004), 170.

10. See, for example, Hannah Bryant, "Betty and Eunice and Their Guests," *SN* 38 (February 1911): 312; Katherine Carleton, "Dorothy the Motor Girl," *SN* 38 (May 1911): 627; and Augusta Huiell Seaman, "The Sapphire Signet," *SN* 43 (November 1915): 35.

11. Carol Billman, *The Secret of the Stratemeyer Syndicate: Nancy Drew, the Hardy Boys, and the Million Dollar Fiction Factory* (New York: Ungar, 1986), 5.

12. Priscilla Ferguson Clement, *Growing Pains: Children in the Industrial Age, 1850–1890* (New York: Twayne, 1997), 105, 107, 109.

13. David I. MacLeod, *Building Character in the American Boy* (Madison: University of Wisconsin Press, 2004), chap. 1; Benjamin G. Rader, *American Sports: From the Age of Folk Games to the Age of Televised Sports* (Englewood Cliffs, N.J.: Prentice Hall, 1996), 98–104.

14. Mary Lynn Stevens Heininger, *A Century of Childhood, 1820–1920* (Rochester, N.Y.: Margaret Woodbury Strong Museum, 1984), 19; Bernard Mergen, *Play and Playthings: A Reference Guide* (Westport, Conn.: Greenwood, 1982), 82.

15. See, for example, Rose Terry Cook, "A Midsummer Madness," *YC,* September 27, 1877, 307; Rufus Sargent, "'Piggy,'" *YC,* May 8, 1873, 143; and Julia A. Eastman, "The Boys at Beechwood," *YC,* August 27, 1874, 277.

16. John Townsend Trowbridge, "The Pocket Rifle," *YC,* January 6, 1881, 1. For further discussion of the growth of competitive school environments during this period, see Clement, *Growing Pains,* 89.

17. See also Sarah Winter, "A Prize for Compositions," *YC,* February 14, 1884, 58; J. L. Harbour, "The Dilloway Prize," *YC,* September 17, 1885, 365; and "Dux," *YC,* December 23, 1886, 525. For examples of such behavior in hazing activities, see H. A. Gordon, "Hazing Freshman Solzberg," *YC,* July 5, 1883, 274; and John Townsend Trowbridge, "Peter Budstone: The Boy Who Was Hazed," *YC,* July 7, 1887, 293.

18. Noah Brooks, "The Fairport Nine," *SN* 7 (May 1880): 562.

19. William O. Stoddard, "Saltillo Boys," *SN* 8 (May 1881): 560. See also Frank R. Stockton, "A Jolly Fellowship," *SN* 6 (November 1878): 13; and Edward Eggleston's "The Hoosier School Boy," *SN* 9 (December 1881): 145.

20. Mrs. Frank Lee, "Redmond, of the 'Seventh,'" *YC,* January 5, 1888, 1.

21. Ibid., February 10, 1888, 74.

22. "Mystery in a Mansion" *SN* 8 (November 1880): 42. Given the prevalence of

their contributions to the magazine and the subversive humor of the story, I suspect it was written by Dodge or Stockton.

23. "Ibid., 42–47. For a more traditional *St. Nicholas* parental figure, see Uncle Alec in Louisa May Alcott, "Eight Cousins," *SN* 2 (January 1875): 132.

24. The author makes it clear that the Bairds are contented and intelligent children, highlighting the latter quality through similar wordplay. In *St. Nicholas,* such wordplay became an indicator of modern juvenile intelligence. See "Mystery in a Mansion," 42–43; and John Townsend Trowbridge, "The Tinkham Brothers' Tide Mill," *SN* 10 (April 1883): 409.

25. For more sinister implications of such knowledge, see Mary Mapes Dodge, "Donald and Dorothy," *SN* 9 (December 1881): 96. The story features a group of bantering young people, one of whom spreads a piece of gossip that he does not understand, which triggers a family crisis.

26. See, for example, Susan Coolidge, "Uncle and Aunt," *SN* 13 (November 1885): 30; and Laura Richards, "Oh, Dear!" *SN* 12 (July 1885): 646.

27. Richard Ohmann, *Selling Culture: Magazines, Markets, and Class at the Turn of the Century* (New York: Verso, 1996); Ellen Gruber Garvey, *The Adman in the Parlor: Magazines and the Gendering of Consumer Culture, 1880s to 1910s* (New York: Oxford University Press, 1996).

28. Stephen M. Frank, *Life with Father: Parenthood and Masculinity in the Nineteenth-Century American North* (Baltimore: Johns Hopkins University Press, 1998), 140–60.

29. A plethora of "success manuals" emerged during the decades after the Civil War to help young men "choos[e] a calling." See Judy Hilkey, *Character Is Capital: Success Manuals and Manhood in Gilded Age America* (Chapel Hill: University of North Carolina Press, 1997), 100–125.

30. George J. Manson, "Ready for Business; or, Choosing an Occupation: A Series of Practical Papers for Boys," *SN* 12 (November 1884): 49.

31. Oliver Wendell Holmes, Jr., "Just the Boy That's Wanted: II. In the Law," *YC,* February 7, 1889, 73; E. L. Godkin, "Just the Boy That's Wanted: IV. In Journalism," *YC,* February 21, 1889, 97; Lyman Abbot, "Just the Boy Wanted for the Ministry," *YC,* June 6, 1889, 297.

32. On magazines that presented themselves as sources of cultural authority rather than as ways to convey that information, see Ohmann, *Selling Culture,* 1–10.

33. Sophie Swett, "How Johnnie's Men Struck Work," *SN* 10 (July 1883): 643; Sophie Swett, "The Great Financial Scheme," *SN* 12 (September 1885): 846.

34. Thomas A. Janvier, "W. Jenks's Express," *SN* 16 (October 1889): 824; John Townsend Trowbridge, "Toby Trafford," *SN* 18 (November 1890): 3; and J. L. Harbour, "Jack Dilloway's Scheme," *SN* 20 (November 1892): 58.

35. Hjalmar Hjorth Boyesen, "Against Heavy Odds," *YC,* January 2, 1890, 1; Edward William Thomson, "The Young Boss," *YC,* October 3, 1895, 461; "Kent Hampden," *YC,* January 1, 1891, 1.

36. Hilkey, *Character Is Capital,* 111–12.

37. Z. A. R., "Jack's Treadle," *YC*, April 10, 1873, 113; "What Shall the Boys Do?" *YC*, February 26, 1880, 68.

38. George H. Bassett, "What One Man Can Do," *YC*, September 14, 1882, 367. See also Geo. Manville Fenn, "Iron Trials," *YC*, July 8, 1886, 261; and Homer Greene, "Blind Brother," *YC*, January 6, 1887, 1.

39. W. C. Grinnell, "Perils of a Linesman's Life," *YC*, March 2, 1882, 79.

40. See, for example, Frederic Palmer, "Stories by Clergymen. No. 1: Aaron's Wife," *YC* January 14, 1897, 13; Henry A. Beers, "Stories by Professors. No. 1: The Third Stage of Discipline," *YC*, April 29, 1897, 197; and Charles W. Harwood, "Stories by Doctors. No. 1: A Wayside Patient," *YC*, May 27, 1897, 245.

41. P. Y. Black, "A Young Savage," *YC*, April 1, 1897, 145; Homer Greene, "Starry Vint's Defence," *YC*, March 18, 1897, 121.

42. Fanny M. Johnson, "Young Knight of Honor," *YC*, July 7, 1892, 346; Hayden Carruth, "Track's End," *YC*, January 7, 1897, 1.

43. See, for example, Fanny M. Johnson, "On His Own Merits," *YC*, July 3, 1890, 360; Manley H. Pike, "The Extra Freight," *YC*, December 17, 1891, 655; and F. E. C. Robbins, "The Adelphian Society," *YC*, April 7, 1892, 169.

44. For an analysis of popular exaltation of the "Great Independent American inventor" during this period, see Glen Scot Allen, *Master Mechanics and Wicked Wizards: Images of the American Scientist and Hero and Villain from Colonial Times to the Present* (Amherst: University of Massachusetts Press, 2009), 50–58.

45. Major Traverse, "Something about Railroads," *SN* 3 (March 1876): 81; John Townsend Trowbridge, "The Young Surveyor," *SN* 2 (January 1875): 169. See also Rossiter Johnson, "Phaeton Rogers," *SN* 8 (December 1880): 153; and George Whittlesey, " 'Ham' Estabrook's Can-Opener," *SN* 15 (April 1888): 453.

46. Brander Matthews, "Tom Paulding (A Tale of Treasure Trove in the Streets of New York)" *SN* 19 (November 1891): 15. See also Clement Fezandie, "Through the Earth," *SN* 25 (January 1898): 179.

47. F. Lovell Coombs, "The Boy Who Knew How," *SN* 37 (December 1909): 117.

48. F. Lovell Coombs, "Race Through the Flames," *SN* 37 (March 1910): 402.

49. Allen, *Master Mechanics and Wicked Wizards*, 58–62; Terry S. Reynolds, ed., *The Engineer in America: A Historical Anthology from Technology and Culture* (Chicago: University of Chicago Press, 1991), 25–26.

50. See, for example, Brooks, "The Fairport Nine," 562; and Stoddard, "The Saltillo Boys," *SN* 8 (August 1881): 798. Nonfiction articles included Samuel Van Brunt, "Snow Sports for Girls and Boys," *SN* 7 (February 1880): 320; Charles Barnard, "A Talk about the Bicycle," *SN* 7 (May 1880): 887; and Charles Barnard, "Lacrosse," *SN* 8 (November 1880): 64.

51. "Dangers of Athletic Sports," *YC*, October 5, 1876, 324; "Base-Ball Playing," *YC*, August 16, 1877, 264; and "Athletic Sports," *YC*, March 4, 1880, 76; January 27, 1881, 28.

52. George B. M. Harvey, "How Science Won the Game," *SN* 12 (October 1885): 924.

53. Mrs. Burton Harrison, "Washington as an Athlete," *SN* 16 (March 1889): 337.

54. Richard Harding Davis, "Richard Carr's Baby," *SN* 14 (November 1886): 50.

55. Walter Camp: "Intercollegiate Football in America," *SN* 17 (November 1889): 36; "Bat, Ball and Diamond," *SN* 17 (May 1890): 555; "A Remarkable Boat Race," *SN* 17 (Aug. 1890): 832. Theodore Roosevelt's articles include "Buffalo Hunting," *SN* 17 (December 1889): 136; "Daniel Boone and the Founding of Kentucky," *SN* 22 (May 1895): 599; and "George Rogers Clark and the Founding of the Northwest," *SN* 22 (June 1895): 639.

56. "Girls Who Can Skate," *YC*, January 6, 1887, 4; "Swimming Girls," *YC*, July 26, 1888, 364. On the other hand, "Why Girls Cannot Throw" (*YC*, April 9, 1891, 215) blame their shortcomings on anatomical differences. On the mixed reaction to girls who played sports in the late nineteenth-century United States, see Dwight W. Hoover, "Roller-Skating Toward Industrialism," in *Hard at Play: Leisure in America, 1840–1940*, ed. Kathryn Grover (Amherst: University of Massachusetts Press, 1993), 65–72; and Martha H. Vebrugge, *Able-Bodied Womanhood: Personal Health and Social Change in Nineteenth-Century Boston* (New York: Oxford University Press, 1988).

57. Albertus T. Dudley, "That Hilton Game," *YC*, October 20, 1892, 517; Charles Asbury Stephens, "The Kind of Boy Len Was," *YC* 65, June 30, 1892, 329.

58. Helen M. North, "About Baseballs and Baseball," *YC*, March 20, 1890, 154; "The Football Question," *YC* 69 (March 14, 1895): 130. On controversies surrounding football during this period, see John Sayle Watterson, *College Football: History, Spectacle, Controversy* (Baltimore: Johns Hopkins University Press, 2002), 26–98.

59. Clifford Putney, *Muscular Christianity: Manhood and Sports in Protestant America, 1880–1920* (Cambridge: Harvard University Press, 2001), especially 25–72; Gail Bederman, *Manliness and Civilization: A Cultural History of Gender and Race in the United States, 1880–1917* (Chicago: University of Chicago Press, 1995); Kim Townsend, *Manhood at Harvard: William James and Others* (New York: Norton, 1996).

60. William Blaikie, "Is American Stamina Declining?" *Harper's* 79 (July 1889): 241.

61. On the complicated stance of white Protestant Americans toward "less civilized" races during this period, see Bederman, *Manliness and Civilization;* and Putney, *Muscular Christianity.* During the 1870s, the *Companion* was especially vehement about the inherent inferiority of other races. See "Chinese Gamblers" *YC*, January 9, 1873; 11; "Among the Gipsies," *YC*, Oct. 15, 1874, 332; and John Brownjohn, "'Ki Bono,'" *YC*, February 15, 1877, 49. *St. Nicholas* focused on the inferiority of Native Americans during this period, portraying them as cruel and undeserving of the land that whites had taken from them. See Samuel Woodworth Cozzens, "The Comanches' Trail," *SN* 2 (December 1874): 94; and Kate Foote, "An Indian Story," *SN* 2 (September 1875): 705. In the early twentieth century, *St. Nicholas* took up the subject of race suicide in stories such as Bradley Gilman, "Son of the Desert," *SN* 36 (November 1908): 3; and Bradley Gilman, "A Young Wizard of Morocco," *SN* 37 (March 1910): 422.

62. Rader, *American Sports*, 101; David I. MacLeod, *Age of the Child*, 121–27.

63. Frank H. Spearman, "Captain Benson's Last Rally," *YC*, January 26, 1899, 37.

64. Robert Thomson, "'Professor,'" *YC*, June 29, 1899, 326; Albertus Dudley, "The Professional," *YC*, October 5, 1899, 482; Samuel Merwin, "Cupid the Fresh-man Manager," *YC*, March 15, 1900, 129.

65. Jesse Lynch Williams, "The Man in the Window," *YC*, December 8, 1898, 614.

66. Ray Stannard Baker, "Tales of the Toilers: At the Whitstone Mill," *YC*, January 5, 1899, 1.

67. Arthur Stanwood Pier, "A Young Savage," *YC*, December 3, 1903, 608.

68. Arthur Stanwood Pier: "The Leader of the Cheering," *YC*, May 7, 1903, 222; "Whippet Boy," *YC*, April 7, 1904, 172; "The Musical Short-Stops," *YC*, May 1, 1913, 225.

69. See, for example, Holman F. Day, "The Rainy Day Railroad War," *YC*, September 7, 1905, 409; Hollis Godfrey, "For the Norton Name," *YC*, February 25, 1909, 83; and Holman F. Day, "On Misery Gore," *YC*, April 3, 1913, 174.

70. See, for example, James Otis, "Teddy and Carrots: Two Merchants of Newspaper Row," *SN* 22 (May 1895): 539; and F. Lovell Coombs, "The Young Railroaders," *SN* 37 (November 1909): 19.

71. Henry James, "The Speech of American Women," *Harper's Bazaar* 41 (November 1906–February 1907): 17.

72. Hunter, *How Young Ladies Became Girls*, 3–5.

73. Jennie June, "The Girl's Problem," *YC*, April 11, 1880, 194; "What She Did Not Know," *YC*, February 19, 1885, 64.

74. Alice Manzell, "Elizabeth Butler," *SN* 10 (January 1883): 185.

75. Elizabeth Stuart Phelps, "Supporting Herself," *SN* 11 (May 1884): 517.

76. Rose Lattimore Alling, "Nan's Revolt," *SN* 13 (August 1886): 682. See also Kate Douglas Wiggin, "Polly Oliver's Problem," *SN* 20 (November 1892): 6.

77. Jessie M. Anderson, "Three Freshmen: Ruth, Fran and Nathalie," *SN* 22 (January 1895): 191.

78. Priscilla Murolo, *The Common Ground of Womanhood: Class, Gender, and Working-Girls Clubs, 1884–1928* (Urbana: University of Illinois Press, 1997); Kathy Peiss, *Cheap Amusements: Working Women and Leisure in Turn-of-the-Century New York* (Philadelphia: Temple University Press, 1986); Susan Porter Benson, *Counter Cultures: Saleswomen, Managers, and Customers in American Department Stores, 1890–1940* (Urbana: University of Illinois Press, 1986).

79. See, for example, Margaret Sangster, "Stories of Working Girls: Christine's Way Up," *YC*, May 12, 1898, 225; and Laura Richards, "Stories of Working Girls: Blue Egyptians," *YC*, May 19, 1898, 237.

80. Theodora R. Jenness, "An Off Wheat Year," *YC*, January 3, 1895, 1; Edward William Thomson, "Alice Adams: Surveyor," *YC*, September 4, 1902, 421.

81. Mabel Earle, "The Probationer," *YC*, October 22, 1903, 490; Mabel Earle, "The Snowside Hospital," *YC*, April 8, 1909, 168; Marguerite Tracy, "The Hanover

Inheritance," *YC*, February 11, 1904, 66, Edith Wharton, "Friends," *YC*, August 23, 1900, 405.

82. Alice Balch Abbot, "How Cousin Marian Helped," *SN* 24 (May 1897): 533.

83. Grace Margaret Gallaher, "The Good Cause," *YC*, August 3, 1905, 364; Grace Margaret Gallaher, "A Real Player," *YC*, May 10, 1906, 234; Gardner Hunting, "The Muscles of Marcia," *YC*, May 5, 1910, 229; "Camping and Tramping for Girls," *YC*, May 25, 1911, 275; C. H. Claudy, "Betty and the 'White' Water," *YC*, January 5, 1911, 2.

84. Reverend James M. Taylor, "What College Does for Girls," *YC*, June 26, 1902, 323; L. Clark Seelye, "Why Girls Should Go to College," *YC*, May 26, 1907, 235.

85. J. Mervin Hull, "A Hustler's Ambition," *YC*, September 18, 1902, 446; Grace Ellery Channing, "By One-Girl Power," *YC*, February 4, 1904, 53; Katharine Holland Brown, "The House of Philippa: Tales of a College Girl," *YC*, January 7, 1909, 1; Susan Keating Glaspell, "Return of Rhoda," *YC*, January 26, 1905, 40: Marion Dickinson, "Heart's Delight," *YC*, May 11, 1905, 226.

86. "Progress of Education for Women," *YC* 80, March 1, 1906, 106. Beth B. Gilchrist's "The Mixing Bowl" (*YC*, April 23, 1914, 216) argues that "[a] woman's hope of happiness" is "dependent upon the extent to which she makes herself worthy of the blessing of love and motherhood."

87. Marshall Saunders, "Chronicles of the Graveleys: IV. The Heart of the Mayor," *YC*, March 19, 1903, 133.

88. M. A. DeWolfe Howe, *A Venture in Remembrance* (Boston: Little, Brown, 1941), 109.

89. See Benson Knipe and Alden Arthur Knipe, "The Lucky Sixpence," *SN* 39 (February 1912): 290; and its sequels "Beatrice of Denwood," *SN* 40 (November 1912): 21; and "Peg o' the Ring," *SN* 42 (November 1914): 25. Also see Seaman, "The Sapphire Signet," 35; Mary Constance Dubois, "Lass of the Silver Sword," *SN* 36 (December 1908): 126; and Mary Constance Dubois, "League of the Silver Ring," *SN* 37 (May 1910): 579.

90. Bryant, "Betty and Eunice and Their Guests," 312; Carleton, "Dorothy the Motor Girl," 627; Seaman, "The Sapphire Signet," 35.

91. Cutting, "The Doings of the Harlows: II. Waiting for a Partner," *YC*, October 8, 1903, 465; Margaret Ashmun, "Stories of the Carleton Family: I. The Chrysophrase Ring," *YC* 90, January 6, 1916, 2.

Epilogue

1. "For Country and for Liberty: Patriotic Service for American Boys and Girls," *SN* 44 (July 1917): 771–72; Margaret Dadmun, "The Girls in Khaki," *SN* 44 (April 1917): 520.

2. C. H. Claudy, "In a Certain Well-Known Ocean," *SN* 45 (July 1918): 771; Grace E. Craig, "The Ambulance-Girl: A Story of the French Front," *SN* 44 (July

1917): 783; Mabel Louise Mountsier and Robert DeMain Mountsier, "Three Loyal Children of France," *SN* 44 (July 1917): 780.

3. "General Bridges' Message to American Boys and Girls," *SN* 44 (July 1917): 779.

4. "Calling Out the Boys," *YC,* March 14, 1918, 130.

5. The *Companion's* few stories focused on young military men serving inside the United States. See Arthur Stanwood Pier, "The Plattsburgers," *YC,* April 19, 1917, 217; Homer Greene, "The Guardsman," *YC,* October 10, 1918, 509; and Fisher Ames, "Sergt. Warren Comes Back from France," *YC,* August 1, 1918, 385.

6. See, for example, Holman F. Day, "The Rainy Day Railroad War," *YC,* September 7, 1905, 409; and Hollis Godfrey, "For the Norton Name," *YC,* February 25, 1909, 83.

7. "For Country and for Liberty," 771.

8. Lisa Jacobson, *Raising Consumers: Children and the American Mass Market in the Early Twentieth Century* (New York: Columbia University Press, 2004); William Leach, *Land of Desire: Merchants, Power, and the Rise of a New American Culture* (New York: Vintage, 1993), 85–90, 248–60.

9. Deirdre Johnson, *Edward Stratemeyer and the Stratemeyer Syndicate* (New York: Twayne, 1993), 2–6. See also Emily Hamilton-Honey, *Turning the Pages of American Girlhood: The Evolution of Girls' Series Fiction* (Jefferson, N.C.: McFarland, 2013), especially chap. 3.

10. Johnson, *Edward Stratemeyer,* 7.

11. Franklin K. Mathiews, "Blowing Out the Boy's Brains," *Outlook,* November 18, 1914, 652–53. Mathiews did not single out Stratemeyer's work, but it clearly falls within the genre he castigates. For more on this opposition, see Hamilton-Honey, *Turning the Pages,* 93–99.

12. Edward Stratemeyer, *Under Dewey at Manila; or, The War Fortunes of a Castaway* (Boston: Lee and Shepard, 1898).

13. Arthur M. Winfield, *The Rover Boys at School; or, the Cadets of Putnam Hall* (New York: Grosset and Dunlap, 1899); Arthur M. Winfield, *The Rover Boys on the Ocean; or, A Chase for Fortune* (New York: Grosset and Dunlap, 1899); Arthur M. Winfield, *The Rover Boys in the Jungle; or, Stirring Adventures in Africa* (New York: Grosset and Dunlap, 1899). "Arthur M. Winfield" was one of Stratemeyer's many pseudonyms.

14. On the decline of families reading aloud and the separation of children's and adult literature, see Anne Scott MacLeod, *American Childhood: Essays on Children's Literature of the Nineteenth and Twentieth Centuries* (Athens: University of Georgia Press, 1994), 123–26.

15. Scot Guenter, "*American Boy*—The Open Road," and Nancy Dahlstrom, "*The American Girl,*" in *Children's Periodicals of the United States,* ed. R. Gordon Kelly (Westport, Conn.: Greenwood, 1984), 7–21.

16. Jacobson, *Raising Consumers,* 13. Jacobson suggests here that this process was largely complete by the end of the Depression, but her argument throughout

the rest of the book suggests that she agrees with my assessment of this pattern of gradual decline.

17. *Highlights* was predominantly the product of Garry Cleveland Myers, a doctor of psychology who always included "Ph.D." after his name on the masthead and used the magazine as a testing ground for his academic principles. *Cricket* proclaimed its intention to "bridge the gap existing in children's publishing since *St. Nicholas* ceased publication," and it has maintained high literary standards throughout its run. However, its contributors' list largely reflects the contemporary divide between authors of children's and adult fiction that did not exist during the late nineteenth-century heyday of *St. Nicholas*. See R. Gordon Kelly, "*Highlights for Children,*" and Mary D. Manning, "*Cricket: The Magazine for Children,*" in *Children's Periodicals*, 203–9, 132–36.

INDEX

PAUL RINGEL is an associate professor of history at High Point University in High Point, North Carolina. He was born in Boston, graduated from Princeton University and Boston College Law School, and earned a doctorate in history from Brandeis University. His previous employment includes a position as historical consultant for the children's television show *The Time Warp Trio,* and he currently serves as the director of The William Penn Project, a collaborative research endeavor dedicated to discovering and circulating information about the African American high school in High Point before desegregation. He lives in Greensboro, North Carolina, with his wife, Erica, and their children, Julia and Sam. *Commercializing Childhood* is his first book.